AF668894

# Informal Employment in India
## Issues and Challenges

# Informal Employment in India

## Issues and Challenges

*Edited by*
**Seepana Prakasam**
MA, Phd, M.Phil, LLB, MEd, B.Lib, NET, FDP (IIM I)
Assistant professor of Economics
PG Department of Economics
PGGCG-11, Chandigarh

**Bookwell Publications**
**New Delhi**

First Published in 2013 by:

**Bookwell Publications**
24/4800, Ansari Road, Darya Ganj,
New Delhi-110002, India
Ph: 91-11-23268786, 23257264
E-mail: bookwell@vsnl.net

**ISBN:** 978-81-92102-36-8

© Author, 2013

All rights reserved. No part of this publication may be reproduced or transmitted in any form, or by any means, electronic or mechanical, including photocopying, recording, or any information storage and retrieval system, without permission in writing from copyright holder.

*Typeset by:*
A.R. Typeset Processing
New Delhi

*Printed at:*
D.K. Fine Art Press (P) Ltd., Delhi

# Disclaimer

The aim of this publication is to supply information taken from sources believed to be valid and reliable. This is not an attempt to render any type of professional advice or neither analysis nor it is too treated as such. While much care has been taken to ensure the veracity and accuracy of, the information presented with in. Neither the publisher nor the authors/editor bears any responsibility for any damage arising from inadvertent omissions, negligence or inaccuracies (typological or factual ) that may have found their way into this book.

# Acknowledgements

It is my pleasant duty to express my sincere thanks and indebtedness to many individuals who have extended their help at various stages of the completion of this work.

I deem it a great privilege to express my profound respect and sincere thanks and deep sense of gratitude to my beloved teacher and research director Prof. G.Ramachandrudu , who inspired me throughout the period of this study .

I would like to say special thanks to Prof. Bikram K Pattanaik Professor, Director, School of Extension and Development Studies, Indira Gandhi National Open University, New Delhi. Prof. Gurmail Singh chairperson Dept. of Economics Panjab University Chandigarh and Prof Sucha Singh Gill Director General CRRID Chandigarh, for the encouragement and valuable suggestions at every stage of completion of this task.

I will be failing in my duty if I do not acknowledge my profound gratitude to Mrs.Achila Dogra, Principal of the college, Mrs. Anita Kosla Dean of the college, Vice Principal Vinita Dogra , Mrs Kusum Lata Garg , Head of the department and my learned senior colleagues Mrs. Vandana Shegal, Shri. Shashi Kant, Mrs. Gurupreet Kaur, Mrs.Vanita Rao, Mrs. Meena Kumari of the Post Graduate Department of Economics and Mrs. Shashi Joshi convener, UGC cell of the college for their inspiration and valuable suggestions, stimulating discussions, analysis and critical evaluation of the work under reference .

I am thankful to all the intellectuals who hails from various parts of the country, and have timely contributed their well thought research papers for duly completion of this book.

As I have drawn upon and assimilated a great amount of materials from the standard works of the well-known authorities, I acknowledge, with gratitude, my indebtedness to the authors and publishers whose works I have referred to with mention or without mention in the course of writing this work.

I am indebted to my parents and thankful to my wife and children for their support during the busy hours of my work.

Last but not least I am thankful to the Bookwell Publications for publishing this book within in a stipulated period of time.

**Seepana Prakasam**

October 2012

# Contents

# Title of Table & Figures

## List of Tables

**Table No.**

## List of Figure

**Figure No.**

# Acronyms

| | |
|---|---|
| BSUP | Basic Services to the Urban Poor |
| BS | Budgetary Support |
| BPL | Below Poverty Line |
| BMS | Basic Minimum Services |
| CDS | Current Daily Status |
| CSS | Centrally Sponsored Schemes |
| CDD | Community Driven Development |
| CMP | Common Minimum Programme |
| C P I | Capability Poverty Index |
| CPIIW | Consumer Price Index of Industrial Workers |
| DWCRA | Development of Women and Children in Rural Areas |
| EAS | Employment Assurance Scheme |
| EGS | Employment Guarantee Scheme |
| EPS | Employees' Pension Scheme |
| EAS | Employment Assurance Scheme |
| EIA | Environment Impact Assessment |
| EGS | Employment Guarantee Scheme |
| EQI | Employment Quality Index |
| EPS | Employees' Pension Scheme |
| EUS | Employment-Unemployment Survey |
| EWS | Economically Weaker Sections |
| FWP | Food for Work Programme |
| HPI | Human Poverty Index |
| HCR | Head Count Ratio |
| HDI | Human Development Index |
| I L O | International Labor Organization |
| INRLF | Indian National Rural Labor Federation |
| ICDS | Integrated Child Development Scheme |
| ICPS | Integrated Child Protection Scheme |
| IAAP | Intensive Agriculture Area Programme |
| JSY | Janani Suraksha Yojana |
| JRY | Jawahar Rozgar Yojana |

| | |
|---|---|
| JGSY | Jawaharlal Gram Samridi Yojana |
| KGBV | Kasturiba Gandhi Balika Vidyalaya |
| KSY | Kishori Shakti Yojana |
| LFPR | Labor Force Participation Rate |
| MPCE | Monthly Per capita Consumption Expenditure |
| MMR | Maternal Mortality Rate |
| MDG | Millennium Development Goals |
| MNP | Minimum Needs Programme |
| MDMP | Mid-Day Meal Programme |
| MNREGA | National Rural Employment Guarantee Act |
| NFSM | National Food Security Mission |
| NUIF | National Urban Infrastructure Fund. |
| NRHM | National Rural Health Mission |
| NPAG | Nutrition Programme for Adolescent Girls |
| MNREGA | National Rural Employment Guarantee Act |
| NCRPA | New Centaury Rural Poverty Alleviation Plan |
| NCRL | National Commission on Rural Labor |
| NBS | National bureau of statistics |
| NSSO | National Sample Survey Organization |
| NSAP | National Social Assistance Programme |
| NSDP | National Slum Development Programme |
| NAFUS | National Fund for Unorganized Sector |
| NAIS | National Agricultural Insurance Scheme |
| NCEUS | National Commission on Enterprises in the Unorganized Sector |
| NCF | National Commission on Farmers |
| NCL | National Commission on Labor |
| NSSO | National Sample Survey Organization |
| NSAP | National Social Assistance Programme |
| MGNREGS | Mahatma Gandhi National Rural Employment Guarantee Scheme |
| OAP | Old age Pension Scheme |
| PMRY | Prime Minister Rojgar Yojana |
| NSAP | National Social Assistance Programme |
| NREP | National Rural Employment Programme |
| PPP | Public Private Partnership |
| PPP | Purchasing Power Parity |
| PQLI | Physical Quality of Life Index |

| | |
|---|---|
| PDS | Public Distribution System |
| RLE | Rural Labor Enquiry |
| RCS | Ryot Cooli Sangam |
| RLH | Rural Labor Households |
| SEWA | Self Employed Women Association |
| SEPUP | Self Employment Programme for Urban Poor |
| SFDA | Small Farmers Development Agency |
| SGRY | Sampoorna Gram Swarojgar Yojana |
| SGSY | Swarna Jayanti Gram Swarojgar Yojana |
| SHGs | Self Help Groups |
| SEAG | Self Employed in Agriculture |
| SENAG | Self Employed in Non-Agriculture |
| TFR | Total Fertility Rate |
| UPS | Usual Principal Status |
| USEP | Urban Self Employment Programme |
| UPSS | Usual Principal and Subsidiary Status |
| VSE | Village and Small Enterprises |
| VAMBAY | Valmiki Ambedkar Awas Yojana |
| VKGUY | Vishesh Krishi and Gram Udyog Yojana |
| VRC | Village Resource Centers |
| WPR | Worker Participation Rate |

# List of Contributors

1. **Bikram K Pattanaik**, Professor , Director ,School of Extension and Development Studies, Indira Gandhi National Open University, New Delhi.
2. **Halima Sadia Rizvi**, Professor, Department of Economics, Jamia Millia Islamia university , New Delhi,
3 **Abhishek Jain**, IAS, Director, SC, OBC & Minority Affairs, Govt. of Himachal Pradesh, Shimla
4 **Mehta.G.S**, Senior Fellow, Giri Institute of Development Studies, Lucknow.
5 **Kailas C. Thaware**, Reader, Gokhale Institute of Politics & Economics, Deemed to be University, Pune.
6. **Jesma J, Macedo**, Senior Software Engineer, iGate Patni Global Solutions Ltd., Bangalore
7. **James M,Antony**. Associate Professor, Department of Economics (Centre for Research), Arul Anandar College, Karumathur .
8. **Dnyandev Talule**, Associate Professor & Head Post Graduate Department of Economics, Ahmednagar College, Ahmednagar, University of Pune
9. **Shinde M.H**, Assistant professor Post Graduate Department of Economics, Ahmednagar College, Ahmednagar, University of Pune
10. **Prakasam.S**, Assistant professor of Economics, P.G. Dept of Economics, PG Govt College for Girls, Chandigarh .
11. **Meena Kumari**, Assistant Professor of Economics P.G. Dept Economics, P G Govt College for Girls, Chandigarh.
12. **Sheena Krishnan U.**, Assistant Professor Post Graduate Govt College for Girls, Sector-11, Chandigarh,

13. **Hastimal Sagara**, Assistant Professor of Economics, GLS Institute of Commerce, Ahmedabad
14. **Isha Jaswal**. Doctoral fellow at Department of Economics, Jamia Millia Islamia, Central University, New Delhi, India,
15. **Satinder Rana**, Doctoral fellow at Dravidian university Kuppam
16. **Shanno Thakur** Doctoral fellow, at Dravidian university Kuppam
17. **Narendra Jena**, Doctoral fellow at (CSRD), School of Social Sciences, Jawaharlal Nehru University, New Delhi.
18. **Sudipta Sarkar**, Doctoral fellow at (CSRD), School of Social Sciences, Jawaharlal Nehru University , New Delhi.

# Prologue

Globalization intensified privatization of public sector, decentralized production through sub contracting, and deregulation of labor markets which lead to transfer of jobs from formal to informal sector . Labor reforms incorporated into economic reforms have resulted in an abnormal expansion of informal sector in most of the developing nations. The larger segment of the population is working in unorganized sector of the economy, as informal labor (unorganized labor). The composition of employment between formal and informal sectors had changed. Fiscal consolidation policy adopted by the government, reduced formal employment generation capacity of public sector; on the other hand, private manufacturing sector adopted labor saving and capital intensive methods of production as a part of strategy to win competitive advantage over others . Workers who lost their jobs in import substituting industries are also forced to join in informal sector.

During globalization wage inequalities are increased between formal and informal jobs , because more skilled and highly educated workers are absorbed in formal sector. There are earnings differentials among informal jobs also i.e. Casual, regular, home workers, contract workers and self employed workers. Liberalization which made easier to import technological equipment and knowhow by manufacturing sector, further aggravated capital intensive techniques. Employment in informal sector is more flexible, such as casual, contract and temporary forms as a result , the decent work deficit has increased and coverage of social protection to workers has declined , which may endanger our aim to achieve inclusive growth if timely appropriate measures are not undertaken.

Liberalization was predicted to increase participation of women, it become true but demand for women labor increased because it is cheaper than male labor. Most of women compelled to do low productive, unskilled and insecure jobs , either to supplement family income or due to loss of jobs by the male bread earner. Informality can impose considerable costs on the economy, hence policies will be needed to encourage informal sector to become formal. Hence, provide supporting environment for the growth of productivity and improvement in working conditions in the informal sector.

In the second chapter **Bikram K Pattanaik,** in his well articulated research paper entitled *'Migrant Laborers In The Urban Informal Sector' A Socio-Economics Analysis'*, rightly made comparative analysis of the lives and livelihood of inter-state migrant construction laborers. The sample comprises of 800 migrant laborers, out of which 400 are male and 400 are female construction laborers. Various aspects covered in this paper are their education and caste profile; quality of living and gender disparities in wages and income. Further the author felt that there is greater violation of human rights of these internal migrant laborers engaged in the construction activities in urban informal sector, more particularly those of women laborers. Neither the government nor the agencies are serious about the well-being of there workers. The laws formulated for their well-being are mere paper exercises and hardly found implemented. The country has to go a long way to promote the well-being of these internal migrant workers with a gender perspective.

**Halima Sadia Rizvi and Isha Jaswal,** in their thought provoking paper entitled *'Social Protection Status of Women Workers In Special Economic Zones In India'* expressed that high economic growth is expected to solve the problems of poverty and inequality in our economy; but in reality a situation contrary to the same exists. Number of social security schemes are introduced by the governments at central and state level ,but vulnerable women not adequately protected. For the development of Special Economic Zones (SEZs) the contribution of informal women workers is enormous. In fact, women workers, who constitute the major share of workforce in SEZs, are employed on contractual basis so that it is easier to hire and fire them. There is a huge gap between social protection policy and its availability to women workers in Special Economic Zones. In order to minimize the cost of production and to sustain the pressure of international competition, the labor laws and policies governing these SEZs are made invariably flexible. Women workers are preferred in these zones since they are hard-working and diligent and more importantly they are too docile to form trade unions and press for higher wages. In return, women are rewarded by minimal wages, 10-12 hours of average work per day and sexual exploitation by the employers or supervisors. Besides the hazardous working conditions, basic facilities are inadequate or not available at all and they face economic disparity in terms of being paid less than their male counterparts. Finally the authors suggested measures to bring the women workers within the frame of social protection policy in the emerging macro-environment.

**Abhishek Jain,** in his well designed paper entitled '*Gender Inequalities and Human Rights Violations of Women Workers in Unorganized Labor Sector*' viewed that human rights of women workers are being violated. Women in the rural areas are many times forced to work for meager wages without social security. Women have to work beyond working hours, even in advanced stages of pregnancy, and there is no leave facility. Most of the employed in the unorganized sector face an array of uninsured risks that render them highly vulnerable to shocks. Moreover they face a lot of problems such as low wages, longer hours of work, irregular payment of wages, unauthorized deductions from wages, non-availability of social security measures, precarious working conditions and sexual harassment at work place etc. Women tend to work longer hours than men and still earn less. The author suggested measures like need of creating awareness about the legal rights of women workers in unorganized sector. Regulatory reforms need to be complemented with effective and active labor market policies that can help such women workers to become more productive to obtain more protection against unemployment, and enhance skills. Ultimately, it is imperative to work towards the goal of decent and remunerative work for all.

**Mehta, G.S,** in his well organized research paper entitled '*Impact of MNREGA on The Rural Labor Market (A micro study)*', which is based on sample of 320 beneficiary and 240 non-beneficiary households spread over 16 Gram Panchayats of four districts in UP. The author examined the effectiveness of implementation of MNREGA with regarding the condition of employment, job security, income security and working conditions at the work place. Except the facility of drinking water, the other facilities which are to be made available according to MNREGA norms were hardly provided at any of the worksite. Even the facility of drinking water and first aid was only seen available by a little over 41 beneficiaries and 21 percent respondents respectively. Due to lack of crèche at the worksites a half of women were leaving their children at home and the remaining were forced to bring their children with them at the worksite, which were look after by themselves along with working at the sites. The benefit of creation of employment opportunities under the MNREGA has mostly gone in favor of landless laborers followed by marginal and small farmers than the other categories of farmers. The fixation of high wage rates under MNREGA has directly influenced the increasing trends of wages of both for agricultural and non- agricultural labors. But the wage rates of agricultural labors were lagging far behind to the non-agricultural labors. However, the wage rates of latter category of labors has been picking up more sharply than the case of former category of labors. Similarly, the wage rates of women were at much lower order than their male counterpart in both agricultural sector and non-agricultural sector.

**Kailas C. Thaware,** in his research paper entitled '*Impact of Urbanization on Informal Labor Migration In India*', rightly said that Various developmental schemes failed to make effective impact on improvement of the socio-economic condition of the rural poor people, despite huge budgetary allocation of the Central Government under central financial assistance programmes, which caused out-migration of labor. The author conducted field study in Pune city of Maharashtra with about 100 sample households, who were migrants. Migrants are engaged mostly in unskilled and semi-skilled activities. Labor migration took place because of their vulnerable socio-economic conditions, lack of availability of employment opportunities, low wage rates and poor basic amenities at their home place. The decision of out-migration is usually taken after getting information on wage rates, regular employment opportunities, and connectivity to migration destination by road, and rail. Workers migrate to Pune; they are paid wages higher than what they get in the local areas. The study has found that the migrants make systematic plan for spending their income. Some of them live together in a group and share expenses on rent and food. This reduces the total monthly personal expenditure and increases the saving. The author advised that the government should take protective measures in villages through regional planning and development so that local work force will be retained hence it will be easier to reduce urban poverty.

**Jesma J Macedo and M. James Antony,** in their paper entitled *' Problems of Domestic Female Workers(A Micro Study)'* stated that domestic work remained unrecognized as a legitimate form of activity. It was thus 'invisible' even within the domain of unorganized work. Even today, it is no surprise that domestic workers are not addressed as a group of workers who need support from the state- in the form of regular and fair wages, holidays, safe conditions of work, pension benefits. This paper is based on the primary data collected from randomly selected 130 female domestic workers both full time and part time. In his study he stated that comparatively workers of SC category are poorly paid than other community workers. Being within the four walls of the employer's house and often being the sole worker in the household, puts the women in a particularly vulnerable position. Abuses could take oral, physical and sexual form, besides curtailment of basic human rights of the workers. Verbal abuse refers to inconsiderate and indiscriminate scolding of workers by employers as a way of exercising authority. The author felt that the governments have a long way to regularize and protect this section of workers in the unorganized category.

**Dnyandev Talule and M.H.Shinde,** in their paper named *'Determinants of Self Employability of Female Informal Entrepreneurs (A field level investigation)'*, expressed that, Feminization of workforce and self-employment activities amongst women are the predominant outcomes of post reforms economic policy. The number of women in self-employment is continuously increasing. Education, financial abilities of families, banking facilities and state policies towards small scale industries after the 1980s have increased the number of self employed women in urban areas. His paper is an attempt to study the determinants of self-employability of 150 female informal entrepreneurs from Pune district of Maharashtra, where the concentration of women entrepreneurial activity of various kinds is more. The author revealed that the level of education and the probability of getting in to a self-employment are positively correlated. It was observed that the family background of all surveyed women entrepreneurs' has been well educated and in most cases their education attainment was of higher order. Most of the women entrepreneurs were housewives, and at the latter stage they entered into the business which is very positive change in case of such women. Encouragement and financial support given by family members can be identified as the major factor influencing to start the enterprise by a woman entrepreneur.Possessing technical expertise through education could be a most prompting reason for starting an enterprise as one feels compulsory to utilize the skills one possesses.

**Satinder Rana, and Shanno Thakur,** in their paper entitled *' Impact of Climate Change on Informal Labor Migration'* described that, in many poor countries, climate change has aggravated the problem of water, access to energy, food security, infrastructure, loss of livestock, indebtedness, hunger and loss of lives. People who have no adaptability and less immune to cope with climatic changes prone to distress displacement for survival elsewhere. Climates changes are a significant cause of livelihood insecurity and it is one among the push factors for forced displacement of labor. Distress migrants are poor and generally in a week position to negotiate the terms of their displacement. Forced displacement hinders development by increasing pressure on urban infrastructure and services, undermining economic growth, increasing the risk of conflict and leading to worse health, educational and social indicators. Environmental degradation therefore undermines sustainable livelihoods and affects the rural poor by disproportionately affecting their health, livelihoods and security, and can aggravate poverty in already stressed urban environments. Stabilizing Greenhouse emissions to limit climate change is an insurance strategy for the world as a whole. Emission targets and energy efficiency targets are to be achieved with rational price policy. Successful adaptation coupled with stringent mitigation holds the key to human development. Rich countries have moral obligation to support adaptation in developing nations.

**Seepana Prakasam,** in his research paper entitled '*Income Levels of Migrant Informal labor in India (A field level investigation)*' analyzed that, rural urban migration is the fastest growing type of migration in India. Migrant workers are the most vulnerable section and they are more likely to be found working at very low wages in hazardous physical conditions. Instances of exploitation by employers and contractors are also widespread in the absence of any effective monitoring by government agencies. Poor people migrate from village economy with the hope that the towns and cities have enough opportunities to make them live happy, but what ultimately happened was that, they were moved from rural poverty to urban poverty. The author analytically examined wages, income levels and poverty among the informal migrant labor in Jammu and Visakhapatnam cities during pre and post migration scenarios. Even post migration, 35% of the households in Visakhapatnam and 30% of the households in Jammu are living below poverty line. The level of poverty is more than that of national poverty line because migrant labor wages are less than national minimum wages, moreover they don't have work on regular basis, and also cost of living is high in urban areas. Further the author suggested measures for the improvement of living conditions of migrant labor.

**Sheena Krishnan, U. and Meena Kumari,** in their paper entitled that *'Informal Labor in India (A Historical Perspective)'* described the socio economic conditions of informal (unorganized) labor during ancient times. A description is made on transformation of the labor class in various periods such as Indus valley, early Vedic, later Vedic, epic period, Buddhist period, period of Alexander's invasion, Mauryan period, Gupta period etc. A focus is made on the activities of the agricultural laborers in various regions of south India . Further the authors viewed that the labor centered activities contributed much to the development of trade relations between Kerala and other European countries .

**Narendra Jena,** in his paper entitled *'Emerging Employment Pattern In Unorganized manufacturing sector In India'*, stated that the globalization process has deregulated and liberalized the labor market in developing countries. He analyzed changing trend, pattern of employment in the unorganized manufacturing sector based on three rounds ($51^{st}$, $56^{th}$ & $62^{nd}$) of National Sample Surveys on unorganized manufacturing sector. Although there has been increase of employment in the unorganized manufacturing during the first study period i.e. 1994-95/2000-01, but it has declined during the second period i.e. 2000-01/2005-06. Further, there is a positive growth of female employment in both the periods. There is evidence of feminization of workers in unorganized manufacturing sector both in rural and urban areas The female employment has largely been concentrated in low-productive and labor intensive industry groups. Large part of female employment are of part-time and contractual in nature and the majority of female are engaged in tiniest enterprises. Thus it reflects the precarious conditions of women in the unorganized manufacturing sector. The optimism about the current pattern of female employment is cause for concern and rather than cheer.

**Sudipta Sarkar,** in her paper entitled *'Part-Time Paid Domestic Workers: An Exploration of their gendered relations At Home Sphere in Delhi '*, felt that informal sector in urban areas provides several work opportunities for the women who are unskilled, illiterate and poor. The irregular nature and low earnings of male members in the family compel women to enter in several low paid and insecure (work and environmental status) occupations, which serves as the only source of a supportive earning for the entire family. This paper is based on randomly selected 152 female domestic workers in Delhi. Majority of them belong to lower caste and the proportion of Hindus are highest than any other religious category in Delhi. Currently married women constitute the highest proportion of domestic workers followed by the widowed women in the study area. Illiteracy among the workers is very high and majority of the workers, in spite of their significant contributions, do not have any decision making power in their households and domination of husbands is more prominent. Much of the household income of these workers is spend on alcohol consumption of male members of the house.

In the last chapter **Hastimal Sagara,** in his paper entitled *'Working conditions of informal labor in IT &BPO sector (A case study of Gujarat)'*, stated that India is at the forefront of the rapidly evolving global IT-Business Process Outsourcing (BPO) market and is well established as a 'destination of choice'. The author explained the emergence and transformation of the IT sector in India in general and Gujarat in particular in the context of economic reforms which caused informalization of the labor force in IT sector. The focus of the study would be to identify the complex issues related to work and workers revenue, etc in the computer hardware, software services and IT-BPO sector in Gujarat. This paper is based on primary as well as secondary data sources. Employment in IT industry implies a host of insecurities and vulnerabilities. The work is too demanding, depressing and demeaning. Most of these youngsters are in fact burning out their formative years as 'cyber coolies'. The process of in-formalization in the IT/ITES sector which is characterized by flexible labor laws, absence of job/old age/social security, absence of trade union activities etc. Therefore, there is job dissatisfaction and attrition rate in BPOs, is around 25% on annual basis. There is increasing number of cases among the IT/ITES workers related to loss of sleep and appetite, indigestion, depression, break up of friend/ social circle etc. The employees seem frustrated, showing lack of interest in social activities, narrowing their friend circle and so on.

**Seepana Prakasam**

# 1

# Introduction

Despite its ameliorative stances, globalization accentuates the stark divide between the privileged class and the common man. There is no doubt that capital in the globalized economy perpetuate itself at the cost of labor. Considerably the large number of informal jobs are created in formal and informal sectors in all most all the developing economies. Wages and employee benefits are lower for informal workers when compared to formal workers. In India most of the credit goes to service sector and less credit goes to manufacturing sector and discredit goes to agriculture sector in generating informal employment during reforms. Underemployment has also increased in urban and rural areas among males and females. Female labor force participation is warranted by lose of jobs by male counter parts in formal sector or inadequate earnings of male members . Difficulty in getting regular jobs lead to actualization of labor force . The wage gap between regular and casual workers has increased considerably. Casual jobs are often at the bottom of the pile in terms of wages and job security. Implementation of new education policy lead to increase in gross enrolment ratio and level of education among workers. Most of the educated workers who lost their jobs in formal sector are settled in self employment activities. Self employment gives mixed income which is inclusive of operating surplus and wage income which will be more than simply employed for wages elsewhere.

Fiscal consolidation policy adopted by the government, reduced formal employment generation capacity of public sector, on the other hand private manufacturing sector adopted labor saving and capital intensive methods of production as a part of strategy to win competitive advantage over others. Liberalization is associated by earning profits which is possible mainly by reducing wage bill in total cost of production is became winning strategy of enterprises. All these factors caused to increase supply of labor in informal sector further imposed pressure on earnings and employment period of the existing labor. During globalization wage inequalities are increased between formal and informal jobs , because more skilled and highly educated workers are absorbed in formal sector. There are earnings differentials among informal jabs also i.e Casual, regular, home workers, contract workers and self employed workers. Liberalization which made easier to import technological equipment and knowhow by manufacturing sector, further aggravated capital intensive techniques, which reduced the necessity of uneducated, semi educated and low skilled labor force. Hence during reforms period the maximum number of army of unskilled labor force are absorbed in subsectors of service sectors i.e construction, trade, hotels, restaurants, transport, storage, communication, distribution, financial, personal , IT and IT enabled services. However all the forms of Informal employment fails to provide social security , minimum wages and decent work for labor , which may endanger our aim to achieve inclusive growth.

Informal sector represents an important part of the economy and the labor market in many countries, especially developing and transition countries in sub-Saharan Africa, Asia and Latin America. The term informal was introduced by Keith hart in his article on informal income opportunities in Ghana in 1970. Informal economy is comprised of all forms of informal employment i.e. employment without social protection in both the cases of self-employment and wage employment .There is widespread miss conception that the informal economy is somehow illegal or is the equivalent of the underground , or even criminal economy (Chen .M.A. 2006).

National Commission for Enterprises in Unorganized Sector defines[1] unorganized sector as " the unorganized sector consists of all un incorporated private enterprises owned by individuals or households engaged in the sale and production of goods and services operated on a proprietary or partnership basis with less than ten workers'. Whereas it defines informal workers "Unorganized/informal workers consists of those working in the informal sector or households, excluding regular workers with social security benefits provided by the employers and the workers in the formal sector without any employment and social security benefits provided by the employers'(NCEUS 2008, CH. 2).

Workers working in the informal economy can be classified according to the following employment status categories (1) Non-wage workers i.e. employers including owners of informal enterprises, operators of informal enterprises , self-employed heads of family business, own account workers , un paid family workers (2) wage workers i.e. employees of informal enterprises , domestic workers , casual workers, home workers (industrial out workers) temporary and part time workers, unregistered workers (Chen et al 2002). Informal sector can be further classified into two subsectors (1) The irregular sector and (2) the informal sector proper.

Unorganized sector is characterized by the temporary, seasonal and changing nature of employment often resulting in long periods of unemployment, absence of a fixed employer and employee relationship , wages are lesser than minimum and not fixed on the basis of collective bargaining or backed by law. Poor working environment, long working hours, irregular incomes and poor or no security of employment ,low productivity, low earnings, low quality jobs ( bad jobs), no decent work conditions, no social security, no job satisfaction , no fringe benefits, hence suffering from chronic poverty .An increase in the share of informal sector implies a deterioration in the quality of employment. Mostly workers displaced from jobs have found employment in informal sector and most new workers have also to resort to this sector for earning their livelihood either as self-employed or wage earners ( Papola 2004). The larger percentage of the informal labor are illiterates and living below poverty line. Moreover to seek employment in informal sector, requires lesser amount of skill, capital and education , hence it is relatively easy to get employment.

Transaction costs of entering into formal sector ( long procedure, bribes, time consumption, fees , red tapism ) ,encourages to prefer and join the informal sector ( Siddhartha and Mitra 2005). Workers who settled in informal sector are belongs to socially backward groups. The variety of work force including agriculture labor, construction labor and labor in traditional industries including leather tanning , handloom, fishing , forestry , salt making , street vending and household industry and also village artisans who fall under the broad generic categories of the unorganized sector.

Informal sector is an important source of employment for women than formal employment. Women are collaborative and self-help and traditional practices and initiatives in the informal sector are vital economic resource (The world's women, UNO 2005). In India and Indonesia the informal sector accounts for nine out of every ten women working outside agriculture. This sector is larger source of employment for women than for men (UN 2000) . Women are poorer than men working in this sector. The majority of women in the informal sector are own account traders and producers or casual and contract workers, relatively few are employers who hire paid workers .The gender gap in income / wages appears higher in the informal sector than in the formal sector.

**Growth of Informal/Sector and Employment**.

In developing nations , Globalization intensified labor market dualism and most of the jobs are created in informal sector. The composition of employment between formal and informal sectors had changed. Greater competition pressures forces, formal sector firms to outsource labor and production to the informal sector and workers who lost their jobs in import substituting industries are also forced to join in informal sector. Shift of labor from formal to informal, the demand and supply forces caused reduction in wages and increase in wage inequalities between the sectors. Firms are responded for hiring more temporary or contract workers who are outside the purview of job security regulations , and free from labor market institutions ( Ramaswamy 2008).

The model of flexible work which has become the hall mark of globalization, has profoundly altered the way workers live and relate to each other (D.N. Reddy 2005). Commenting against the argument, that the flexibility leads to more efficiency and increased investment , Stieglitz viewed that " the mantra of increased labor market flexibility was only a thinly disguised argument to roll back under the guise of economic efficiency- gains that workers had achieved over years and years of bargaining political activity". This flexibility enhances the welfare of capital class at the expense of workers. If labor is treated like other commodities it leads to bad consequences, on the other hand competitiveness strategy leads to a reduction of workers living standards( Paul Burkett quoted in Bina et al 1996 ). Reduction in subsidies , and decline in public investment on agriculture , lifting of quantitative restrictions , commercialization of agriculture , crop failure , high cost of credit badly affected earnings of rural informal labor in general and women labor in particular.

**Magnitude of Informal Employment.**

Over the past two decades employment in the informal sector has risen rapidly in all regions in the world. The share of informal sector in non-agricultural GDP is between 45 to 60 percent in developing nations. Informal employment comprises 50 percent to 75 percent of non-agricultural employment in developing nations. 65 percent in Asia, 51 percent in Latin America , 48 percent in north Africa, 72 percent in Sub Saharan Africa. If employment in agriculture also included in the informal employment , the share of informal employment in India will increase from 83 percent to 93 percent, from 55 to 62 percent in Mexico, from 28 to 34 percent in south Africa ( Santos Mehrotra and Maruio Biggeri, 2008). A higher % of people working in the informal sector, relative to formal sector are poor. The average income of both men and women are lower in the informal sector than in the formal sector.

### Informal Employment In India

Unorganized sector in India, contributes around 60 percent of total net value added, and 60 percent of the total household savings originates from the unorganized sector. Around 30 percent of exports and 41 percent of manufacturing exports is contributed by this sector (Ghatate 1999). Table 1.1 reveals that the un organized sector accounts for 92 percent of the total work force of about 457 million (NCEUS 2007). Total employment in India has increased from 397 million to 457 million between 1999-2000 and 2004-05. Informal employment has increased from 361.7 million to 422.6 million, whereas formal employment has declined from 35 million to 34.9 million during the same period. The change in the organized or formal employment has been marginally negative. The entire increase in the employment in the organized sector over this period has been informal in nature, and the terms and conditions of employment are usually precarious.

That the annual growth of employment in the organized sector has declined from 1.2 percent during 1983-94 to –o.38 % during 1994-2004. Even in the organized sector the proportion of unorganized workers has increased from 20.5 (37.8percent) million to 29.1 (46.4percent) million in the same period. So the broad trends in the labor market seem to point towards normalization. (Economic survey 2007).The failure of public and private organized sectors to provide employment to the growing labor force , the responsibility unwontedly delegated to the informal sector (Amitab Kundu).

There is significant increase in the self-employment category during the period 1999-2000 to 2004-05 in both rural and urban areas ,but this kind of employment is not remunerative. Self-employment is also seen as an index of marketisation of the economy. Now the market is gaining importance over the state .The 61 round NSSO data reveals that nearly 2/3 of the jobs are in the category of self-employment in which there is no direct employer . This has led (Chandrasekhar and Ghosh 2007) to ask the question, how one ensure decent work conditions when the absence of a direct employer? The dangerous consequence of growing self-employment is the self-exploitation by workers in a competitive market.

The regional concentration of informal workers are concerned, out of total workforce, 94% are informal workers in the states like Bihar, UP. MP, Orissa and Rajasthan. In industrially advanced states like Maharashtra, Gujarat, Tamil Nadu ,West Bengal the share of un organized workers close to 90% of the total work force . In Goa, Delhi, and Kerala accounted for ¾ of the total work force are informal workers. Lower the level of urbanization , higher the percentage of informal sector employment and a positive association between incidence of poverty and informal sector employment ( Anup Metra 2001).

The number of migrated urban workers is increasingly being pushed into the informal sector. These working poor are not entitling to social security and job security benefits hence generally face greater vulnerability. In India among the working population 29 percent belongs to poor households in 1999-2000 in the prime age groups (15-60) in urban areas fell from 40% .In spite of falling poverty , the highest proportion of poor was among the casual workers , it is being 52% among men and 62% among women (urban poverty report 2009).

Informality can impose considerable costs on the economy, hence policies will be needed to encourage informal sector to become formal. Informality is encouraged in an economy when firms seek to avoid the transaction costs of complying with regulations concerning registration, licensing and taxation. In the long run , however , the costs of informality can be high for firms and for the economy. Firms may avoid official taxes but pay bribes to corrupt officials (World Bank , 2010). Informal sector firms are less access to low cost capital, reliable electricity supply and other business services because of lack of legal status. Hence government need to take steps to encourage firms to become formal. Provide supporting environment for the growth of productivity and improvement in working conditions in the informal sector. Impose penalties for non compliance with formal sector regulations.

**Footnotes**

[1] The terms 'unorganised sector' and 'informal sector' are used in this report interchangeably, which is a general practice followed in India. Accordingly, informal employment is referred to as unorganised sector employment. Whenever, reference is made to informal/unorganised sector and informal/ unorganised sector conjointly, the term 'informal economy' is used. These concepts are in accordance with the definitions followed by the National Commission for Enterprises in the Unorganised Sector (NCEUS) in India.

## References

Arjun Sen Gupta et .al (2005); India's common people – who are they , how many are they and how do they live ? *Economic and political weekly*. March 15- 2008..

Amitab Kundu and Niranjan Sarangi (2007); Dynamics of labor market under globalization . changing characteristics of informal employment in India . *Indian Journal of Labor Economics* . Vol 50. No 2.

Amitab Kundu and Alak N Sharma (2001); edit. Informal sector in India perspectives and policies . Institute of human development and institute of applied manpower research. New Delhi.

Chen. M.A.(2007); Rethinking the informal economy linkages with the formal economy and the formal regulatory environment. *Linking The Formal And Informal Economy , Concepts and Policies,* edit Basudeb, et .al. oxford University press, New Delhi

Jeemol Unni (2008); Women workers in the new economy . *The Indian Journal of Labor Economics* . Vol 51, No. 4.

Jyati Ghosh and C.P.Chandrasekhar (2006); Employment growth ; the latest trends (17 th November 2006), the results of the latest suvey of the 61st round covering 2004-05.

Kannan. K.P (2008); Dualism , informality and social inequality . Presidential address at golden jubilee conference of Indian society of labor economics . Dec 13-15

Kundu Amit (2006); wage employment relationship in the agriculture ;labor market of West Bengal . *Indian Journal of Labor Economics* . vol 49, no. 4, PP 681-690.

Mahendradev.(2002); Growth mediated and support led social security in the un organized sector in India . *The Indian Journal of Labor Economics*. Vol. 45. No. 2.

Narasimha Reddy D.(2005); Challenges of decent work in the globalizing world. *Indian Journal of Labor Economics* . Vol 48. No.1.

NCEUS (2008); Report on conditions of work and promotion of livelihoods in the unorganized sector . govt of India , New Delhi . also published by academic foundation , New Delhi.

Paola .T.S. (2004); Globalization, employment and social protection, emerging perspectives for the Indian workers. *Indian Journal of Labor Economics* .vol. 47. no.3.

Patnaik, Utsa, (2006); poverty and neo liberalism in India , based on Rao Bahadur kale memorial lecture delivered at Ghokale institute of politics and economics Pune, Feb.3.

Ruddar Datt.(2002); Employment policies and the un organized sector . *Indian Journal of Labor Economics* . Vol. 45, No.2.

Ramaswamy .K.V (2008); Globalization , employment and labor market flexibility . India development report 2008. oxford.

UNO (2005); *The world's women*.

World Bank (2010) India's employment challenge, creating jobs, helping workers. Oxford University Press , New Delhi.

# 2

# Migrant Laborers in the Urban Informal Sector ( A Socio-Economics Analysis)

**Abstract**

*This paper does a comparative analysis of the live and livelihood of inter-state migrant construction laborers. The sample comprises 800 migrant laborers, 400 each of male and female construction laborers. Various aspects covered in this paper are their education and caste profile; quality of living and gender disparities in wages and income. The study finds that the human rights of these internal migrant laborers engaged in the construction activities in urban informal sector are grossly violated, more particularly those of women laborers. Neither the government nor the agencies involved in the welfare of these informal workers are serious about their well-being. The laws formulated for their well-being are mere paper exercises and hardly found implemented in the ground to raise their well-being. The country has to go a long way to promote the well-being of these internal migrant workers working in the urban informal sector with a gender perspective.*

## Introduction

Migration has now become an essential characteristic feature of modern society, as it consists of a variety of movements that can be described in aggregate as an evolutionary and development fostering process operating in time and space to correct rural-urban, inter-urban and inter-regional imbalances (Joshi, 1994). Migration in general and internal or inter-state migration of labor in particular is an age-old phenomenon in India. The Government of India has defined inter-state migrant workman as "any person who is recruited by or through a contractor in one state under an agreement or other arrangement for employment in an establishment in another state, whether with or without the knowledge of the principal employer in relation to such establishment."[1] While analyzing 1991 census data Srivastava (1998) found that Uttar Pradesh and Bihar constituted one-third of inter-state migration. On the contrary, the agricultural and industrial development of Punjab has created an additional demand for labor force, which has been met by the migrant labor hailing from backward areas of states of Uttar Pradesh, Bihar, Himachal Pradesh, Haryana, Rajasthan, Jammu and Kashmir and Orissa (Chand and Others, 1998). Really Punjab has been demanding labor for various activities through pull factors from the neighboring states of Uttar Pradesh, Jammu and Kashmir and Rajasthan since long (Sidhu and Rangi, 1998). In recent years, it is observed that the youth in rural areas of Punjab are not adequately motivated to work in the agricultural sector as laborer, therefore, the large and even medium scale land holders are seeking laborers from Uttar Pradesh and Bihar during the sowing and harvesting season of the crops. This seems, Punjab is dependent of migrant labor both in urban as well as rural areas to perform menial laborer activities. Sighting the reasons for inter-state migration, Kumar and others (1998) said that there is exodus of rural youth not only from landless families but also from land owning upper castes from villages of Bihar. This is happening because of land-man ratio has deteriorated and economic hardship has grown. Similarly, the out-migration from rural areas of Orissa is due to the absence of assured irrigation, small operational holding accompanied by the use of mono-cropping and absence of non-farm opportunities (Mahapatra, 1998). The push and pull factors play key role in determining the extent of internal migration (Narasimhan and Chandra, 1998). The economic reform process, commonly labeled as 'LPG'-Liberalization, Privatization and Globalization initiated in early 1990's in India abetted not only the pace of urbanization but also fostered the velocity of internal migration mostly from rural to urban areas in the country. It is rightly remarked that although the migration has become a worldwide phenomenon and the process of industrialization and urbanization has made it inevitable (Joshi, 1994).

**Inter-state Migration and Informal Sector**

1980s has been the romanticism of the informal sector as a vehicle for labor absorption and means of redistribution (Standing, 1999) and informalization was recognized as one of the critical components of capitalist globalization (Munch, 2002). After 1980s and particularly after 1990s, most of the laborer migrated to the urban areas absorbed in the informal sector, characterized by long working hours, absence of any social security and wage payments, which are generally below the legal minimum (Srivastava, 1998). Logically, in the developing countries including India, where there is surplus of labor and dearth of employment opportunities in organized sector, informal sector will continue to play a pivotal role in the labor absorption and employment. Moreover, the economic liberalization, privatization and globalization would make this sector more vibrant from the stand point of production of goods and services, employment and income generation. Pais (2002) remarked that the growing size of informal employment of which casual employment forms a subset, current concern becomes important due to growing casualization of the workforce and its links with the quickened pace of liberalization all through the 1990s.Thus, given the country's economic dynamics, the issues related to unorganized sector in India in terms of employment and income as well as social well-being of the population depending on this sector assumes great importance (Sen,

2002). However, Rani and Unni (2004) argued that the ongoing flexibilization process world over has no doubt created new jobs, most of them informal, but they lie beyond the reach of labor legislation and social protection and are characterized by low incomes and high levels of insecurity.

The unorganized or informal sector plays a crucial role in India's employment and production front. It accounts for over 90 percent of workforce. According to available statistics, there are more than 400 million working people (employed persons above the age of 15) in our country. Out of these, only 28 million (7 percent) belong to the organized sector. Putting it differently, 9 out of 10 Indians belong to the sectors that are not organized (Monteiro, 2006). According to a recent study, a staggering 394.9 million workers or 86 percent of India's working population, work in the unorganized sector without a social security cover. The report has also envisaged that between 1999-2000 and 2004-05 there has been increase in the informal employment both in organized and unorganized sector. [2] The unorganized sector of the urban economy provides an easy access to opportunities of work and thereby a means of livelihood for the deprived segments of the urban society as well as the migrants from the rural sector (Reddy and Vinodini, 2005). Despite its contribution, unorganized labor has been left aside both by their employers and even by the government. The degree of socio-economic conditions of unorganized workers deployed in the informal sector varies from state to state and cities to cities, yet as commonly understood many of them are subject to the stereotypes of apathy and misery. In spite of misery, migration can generate substantial benefits not only for migrants themselves but also for areas of origin and destination (Oberai and Sardana, 1989).

**Internal Migration and Urban Problems**

As the process of urbanization have been taking place ahead of industrialization in the Third World countries, a substantial part of the enhanced labor force is being absorbed not in the formal organized sector, but in a sector called 'informal or unorganized sector', where they created their own employment to the extent their capital and skill would permit (Chakarbarti, 2002). The experience of developing countries like India reveal that the modern sector, due to its relatively slow pace of growth and emphasis on highly capital intensive techniques, cannot absorb the natural growth of the urban workforce (Singh and Aggarwal, 1998). The internal migration of unskilled and semiskilled workforce from the rural areas to urban areas with the urge for employment and higher earning has vitiated many urban problems such as housing, health care, drinking water, sanitation and education.

The rural-urban migration is persisting in spite of high rates of urban unemployment (Oberai and Singh, 1983).The migrants may simply burden the urban economy through increased unemployment and under-employment, lower levels of productivity and a greater demand for urban services (Obrien and Sardana, 1989). Truly, rural-urban migration is now seen as a major factor contributing to the ubiquitous phenomenon of urban surplus labor, as a force, that continues to exacerbate already serious urban unemployment problems caused by economic and structural imbalances between urban and rural areas (Tadaro, 1993). Mukherji(2006) commented that the metropolises are very fast becoming the scenes of extreme social and economic inequalities where in abundant affluence among a handful few stand hanging and overlooking abject poverty among the masses down below. These kinds of situation may create a dangerously eruptive situation-which is conducive to unleash in the near future extreme social disorder, severe class conflict, crimes, widespread violence and urban civil war.

It is not flight of fancy, but delicately the economic system and urban development of a country copiously bank on unorganized sector and unorganized workers. It is said that migration and urbanization act as a catalyst for economic and social advance (Oberai and Sardana, 1989). In a labor surplus economy like India, rural-urban migration on sufficient scale may also reduce under-employment and disguised unemployment in the rural areas, improve distribution through remittances, and waken the traditional, outmoded, semi-feudal agrarian structure (Oberai and Sardana, 1989).

**Informal Sector and Migrant Workers**

Formal-Informal distinction is the most recent development in dualistic thinking, that is, it can be considered a theoretical reaction to the stagnation in socio-economic development in countries like India, a stagnation which undermined the propositions at the base of modernization (Streefker, 1981). In India, the term unorganized sector is of recent origin and has been in use only during the last two-three decades. The First National Commission of Labor, under the chairmanship of Justice Gajendragadkar defined the unorganized sector as that part of the workforce, who have not been able to organize in pursuit of a common objective because of constraints such as:(i) casual nature of employment; (ii) ignorance and illiteracy; (iii) small size of employments with low capital investment per person employed; (iv) scattered nature of establishments and (v) superior strength of employer operating singly or in combination. The unorganized workforce are: (a) contract labor including construction workers; (b) casual labor; (c) labor employed in small scale industries; (d) handloom/power loom workers; (e) beedi/cigarette workers; (f) workers in tanneries; (f) tribal labor; and (g) other unprotected labor.[3] Further, the National Commission on Labor in India in 2002 has commended that unorganized sector is no way independent or exclusive sector but is dependent on the organized sector and the rest of the economy through variety of linkages such as raw material, capital, generation of employment, market facilities and so on. Although, the list is lengthy, it broadly includes, apprentices, causal and contract workers, home-based artisans, a section of self-employed persons involved in jobs such as vending, rag picking, and rickshaw pulling, agricultural workers, migrant laborer and those who perform manual and helper jobs come under this sector. Monteiro (2006) classified the unorganized sector as the sector where a large number are unregistered. Born in village homes, without birth certificates, having dropped out of school without leaving certificates, forced to migrate to distant cities for work, living in unauthorized slum dwellings, very often without any identity card for many their name on the voter list is the only record of their existence as Indian citizen. The occupation he has identified are: (i) worker in small industries; (ii) domestic workers; (iii) auto rickshaw drivers; (v) shop workers; (vi) loading and unloading workers; (vii) construction workers; (viii) sex workers; (ix) hotel and restaurant workers; (x) rag pickers; (xi) hawkers; (xii) small shop vendors; (xiii) security guard and so on. The migrants contribute to the growth of the urban economy through increased supply of unskilled and semi-skilled labor, greater labor productivity, higher incomes and diversification of industry and services (Oberai and Sardana, 1989).

**Construction Activities and Migrant Workers**

Liberalization process started since 1991 has boosted urban infrastructure development and propped up real estate business and construction activities in cities and towns of India. It is remarked that construction is a fundamental, integral part of economic development and provides many of the material benefits of progress: housing, schools, hospitals, transport, infrastructure, irrigation schemes, power stations, industrial plants, etc. (Satya Raju, 1994). With the globalization, construction activities are zooming up in not only metropolis but also in the medium and small cities. Construction accounts for 40-50 percent of the capital expenditure on projects in various sectors such as energy, transport, irrigation, social, communications, defense and rural and urban infrastructure (Roopa, 2004). It has substantially contributed to the gross fixed capital formation in the country. During the period of first three Five Year Plans, its contribution to the gross fixed capital formation in the country was over 60 percent and averaged 66 percent. During the Fourth and Fifth Five Year Plans the contribution averaged 56 percent and during the eighties, its contribution averaged 48 percent. The Tenth Five Year Plan records the main advantage of the construction industry in employment generation as being its ability to: (i) absorb rural labor and unskilled workers (in addition to the semi-skilled and some-skilled); (ii) provide opportunity for seasonal employment, thereby supplementing workers income from farming; and (iii) permit large-scale participation of women workers. However, the Tenth Five Year Plan document has identified lack of skilled workers and training facilities as ills affecting the efficiency of this sector. To redress, the Planning Commission has suggested: (i) training and skill certification progress; (ii) creating a data bank through registration of construction labor and allocating a permanent registration number; and (iii) provision for a stipulation for contracts; for a minimum percentage of trained and certified workers (Roopa, 2004). It was found that industry wise a higher percentage of migrant workers are in construction activities (Oberai and Singh, 1983). Estimates of the number of construction workers in the country vary from three million to 25 million. However, up to 95 percent of them are estimated to be temporary workers and a majority of them are seasonal labor. Despite its critical importance to the economy, this is one of the mostly neglected sectors from the human resource point of view. Sharma (1980) said that inspite of what some good-natured and well-being people may say or at least may desire, about the interests of the employers and the employees being identical, there is absolutely no doubt that, under present industrial system of free competition and of capitalist control, there is a clear conflict between the interests of the employers and of the employees as regards the conditions of service of the latter. Inspite of construction labor having been largely instrumental in bringing about development in Asian societies, its contribution has not been adequately acknowledged in the academic and policy domain (Kannan and Rutten, 2002).

**Women in Informal Sector**

During the past few years, there have been many studies concerning the employment of women, showing that women not only have reproductive tasks, but that they also take considerable part in productive task (Tom, 1989). However, in the productive task and sphere, they are largely marginalized, giving low profile jobs, lower wage rate, unskilled activities, etc. Therefore, it is stated that marginalization of women and the course of economic development are closely related (Tom, 1989). So also the process of division of labor goes hand in hand with process of women's marginalization (Baud, 1985). Considering weekly and daily status of NSSO data set, Kundu (1997) reports that " the growth rate of employment for women by weekly and daily status are higher compared to those by usual status. This could possibly be explained in terms of growth in demand for short duration employment in informal activities where women are generally preferred. For men, too, this has happened but to a lesser extent." Harnessing NSSO data, Mukhopadhyay (1999) reports a high incidence of female work participation in unorganized sectors in both rural and urban areas. Dissecting the issue of female marginalization of labor market in India, Parthasarathy and Nirmala (1999) probe into four aspects which they consider an index for women's marginalization: (i) low work participation rates; (ii) higher unemployment rates; (iii) casualizaiton of female labor; and (iv) shift to low paid occupations. According to Sakthivel and Bhattacharya (2002) female employment is typically characterized by under-recognition and under evaluation of their economic activities in developing economies like India. The United Nations has remarked that of late labor migration is getting feminized especially in developing countries.

The IInd Labor Commission Report has highlighted that women workers are vulnerable because their work is insecure, irregular, and often unrecognized. Besides these, they have to balance the work they have to do with their responsibilities for children and home. Since their income is not commensurate to their work, they do not own any assets and so do not have access to social security. They often have to incur debts to bear expenses for illness or other shocks (IInd Labor Commission Report, 2002). Tripathy (1996) noted "everywhere else, also in the construction work too, there exists the division of work between men and women in the "unskilled" jobs. Although, jobs such as balancing twelve bricks on the head while climbing the ladder and passing the bondlis of mixture along the heights in quick succession require dexterity and skill along with the great stamina and yet they are termed "unskilled" jobs by everyone concerned.....not understanding the fact that women do all the various types of work in many instances, women are always considered to be the lowest in the hierarchy of the system of sub-contract and therefore paid the lowest in the construction work." Further, women working in the unorganized sector lack supportive service like crèches and child care centers where women could leave their children during working hours. Sexual harassment is very acute in the sector. Contractors exploit young girl's even women, and women many a situation circumvents to their last. Banerjee (1985) observes that social neglect of these women as workers is evident from the fact that a large percentage of them never found any organization interested in them as workers. The main concerns of a women worker centers around her family, especially her children. She sacrifices continually for her children and for the family. She takes full responsibility of the children, sick and the old, for feeding the family and for carrying on the family obligations like rituals and ceremonies. She works for long hours, for money and for subsistence. She does all this with only one aim-better life for her family (Jhabvala and Sinha, 2001). Murali Manohar (1983) has remarked that the work situation of women working in the unorganized sector is no better. Nature of work has become burdensome. Manual and physical nature of jobs, encountering hardship in sun and rain alike did not yield any good rewards in return.

## The Study

The present study was carried out on the construction labor working in tri-city of Chandigarh, Puncukula and Mohali, former is a Union Territory and capital of Punjab and Haryana and the latter two are the cities of Haryana and Punjab respectively adjoining to Chandigarh in various construction activities such as roads, public and private building, apartments, shopping complexes, bridges and culverts, public parks, etc. . The sample covered 800 construction laborers, 400 each of male and female laborer.

## Discussion

The migrant unorganized construction laborers are working in the tri-city from dawn to the dusk to earn a livelihood for themselves and for their families. They have largely been migrated from the economically backward states and regions of the country. Besides, a colossal percentage of them belong to the economically impoverished families require their economic contribution for a sustainable livelihood. Sometimes, the natural calamities i.e. flood, cyclone, and severe drought in economically weaker states such as Bihar, Uttar Pradesh and Orissa, pushed many people including the young children less then employable age to the cities to search for work and income. All of them have migrated for many a reasons such as earn sustainable income for the family; repay family debt, give better education and health care to family members, purchase land, construct houses, saving for the future, etc. The data show that male laborers have been migrated mainly from the backward regions of Bihar and Uttar Pradesh; while female laborers have migrated largely from the underdeveloped and tribal areas of Madhya Pradesh and

Chhattisgarh. Because of traditional believes and values, the female from the rural areas of Bihar and Uttar Pradesh are reluctant to migrate along with the male members for performing menial works. Moreover, in these states, in the absence of male members, females are required to look after the agriculture and livestock, grooming children and caring of elderly. On the contrary, the tribal women of Madhya Pradesh and Chhattisgarh are hardworking and do not have much self-ego and least care for community and societal believes and values and in the absence of landed property these women prefer to move along with their male members in search of work to other states. Moreover, many of them have seen both their parents working for earning a livelihood for their families and they are traditionally from the labor class families. Thus pursuing labor work is a born family, societal and economic burden on many of them. They carry infant along with them and leave the adult and grown up children with the parents. Some move seasonally and while other regularly visit their home once or twice in a year for few days and weeks. Largely, these migrant laborers are the floating population in the in-migrating states. One of the studies on impact of migration on women conducted by Dayal and Karan(2003) in Jharkhand have noted that on the one side it leads to greater social and economic freedom, greater empowerment and more autonomy for women and on the other side it affects them adversely as it increases their workload, makes them more dependent and subordinate to men and in some cases causes even their sexual exploitation. While the out migration mainly of male from Uttaranchal has overburdened the women and have put them on increased labor effort on essential activities like cultivation, animal rearing, fuel and fodder collection, etc. apart from other domestic chores (Mamgain, 2003)

Ravenstein (1885) remarked, migrants move from areas of low opportunity to areas of high opportunity and migration accelerate with growth in the means of transport and communication and expansion of trade and industry.

Shrinking of employment; lower wage rate and poor proliferation of non-farm sector in rural areas in rural areas and massive infrastructure development in urban areas has created an environment of rural push and urban pull of internal migration of labor in the country. Chand and et.al (1998) has remarked that because of low level of development, subsistence level of agriculture and severe unemployment in Uttar Pradesh and Bihar, labor from these states forced to seek employment elsewhere. It is obvious that the people do not migrate to new places unless life in these places promises improvement and in a developing country this invariably means economic betterment (Joshi, 1994).The economic necessity is usually the most important single factor which has 'pushed' the migrants from their original abode to the city and among the 'pull' factors having relations in town was the most important for attracting the migrants (Vidyarthi, 1969).

**Social Aspects**

Human identity in Indian society is pre-determined by the caste, which has a strong civilizational root. Najma Khan(1986) said that "in spite of legal equality of opportunity, the institution of caste continues to posit as a decisive influence on the socio-economic and political spheres". Caste guarantees autonomy to a community and at the same time it brings that community into relation with numerous other communities all going on to form a hierarchy (Srinivas, 1952). Further, the occupation of an individual in most of the places and particularly in rural India are determined by caste . The caste system is the pivotal point in the stratification of the Indian society in hierarchical order (Joshi, 1994) .The gender discrimination begins at the community and caste level itself. The data in Table-2.1 depicts that the percentage of male construction laborer belonging to General Caste is significantly higher than the female. On the other hand, the percentage of female construction laborer belonging to

Scheduled Castes is significantly higher than the male. This clearly depicts that the male migration is caste neutral, while the migration of female laborer is caste-biased. The women migrant construction laborers largely belong to the Scheduled Caste and Scheduled Tribe families those are impoverished and landless households in rural areas. Poverty has pushed them out of the frame of traditional believes and values and caste-based obstruction. Further they also face least social criticism as compared to General Caste women. Thus the migration of female labor is largely influenced by caste. The male members of the Upper Caste community do not like to deploy their female members in menial works even if they are impoverished. In pressed circumstances, they even prefer to sale their property to meet the expenses than send and deploy their women in wage earning activities. The family and community members criticize the male members engaging their female members in menial labor work.

**Table-2.1: Caste Profile of Male/Female Migrant Construction Labor**

| Type | Male | Female | Gender Gap (in%) |
|---|---|---|---|
| General Caste | 78 (19.5) | 38 (9.5) | 10.0 |
| Other Backward Castes(OBCs) | 150 (37.6) | 110 (27.5) | 10.1 |
| Scheduled Caste | 158 (39.4) | 220 (55.0) | -15.6 |
| Others(Scheduled Tribes + Muslims) | 14 (3.5) | 32 (8.0) | -4.5 |

Note: Figures in parenthesis show percentages to their respective totals

The rural-urban migrants are likely to have lower levels of education and education and skill acquired in the rural areas may not be as relevant as those acquired in the urban areas (Peek and Antolinex, 1977). Migrants mainly are the illiterate, economically weak and oppressed (Kumar and Prasad, 1998).The illiteracy rate among the women migrant construction laborers is significantly higher compared to male laborers. The female illiteracy rate among migrant construction worker is 81 percent, while in case of male it is 44.5 percent (Table-2.2). Among the literate, the gender gap is significant at primary and secondary and above level of education. Even if educated their level of education is very low and a large percentage of them have elementary education. One of the key reasons for low level of literacy among these women migrant unskilled construction laborers is high dropout rate at different levels of education. Besides, the late start of education, onset of puberty and urge by the parent to give them marriage at an early age are a few among many factors restricted their scope to acquire education. Moreover, with scanty income, the impoverished and illiterate parents prefer to invest in the education of boys than girls, as a result both the illiteracy and low level of literally become a permanent feature of gender discrimination in these laborer class families. The impoverished families prefer to educate their children if it is free and the cost of education including book, copies, and dresses is substantially low. During abject poverty many of them withdrew their children and put them in paltry income earning and household activities. Therefore, even if the education is free for many families still it is a luxury, which they could hardly afford.

**Table-2.2: Educational Profile of Male/Female Migrant Construction Labor**

| Type | Male | Female | Gender Gap (in%) |
|---|---|---|---|
| Illiterate | 178 (44.5) | 324 (81.0) | -46.5 |
| Primary | 130 (32.5) | 44 (11.0) | 21.5 |
| Middle | 80 (20.0) | 28 (7.0) | 13.0 |
| Secondary & Above | 12 (3.0) | 4 (1.0) | 2.0 |

Note: Figures in parenthesis show percentages to their respective totals
Source :-Based on field level investigation

## Human Aspects

Migrant laborers are the genesis as well as victims of urban pollution and insanitation. The Report of the National Commission on Labor has envisaged that temporary residential sheds put up for construction workers lack minimum facilities. Crèche facilities are not available at work sites and social security benefits are virtually non-existent because of various constraints such as lack of stable nexus between employers and employee, instability of employment, poor and uncertain earnings of workers, and unreliable duration of works, etc.

**Table-2.3: Quality of Living of Male/Female Migrant Construction Labor**

| Type | Male | Female | Gender Gap (in%) |
|---|---|---|---|
| Living in Kuchha Houses | 178 (44.5) | 386 (96.5) | -52.0 |
| Using open field for defecation | 70 (17.5) | 388 (97.0) | -79.5 |
| Using safe drinking water | 400 (100.0) | 400 (100.0) | 0 |

Note: Figures in parenthesis show percentages to their respective totals
Source :-Based on field level investigation

The quality of living of women construction laborer is not salubrious as compared to the male laborer. 96.5 per cent of women construction worker are living in the temporary accommodations either in the construction sites or in the slums and 97 per cent of them are using open field for defecation, which is significantly higher than their male counterpart (Table-2.3). The living conditions in these ephemeral structures become dodgy during rainy and winter seasons and precarious during cyclone. This signifies that the male construction laborer is enjoying better quality of live than the female who bear double burden of managing their families and the burden of insanitation. The lower quality of living, coupled with lower nutritional intake and higher amount of physical labor severely affect their health. Most of them look stunted manifesting a gap between their appearances and actual age. The physical work burden without any proper rest and nutrition during pregnancy sometimes resulted in spontaneous abortion of pregnancy and even premature deliveries. Thus women who are surmised to be more secured are in hardship. Rao (1984) also noted that "construction industry without providing for the welfare of the laborers results in slums and worst form of exploitation by middlemen....Though it is believed that migration is means to cross the poverty line for most laborers by increasing their income, their benefit will be offset by not creating better working and living conditions, by suitable programmes." Their paltry income forces them to squeeze their expenditures on food, clothing and shelter. They customarily buy dresses on sale sold at throw away prices; eat low cost simple diet; and their dress code easily personifies them as migrant labor. Their prime objective is to save, save, save and send remittances by forgoing healthy living. The propensity to send remittances was higher among migrants who migrated outside the state than among those who migrated within the state (Bhatia and Kaur, 1998).

### Economic Aspects

The women laborers are also victim of free market forces and are discriminated and marginalized in the labor market. They perform most of the unskilled hard labor such as carrying bricks and cement mixture on their head, breaking the stones, which expose them to health hazard such as backache, body pain and sometimes spontaneous abortion during advanced stage of pregnancy. The wages which they get are not in commensuration to their labor. Besides, their wages are significantly lower than their male counterpart for the same kind and sometime more unskilled hard work. The disgruntled *'mistri'*/sub-contractors pay them lower wage rate than their asking rate and sometimes far below the minimum wage rate prevailing in the in-migrating state. They are the victims of twin hardships such as gender discrimination and market discrimination. These women work eight to nine hours in a day with half an hour launch break in between. Some carries launch boxes along with them; those who stay in the work site quickly prepare their plain launch, which are insufficient in minimum required calories. The *Mistri* stands on their head and hardly allow them to sit for a movement during the working hour. Most of these women migrant laborers are vulnerable and victim of exploitation and discrimination.

**Table 2.4 : Wage Rate of Male/Female Migrant Construction Labor**

| Type | Male | Female | Gender Gap (in Rupees) | Paired 't' values |
|---|---|---|---|---|
| Mean minimum wage rate in the tri-city | 91.94 | 62.15 | 29.79 | 5.64* |
| Mean minimum wage rate in the home place | 42.40 | 35.5 | 6.9 | 3.61* |
| Mean maximum wage rate in the tri-city | 112.86 | 73.5 | 39.36 | 6.45* |
| Mean maximum wage rate in the home place | 50.87 | 44.2 | 6.67 | 2.71* |
| Mean Monthly Income in the tri-city | 2438.78 | 1768.75 | 670.03 | 5.89* |

□ Significant at .01 level of probability
Source: Based on field level investigation

**Table 2.5: SDs and Variances of Male, Female and Gender Gap of different Variables**

| Variables | SD (of %) | | | Variance (of %) | | |
|---|---|---|---|---|---|---|
| | Male | Female | Gender Gap | Male | Female | Gender Gap |
| Caste | 16.92 | 21.87 | 12.46 | 286.21 | 478.50 | 155.21 |
| Education | 17.75 | 38.06 | 30.40 | 315.17 | 1448.25 | 924.17 |
| Quality of Living | 42.06 | 1.89 | 40.37 | 1769.25 | 3.58 | 1630.08 |

Source: Based on field level investigation

The values of variances in Table-2.5 are 155.21, 924.17 and 1630.08 respectively for caste, education and quality of living. The variance value for the quality of living of women is nearly ten times higher than the caste and one and half times higher than the education for women, which clearly reveals that the women migrant laborers are enjoying an astoundingly lower quality of life as compared to their male counterpart. Educationally also the women are more backward than their male counterpart for male variance value is 315.17, while for the female it is 1448.25. As far as quality of life is concerned, the variance value for male is 1769.25 and for female it is 3.58, means the negative indictors like the percentage of women living in *kaccha* houses and open defecation are closer to the positive indicator of their access to safe drinking water.

## Conclusions

These innocent inter-state migrant laborers are marginalized in the in-migrating state; they are being ill-treated and even cheated by the employers/contractors. They live in sub-human conditions and are marginalized both economically and socially. The human rights of migrant construction laborers are violated. Those are: (i) right to equal wage for equal work; (ii) right to access to quality health care services; (iii) right to medical and maternity benefit; (iv) right to education for themselves and for their children; (v) right to access to subsidized food; (vi) right to registration and form union; and (vii) right to access to healthy home and sanitary environment.

The migrant women construction laborers suffer from a lot of hardship and their human rights are mostly violated. Some of the gender discrimination which they face are: (i) they perform strenuous unskilled labor jobs compared to their male counterpart; (ii) maltreated in the open labor market, the *mistri*/sub-contractor pay less than the minimum wage rate and because of fear of losing work they confess more than what they actually get. The female construction laborer get significantly lower wages than their male counterpart for the same work and employed by the same contractors. In other words, they are discriminated in the labor market; (iii) they are not paid any medical benefit for injuries caused during working hour and maternity benefit during delivery; (iv) stay in unsanitary conditions and temporary *kachha* accommodations and (v) they face hardship both in the home as well as in the workplace.

Some of the problems faced by the male migrant construction laborers are follows:

- Migrant laborers do not get regular work and usually remain without work for one half week in a month. They consider it as wastage of time and loss of income. As their sole motto is to earn as much as possible by working as much as days available, the non-availability of work is denial of opportunity.
- Some of them opined that the contractors exploit them mentally, economically and physically. As these workers are not registered, it provides an opportunity to the contractors to exploit them. Many times they pay less what they are agreed, make weakly payment and even delayed payment and some even refuse to pay and instead threaten to beat them and tortured them by lodging false allegation.[5]These marginalized workers have no alternative but to bear these atrocities with the fear that they may be thrown out of the work. One of the features of informal sector is absence of labor unions, which is an advantage for the employers to exploit the workers.
- Neither the employer nor the unscrupulous contractors take care of the causalities happening at the work place. There is no provision of first aid facility on behaves of the contractors or compensation for health hazard during working

hours. In case of causalities, they spend money from their own pocket. It can be remarked that the destinies of the workers are linked with the machinations of a large number of contractors on whose whims and fancies, likes and dislikes, depend the availability of work for this type of labor. These middlemen have the least regard for the health and welfare of the workers, and in fact, exploit them by taking advantage of their economic dependence and ignorance.

- There is no system of registration of these workers and sometimes police personnel harass by asking them to show identity card. Many of them opined that they have to bribe them in order to be free from their clutches. One of the laborers said that all on a sudden a few police personnel started beating them in the 'labor chwak' by saying that you are not entitled to gather here and a few of them severely injured. This happens because these are informal place for labor market. Thus these poor workers are not free from the atrocities of the police. Instead of getting protection from the people, they become victim of their atrocities. Besides, in case of accidental deaths, it becomes difficult on the part of the medical authority and police to handover the dead body to their relatives.[6]
- Many those who have family with them face difficulties in getting their children admission to the schools. Even if admitted, their children do not get equal treatment from the teacher as those of other children. In the public hospitals also, they are not treated equally and many of them have to wait for long times in a queue for getting treatment. They are discriminated and marginalized in the social sphere.

- Most of the youth migrant laborer lamented that they do not have any family life. They squander prime phase of their life by staying away from their family. Their children are deprived of parental care and guidance and proper education and ultimately succumb to the vicious circle of labor in which they are being trapped. Mishra(1999) said that "migration being the movement of human beings in pursuit of better employment, better wages and better quality of life, there is apparently nothing objectionable...It becomes objectionable when human greed, rapacity and exploitations instincts of employers, contractors and sub-contractors take over the finer aspects of human character which may be characterized by the denial of dignity, justice, equity and the inalienable human rights of certain downtrodden sections of the society."[7]
- There is general lack of social security such as old age pension, health insurances, life insurances, etc. and while giving an account, one of the laborer said that their fellow laborer are leading miserable life in their villages. The long absence from the family has created mistrust between husband and wife of many families. As a result, even some of them are leading secluded life.

The inter-state marginalized unskilled migrant laborers are facing discrimination and deprivation in the social and economic spheres in the in-migrating states. Their human rights are grossly violated. Although the migration is somewhat economically beneficial, it is socially detrimental. They are precisely segregated from the urban society and are living in sub-human conditions. They are the victim of labor market elasticity and fluctuations, which is adversely affecting their earnings and living conditions. In addition, women migrant laborers are vulnerable to gender based discrimination and injustices. They are poor but many of them are not recognized as people below poverty line in the in-migrating state and thus denied of benefits under poverty eradication schemes. Moreover, it is observed that the women migrant laborers and gender poverty is synonymous. The urban informal sector and laws enacted for the unorganized workers have failed to protect the rights of these workers.

## Notes

1. The Compact Committee appointed by the Government of India which submitted its report in 1978 recommended enactment of a legislation, the framework of which was furnished along with the report. In accordance with the recommendations of the committee, the Inter-state Migrant Workmen (Regulation of Employment and Conditions of Services) Act 1979 was passed by the Union Parliament. The Act has defined the Inter-state migration as quoted.
2. Finding from a recent survey (2004-05) compiled by the National Commission for Enterprise in Unorganized Sector (NCEUS) in the Report on conditions of work and promotion of livelihood in the unorganized sector, Published in Hidustan Times, August 10, 2007 in the front page.
3. IInd Labor Commission Report , *Report of the National Commission of Labor,* Shri Ravindra Verma (Vol.I Part I) Akalank Publication New Delhi, 2002.
4. *Report of the National Commission of Labor,* Shri Ravindra Verma Akalank Publication New Delhi, 2002.
5. It was reported in the Hindustan Times September, 14 2008 that four laborers were allegedly tortured by their contractors. They beat them up with iron rods and tied their hands and legs with ropes before giving them electric shocks. These laborers were working on a bridge on the Panchkula-Hallomajra road.
6. It was reported in the Hindustan Times on 9th April 2008 that unclaimed bodies of the migrant laborers dyeing due to accident poses problem for post-mortem
7. Quoted from L. Mishra, *Unorganized Labor Deprivation and Emancipation,* Manak Publication, New Delhi, 1999.

## References

Banerjee, N (1985), "Modernization and Marginalization", *Social Scientist,* No. 149-150, Oct-Nov, pp 13-25

Bhatia, A S and Kaur, G (1998), "Rural Out-migration and Remittance: A Case Study of Patiala District" *The Indian Journal of Labor Economics,* Vol.41, No.4, pp799

Baud, I S A (1985), *Industrial Sub Contracting: The Effect of Puttigout Systems on Poor Working Women in India,* Onge Publicerde Versie.

Chakraborti, S (2002), "Informal Labor Market in India: The Post-Liberalization Scenario" in R K Sen (ed) *Indian Labor in the Post-Liberalization Period*, K P Bagchi &Co. Kolkata, pp101-121.

Chand, K, K.C Singhal and S, Modi (1998), 'Socio-economic Variables and Process of Migration in Sugar Industry of Punjab', *The Indian Journal of Labor Economics*, Vol.41, No.4, pp675-694

Dayal, H and Karan, A K (2003), "Labor Migration from Jharkhand" *Labor and Development*, Vol.9 No.2, pp223-258

Heggade, O D(1998) "International Labor Standards and India-The Case of Women Labor" *The Indian Journal of Labor Economics*, Vol.41, No.4, pp1035-1043

Jhabvala, R and Sinha, S (2001), "Social Security for Women Workers in the Unorganized Sector' *Indian Journal of Labor Economics*, Vol. 44, No.4, pp577-584

Joshi, H and V, Joshi (1976), *Surplus Labor and City*, Oxford University Press, New Delhi

Joshi, S C (1994), *Migration to a Metropolis*, RBSA Publishers, Jaipur

Joshi, SC, *Migration to a Metropolis*, RBSA Publihsers, Jaipur, 1994

Kannan, K.P and M Rutten (2002), 'Labor and Capitalist Transformation in Asia Report on a Conference', *Economic and Political Weekly*, May 25, pp.1981-85

Kumar, B; Singh B P and Singh R (1998) "Out Migration from Rural Bihar: A Case Study", *Indian Journal of Labor Economics*, Vol. 44, No.4,pp729-36

Kumar, N and Prasad, A (1998) "Rural Out Migration in Kurnool District", *Indian Journal of Labor Economics*, Vol. 44, No.4, pp806

Kundu, A (1997), "Trends and Patterns of Female Employment in India: A Case of Organized Informalization", *The Indian Journal of Labor Economics*, Vol.40, No.3, pp 439-451.

Mahapatra, M K (1998) "Labor Migration from Backward Region of Orissa", *Indian Journal of Labor Economics*, Vol. 44, No.4,pp737-44

Mamgain, R P (2003) "Out-Migration among Rural Households in Uttaranchal: Magnitude and Characteristics" *Labor and Development*, Vol.9, No2, pp259-287

Monteiro, V (2006), 'Another India is Possible Basic Needs, The Unorganized Sector and Science in India', in M. Malhoutra (ed), *India the Next Decade*, Academic Publisher, New Delhi, 2006.

Mukhapadhyay, S (1999), "Locating Women within Informal Sector Hierarchies" in Papola, T S and Sharma A K (ed.) *Gender and Employment in India*, Vikas Publishing House Pvt. Ltd.

Mukherji, S (2006), *Migration and Urban Decay Asian Experiences*, Rawat Publications, New Delhi

Munch, R (2002), *Globalization and labor*, Gopsors papers Ltd, New Delhi.

Murali Manohar, K (1983) *Socio-Economic Status of Indian Women*, Seema Publication, Delhi.

Najma Khan (1986), *Pattern of Rural Out migration*, B R Publishing Corporation, New Delhi.

Narasimhan, R L and Chandra, H (1998) "Sources of Data on Migration and Recent Trends" *Indian Journal of Labor Economics*, Vol. 44, No.4,pp633-44

Oberai, A S and H. K Manmohan Singh (1983), *Cause and Consequences of Internal Migration A Study in the Indian Punjab*, Oxford University Press, Delhi.

Oberai, A S, Prasad P S and Sardana M G (1989), *Determinants and Consequences of Internal Migration in India*, Oxford University Press, New Delhi.

Parthasarthy, G and Nirmala, K A (1999), "Marginalization Hypothesis and Post-Green revolution Period" in Papola, T S and Sharma A K (ed.) *Gender and Employment in India*, Vikas Publishing House Pvt. Ltd.

Pais, J (2002) "Casualization of Urban Labor Force Analysis of Recent Trends in Manufacturing", *Economic and Political Weekly*, Feb 16, pp-631

Peek, P and Antolinez, P (1977), "Migration and the Urban Labor Market: The Case of San Salvador", World Development, Vol.5, No.4, pp 291-302

Rani, U and Unni, J (2004), "Women, Work and Insecurity in India", *Labor and Development*, Vol.10, No.2, pp. 104-136.

Rao, MSA, (1995), Seasonal Migrant Laborers, in Proceedings of the National Seminar on Organizing Unorganized Rural Labor for Social Justice- Strategy and Methodology, also see Loes Schenk-Sandbergen(ed) *Women and Seasonal labor Migration,* Sage Publication, New Delhi, pp 74.

Ravenstein, G (1985), "The Law of Migration", *The Journal of Royal Statistical Society,* 52 (June), pp 241-301.

Reddy, G R and Vinodini, J M J(2005), 'Gender-Related Issues of Urban Informal Labor Market', in Saibaba, G and et.al (ed) *Labor and Development in Twenty First Century, Challenges and perspectives,* Serial publication, New Delhi,224-34.

Roopa, M (2004), "Protect Construction Workers", *Labor File,* Sept-Oct,pp44-49

Sakthivel, S and Bhattacharya, Bb (2002) "Feminization of India Labor Force?-Evidence from the Literature", *Labor and Development,* Vol.8, No.1&2, December, pp. 1-26.

Satya Raju S (1994), 'Socio-economic Aspects of Construction Labouer in India', in K Rao, M (ed.) (1994): *Growth of Urban Informal Sector and Economic Development,* Kanishka Publisher, Delhi, pp13-26

Sen, R K (2002), *Indian Labor in the Post-Liberalization Period,* K P Bagchi & Co. Kolkata

Sharma, G K (1982) *Labor Movement in India Its Past and Present: From 1885 to 1980,* Sterling Publishers Pvt. Ltd. New Delhi

Sidhu, M.S and P.S Rangi (1998), 'Out-migration from Rural Bihar: A Case Study', *The Indian Journal of Labor Economics,* Vol.41, No.4.pp717-28

Singh, S P and Aggarwal R K (1998), "Rural-Urban Migration: The Role of Push and Pull Factors Revisited", *Indian Journal of Labor Economics,* Vol. 44, No.4,pp911-16

Srinivas, M N (1952), *Religion and Society among the Coorgs of South India,* Oxford University Press, New Delhi

Srivastava, Ravi (1998), 'Migration and the Labor Market in India' *The Indian Journal of Labor Economics,* Vol.41, No.4,pp 583-616

Standing, G (1996), "Global Feminization through Flexible Labor", *World Development,* Vol.17, No.7, pp 1077-95.

Streefker, H (1981) "The Two Little to Live on, Too much to Die on: Employment in Small Scale Industries in Rural South Gujarat", *Economic and Political Weekly*, April, 11, 659-68.

Tadaro, M P (1993), *Economic Development in the Third World*, Hyderabad, Orient Longman

Tom, Irene (1989), *Women in Unorganized Sector*, Usha Publications, New Delhi,

Tripathy, S N (1996), (ed) *Unorganized Women Labor in India*, Discovery Publishing House, New Delhi.

Tripathy, S K (1998), "Labor Out-migration in Orissa" *The Indian Journal of Labor Economics*, Vol.41, No.4, pp800-802

Vidyarthi L P (1969), *Cultural Configuration of Ranchi*, J N Basu and Co., Calcutta.

# 3

# Social Protection Status of Women Workers in (SEZs) in India

**Abstract**

*Indian economy is undergoing substantial structural transformation which can be witnessed in its broad macro-economic indicators such as, growth rate, employment rate, exports, rate of poverty reduction and so on. High economic growth is expected to solve the problems of poverty and inequality in an economy; but in reality a situation contrary to the same exists in India. Despite the fall in the percentage of the level of poverty, the number of people below poverty line, in absolute terms, has ironically not decreased. Simultaneously it has also been felt that over the decades the fruits of development are not evenly distributed among all sections of the society and especially women are the most deprived of all.*

*In order to resolve the situation the Government of India has adopted several social protection policies and programmes time and again. Social protection can be defined as a host of policies and programmes undertaken with a view to reduce poverty and to emancipate, especially, the aggrieved sections of the society from their persistent state of risks, deprivation and vulnerability. Even though social protection is not a very new concept in India but its scope, vision and coverage has increased over the years. These schemes target numerous sections of the society which face risks and vulnerabilities owing to their socio-economic conditions, caste, health, age, race etc. But women in particular are in the most deplorable situations.*

*The Indian economy is also witnessing major shift through its Export Processing Zones (EPZ) or Special Economic Zones (SEZ) where emphasis is on attainting inward looking inclusive growth opportunities. The contribution of women workers in this particular sub-sector is enormous. However, substantial discrimination is observed when it comes to measuring their earnings, working environment and social functionalities. The social protection programmes adopted and undertaken by different government and private agencies are numerous and far apart; but the same are not available to the women workers most of the time. The present study intends to venture into this gray area and examine the situation first hand and undertake a peep into the studies already carried out by different scholars.*

*On account of enormous competition induced by globalization, SEZs have been accorded significant importance to give an edge and boost the economy's growth. They are also considered instrumental in developing economically backward areas by attracting foreign as well as domestic investment, by providing employment to local inhabitants and by promoting technical advancement. Consequently, India has witnessed a rapid increase in the SEZs. In return, these zones have been instrumental in enhancing growth in their related industries, promotion of new production sectors and building India's image in international market.*

*However, the study has revealed that there is a huge gap between social protection policy and its availability to women workers in Special Economic Zones. In order to minimize the cost of production and to sustain the pressure of international competition, the labor laws and policies governing these SEZs are made invariably flexible. Women workers are preferred in these zones since they are hard-working and diligent and more importantly, because they are too docile to form trade unions and press for higher wages. In return, women are rewarded by minimal wages, 10-12 hours of average work per day and sexual exploitation by the employers or supervisors. Besides the hazardous working conditions, basic facilities of toilets, accommodation, crèche, rest room etc. are inadequate or not available at all. The concept of maternity leaves seems to exist only on papers. In fact, women workers, who constitute the major share of workforce in SEZs, are employed on contractual basis so that it is easier to hire and fire them. To add to their plight, studies also reveal that women workers face economic disparity in terms of being paid less than their male counterparts. Such evidences make the arguments, in favor of SEZs in terms of them at least aiding the jobless and being instrumental in empowering women, completely redundant. Moreover, such arguments simply lose their worth in the face of such appalling and atrocious working conditions. Thus, it is viable to assert that labor laws are only theoretically applicable in the SEZs and women workers lose out on a number of counts and bear the brunt of it in big ways.*

*An attempt is made to suggest few measures to bring the women workers within the frame of social protection policy in the emerging macro-environment. For instance, steps should be taken to provide them with appropriate training for their skill development which in turn will enhance their bargaining power. It has also been recommended that government, along with adopting social protection policy covering the entire economy, should aim to adopt social protection measures targeting women workers in SEZs which in turn will help achieve the overall developmental objectives, directly and via its spill over effects.*

## Introduction

Macroeconomic environment broadly refers to the level of total economic activities and fluctuations that an economy is subjected to. In general, macroeconomic environment takes into account the trends in gross domestic product (GDP), inflation, employment, spending, and monetary fiscal policy, fluctuation in business cycles etc.

Economic growth is one of the chief indicators that reflect the macro-economic health of the economy. High rate of economic growth refers to increase in a country's productive capacity and indicates rise in the standard of living of the people as well. As can be seen from Table3.1, India's growth rate in GDP was 1.4% in 1991-92, 5.81% in 2001-02 and rose to 8.6% in 2010-11. Moreover, India's exports grew from -1.5%

in 1991-92 to 29.5% in 2010-11 and gross domestic capital formation as a percentage of GDP increased from 22.1% in 1991-92 to 36.5% in 2009-10 (Table1).

**Table 3.1: India's Macroeconomic Indicators (as on 1st April, 2011)**

| Year | Growth Rate in GDP at Factor Cost* | Exports Growth (US $) | Gross Domestic Capital Formation** |
|---|---|---|---|
| 1991-92 | 1.4 | -1.5 | 22.1 |
| 1992-93 | 5.4 | 3.8 | 23.1 |
| 1993-94 | 5.7 | 20.0 | 22.5 |
| 1994-95 | 6.4 | 18.4 | 25.5 |
| 1995-96 | 7.3 | 20.8 | 26.2 |
| 1996-97 | 8.0 | 5.3 | 24.0 |
| 1997-98 | 4.3 | 4.6 | 25.3 |
| 1999-00 | 6.44 | 10.8 | 26.1 |
| 2000-01 | 4.35 | 21.0 | 24.2 |
| 2001-02 | 5.81 | -1.6 | 24.2 |
| 2002-03 | 3.84 | 20.3 | 25.2 |
| 2003-04 | 8.52 | 21.1 | 26.8 |
| 2004-05 | 7.5 | 30.8 | 32.5 |
| 2005-06 | 9.5 | 23.4 | 34.7 |
| 2006-07 | 9.6 | 22.6 | 35.7 |
| 2007-08 | 9.3 | 29.0 | 38.1 |
| 2008-09 | 6.8 | 13.7 | 34.5 |
| 2009-10 | 8.0 | -3.6 | 36.5 |
| 2010-11 | 8.6 | 29.5 | - |

Source: Reserve Bank of India, Central Statistical Organization, Finance Ministry etc. Available at: Planning Commission (http://planningcommission.nic.in/data/datatable/1705/final_1.pdf)

* Growth rates in GDP from 1991-92 to 2004-05 are on the basis of 1999-2000 prices and that from 2004-05 to 2010-11 are on the basis of 2004-05 prices

**Gross Domestic Capital Formation from

Many studies have established the fact that high rate of economic growth is known to solve the problems of poverty. Even though the percentage of people living below poverty line, as estimated by the Expert Group 2009 (Tendulkar)[1], decreased from 45.3% in 1993-94 but it was as high as 37.2% in 2005. Further, the total number of poor increased from 403.7 million in 1993-94 to 407.1 million in 2004-05 which clearly indicates that the number of large amount of people living below this line of deprivation did not fall in actuality.[2] Moreover, the rate of unemployment as a per cent of labor force increased from 6.06% in 1993-94 to 8.28% in 2004-05.[3] Table 3.2 gives further insight to the extent of employment and unemployment in India and shows that despite the increase in the level of employment, the rate of unemployment increased significantly.

**Table 3.2: Extent of Employment and Unemployment in India**

| Year | Labor Force (in Crore) | Employment (in Crore) | Unemployment (in Crore) | Unemployment Rate (%) |
|---|---|---|---|---|
| 1999-2000 | 36.4 | 33.7 | 2.66 | 7.3 |
| 9th Plan (2001-2002) | 37.8 | 34.4 | 3.48 | 9.2 |
| 10th Plan (2006-2007) | 41.3 | 36.8 | 4.45 | 11 |

Source: Tenth Five Year Plan, Vol. I. Available at: Jain.T.R, Ohri.V.K, and Majhi.B.D. "Economic Development and Policy in India" Edition: 2010-11. Publisher: VK Publications. Page No. 149.

According to NSSO's 66th Round only 2 million jobs were generated between 2004 and 2009 even as the economy grew at the rate of 8.43 per cent annually. In contrast, 62 million jobs were created between 1999 and 2004. Hence the (2004-09) period is often referred as the period of jobless growth. The survey also revealed the wage differentials among the urban and rural workers. Where, on an average, an urban worker earns rupees 365 per day; the rural worker earns rupees 232 on daily basis. The findings also revealed that women workers, both in rural and urban areas, received less remuneration than their male counterparts.

Thus, even after attaining high rates of growth, rise in percentage of exports, and increased capital formation, the corresponding evidence of poverty rates and unemployment depicts a rather dismal situation where the fruits of growth have been reaped by a few. Nevertheless, past experiences show that economic growth is not self-sufficient to deal with the issues of inequality of opportunity in growth and inequalities of benefits of growth. In fact, even with the possibilities to grow more rapidly on account of integration of the world economies, the socio-economic problems seem to endlessly persist.

As it has been realized that economic growth of a country does not alleviate poverty to a great extent, hence, Government intervention becomes indispensable at this stage. The Government ought to assure that social protection to the aggrieved section is adequately delivered. Hence, the need for social protection, in general, is deliberated upon in an elaborate manner in the subsequent segment.

## Meaning and Need For Social Protection

Social protection can be defined as a host of policies and programmes undertaken with a view to reduce poverty and to emancipate, especially, the aggrieved sections of the society from there persistent state of risks, deprivation and vulnerability. The aggrieved sections of the society refer to those placed at a disadvantage owing to their socio-economic status, gender, caste, age, health, race etc.

In all walks of their life, individuals or groups are exposed to an array of contingencies. Hence, risk is a part and parcel of every human life. But, some are exposed to high level risks relative to others and so, they are more susceptible to form the vulnerable sections of the society. An estimated one-third of the world's labor force was found to be insufficient in obtaining material reward from their work to survive and 2 million deaths every year were estimated owing to their unsafe and dangerous working conditions (Garcia A.B. and Gruat J.V. (November 2003)[4]. Social protection is indeed imperative in order to attend the destitute sections of the society. Experiences of a number of countries show that social protection is instrumental in ensuring basic socio-economic securities to individual and society on one hand, and contributing to the long-term goal of sustainable economic development by promoting human development, facilitating cultural change and advancing social justice on the other.

The era of globalization has without a doubt provided tremendous opportunities for human advancement but at the same time it has widened the wage differentials, favoring skilled over unskilled labor. Moreover, on account of intense global competition, employers adopt flexible labor policies, low working standards and less secure forms of employment. In fact, in developing economies a large part of the labor force is employed in the informal sectors where despite the hazardous working conditions the scope of security of employment and income is minimal, thus rendering them and the ones dependent on them highly vulnerable to risks. Social protection, therefore, plays a key role in providing security to enable people not only to just survive but to lead a decent life.

Social protection is a dynamic concept and has evolved with societal changes. For instance, during the period of industrialization, provision of income security became a subject of paramount importance due to the development of the concept of wage labor. As a result, saving schemes, private insurance and legislations requiring employers to cater to the needs of the injured workers emerged. With the passage of time, as labor became more organized, social protection programmes in industrialized countries took the shape of safety net functions to ensure that the essentials needs of the people is met along with coverage of socio-economic risks for all.

As the world has progressed the coverage of social protection schemes has enhanced to incorporate health care needs, housing needs and social services. However, whereas in the developed countries, social protection schemes became universal, a large majority of the population in the developing countries remained outside the purview of the social protection schemes since these schemes cover only those with formal worker-employer relationship. Apart from the inadequate coverage of social protection policies in the developing world, the increase in risks due to change in life cycle patterns of men and women, and the rise of social exclusion caused by globalizing forces accords an ever greater need for social protection.

Social protection measures have often been criticized on account of the financial burden they pose on the public funds and that the public funds are diverted away from investment in the priority sectors. Therefore, traditionally, social protection policies have been considered to thwart economic growth. Economic growth is undoubtedly important for the advancement of the human well-being. However, the rising inequality worldwide in the wake of negative impacts of globalization, economic growth is now not considered to be self-sufficient to reduce persistent poverty. Hence, there is a need to find a balance between economic goals and social protection of the world's population in pursuit of enhancing equity, social cohesion and stability, necessary for sustainable development.

Social protection measures thereby empower the distressed section of the society to live life with human dignity. So having understood the significance and the critical role that social protection measures assume, we further look into the scenario of social protection regime in India.

**Social Protection In India**

India being the second largest nation in terms of population after China has majority of its population still below the poverty line (BPL). Therefore, social security programs in India were introduced as a means of improving well-being of the poor. According to international statistics, over 300 million people in India live in extreme poverty on less than US$1 a day, and over 500 million on less than US$2 a day ( Sülzer R. 2008)[5]. Only half of the population has access to piped water, and most health services (in fact about 92%) are paid for out of pocket, making India's health system the biggest private health service in the world. Such conditions relating to poor availability of facilities to the poor like lack of education, scarce employment opportunities, poor health conditions and inadequate access to productive assets led to the initiation of social security schemes in India.

The Indian social protection system is very complex in terms of its evolution, expansion, administration, and coverage. From early on, India extended social protection measures to workers in the organized sector, which attributed to only about 7% of the total workforce. The early social protection schemes failed to provide a comprehensive national scheme for around 93% or about 370 million unorganized workers who contributed about 60% of Indian gross domestic product (Sakthivel S. et al, 2006)[6].

This fumed the debate between state policies towards industrialization and welfarism as these policies only benefited the organized sector workers, who enjoyed the benefits of secured jobs, price-adjusted salaries, sufficient and reliable access to multiple social protection instruments. Finally with the economic reforms of 1991 the Indian Government moved towards formulation, and visioning of viable social security programs in India. Today, Indian social security programs can be structured and clustered into four categories:

- *Contributory social protection schemes*: These protection schemes fall under the jurisdiction of the Indian State government and are implemented with the help of specially formed boards. The government of Karnataka, for example, has set up more than twenty welfare boards for the benefits of agriculture workers, coir workers, handloom workers, fishermen, motor transport workers, etc. Furthermore, such protection policies also cover accident insurance, medical facilities, old age pension, gratuity, provident fund, maternity benefits, income security and unemployment allowance (Sülzer R. 2008)[7].

- *Welfare schemes*: These schemes form part of the Central government jurisdiction. Under the welfare schemes the center imposes a cess on certain categories of employers. The employers for workers engaged in, for example, lime-stone, dolomite, iron ore, manganese, beedi (local cigarettes) industry, and the film making industry etc serving definite and distinct geographic pockets of the country and its population ensure a fixed income for the Indian state which is then diverted towards welfare policies (Sülzer R. 2008)[8].
- *Social assistance*: These social protection schemes in India are largely sponsored by the central government like the National Social Assistance Program (NSAP). Social assistance as a measure of protection incorporates three components: a) Old age pension scheme, b) National family benefit scheme and c) National maternity benefit scheme (Sülzer R. 2008)[9].
- *Promotional social security*: This led to the formulation of nationwide programs like the public distribution system, the Integrated Child Development Program (ICDS), the Midday Meal Program in primary schools, the Supplementary Nutrition Programs, the Rural Employment Programs (Sampoorna Grameen Rozgar Yojana, SGRY) and many more ( Sülzer R. 2008)[10].

The most recent effort by the Indian government towards social protection has been the National Rural Wage Employment Guarantee Act 2005 (NREGA), which aims to provide 100 days per year of guaranteed employment (unskilled manual work) to one person of each rural household in India, with the Panchayati Raj Institutions as the key implementing body. In 2007, with the tabling of the Unorganized Sector Worker's Social Security Bill (USWSS), which aims to incorporate informal urban workers into a basic social insurance scheme and the Domestic Workers (Registration, social security and welfare) Act, 2008, India has taken a regional leadership role in social protection measures. If successful these schemes are expected to substantially reduce the insecurity of India's vast rural and urban informal labor forces.

Social protection measures in India target numerous vulnerable sections in the society. However, women in particular are considered to be the most vulnerable among all. So, we try to further examine the state of women workers in one of the crucial sub-sectors of the economy i.e. Special Economic Zones in India.

**SEZs and Women Workers in India**

Special Economic Zone (SEZ) refers to a particular area selected by the government for carrying out developmental activities in that area. This area in turn is governed by laws, specially created, for governing its economic activity in lieu of attracting business and industrial investment in this area. Export Processing Zone (EPZ), in particular, are an important policy instrument to accelerate industrialization, generate employment and for regional development, thus, influencing the increasing share of trade flows and employing a growing number of workers. Both these zones are created for developing economically backward areas by attracting foreign as well as domestic investment, by providing employment to local inhabitants and by promoting technical advancement. This, in turn, is most likely to boosts the overall growth of a country.

India's first EPZ came up in Kandla, Gujarat, in 1965 and was followed by one in Santa Cruz Mumbai in 1973. By the mid to late 1980s, a few more zones were added in Chennai, Cochin, Falta, Noida and Vishakapatnam, but, with little impact on national economy. In India, the early 1990s marked a watershed in the country's economic policy framework. *But the economic reforms, especially owing to a slump in the manufacturing sector in the second half of the decade, failed to realise the objective of overall growth of the Indian economy. As a result, the government reverted to EPZs with the expectation that they could provide the "engine of growth" to boost the manufacturing sector.* The government replaced the EPZ scheme with the "SEZ scheme" in 2000. SEZ Act was enacted in 2005 and SEZ Rules were notified in February 2006. The main objectives of the SEZ Act were - (a) generation of additional economic activity (b) promotion of exports of goods and services; (c) promotion of investment from domestic and foreign sources; (d) creation of employment opportunities; and (e) development of infrastructure facilities.

**Table 3.3: List of operational SEZ in India**

| Name of the SEZ | Location | Type |
|---|---|---|
| Kandla Special Economic | Kandla, Gujarat | Multi Product |
| SEEPZ Special Economic Zone | Mumbai, Maharashtra | Electronics and Gems and Jewellery |
| Noida Special Economic Zone | Uttar Pradesh | Multi Product |
| MEPZ Special Economic Zone | Chennai, Tamil Nadu | Multi Product |
| Cochin Special Economic Zone | Cochin, Kerala | Multi Product |
| Falta Special Economic Zone | Falta, West Bengal | Multi Product |
| Visakhapatnam Special Economic Zone | Visakhapatnam, Andhra Pradesh | Multi Product |

Source: Ministry of Commerce and Industry, Department of Commerce (http://sezindia.gov.in/writereaddata/pdf/ListofoperationalSEZs.pdf)

As a result, these zones, for instance, have been instrumental in enhancing growth in electronic industry and contributed to promotion of new production sectors and in building India's image in international market. SEZ accounted for 26 per cent of total hardware exports in 2000-02 and accounted for over 55 per cent to total Indian jewellery exports in 2002-03 (Aggarwal A. 2006)[11]. However, the success story of SEZs pertaining to economic contribution at the national level remained miniscule. The share of SEZs in exports was a mere 5 per cent in 2004-05, they accounted for only 1 per cent of factory sector employment and 0.32 per cent of factory investment in the same year (Brijoy.C.R 2007)[12]. Their contribution to regional economies has also been limited. They have also sparked concerns over the land acquisition process as well as suspicion that in some cases the policy has been a clever way for real estate developers to snag land.

Nevertheless, in their recent survey, OECD viewed India's SEZs favorably in terms of providing an important platform for industrial development (Lahiri T. 2011)[13]. According to the report, India had granted approval to set up 571 SEZs by 2010, and those zones already in operation employed 600,000 people and accounted for a quarter of the country's total exports.

**Table 3.4: Exports from the functioning SEZs**

| Year | Value (Rs. Crore) | Growth Rate (over previous year) |
|---|---|---|
| 2003-04 | 13,854 | 39% |
| 2004-05 | 18,314 | 32% |
| 2005-06 | 22,840 | 25% |
| 2006-07 | 34,615 | 52% |
| 2007-08 | 66,638 | 93% |
| 2008-09 | 99,689 | 50% |
| 2009-10 | 2,20,711.39 | 121.40% |

Source: Ministry of Commerce and Industry, Department of Commerce (http://sezindia.gov.in/about-ep.asp)

A study (Aggarwal A. 2007)[14], across the three largest Indian SEZs (in terms of their contribution to exports and employment): SEEPZ, Madras and Noida, reveals that 'employment generation' has been the most important channel through which SEZs contributes to human development concerns in India. The survey study revealed that the zones have been of particular benefit to females since these zones opened up opportunities for wage employment for women in the formal sector. Furthermore, the usual notion of socio-economic exploitation of women workers in these zones has not been supported by the study.

However, a major problem relating to SEZs is that the government tends to invariably relax the laws relating to labor protection in order to attract investment. Referring to the study conducted by Society for Participatory Research in Asia (PRIA) on the plight of workers in Indian zones, (Sinha S. 2008)[15] noted that the gains generated by SEZs were not long-term since most of the contracts were short-term in nature in lieu of the flexibility to hire and fire and avoid costs like maternity and redundancy pay. The same study also showed that 70-90 per cent of the workforce was constituted by women and it is they who bear the brunt of global competition since these zones on account of being export oriented emphasise on minimising production costs. Consequently, women were seen to work 10-12 hours a day without or with improper overtime payment, social security benefits and maternity leave not in place, and sexual harassment of women being common in these zones. A study on the Cochin Special Economic Zone (CSEZ) constituted by 79 factories depicted similar conditions of women's employment. Wages were as low as rupees 35 to rupees 75 per day and to top it all, rupees 10-15 had to be paid every day to contractors as their commission. The picture of an ideal zone catering to workers need in form of housing, education and medicine seem to remain on papers only. In spite of employing more than 3500 women, the zone had no provisions for accommodation or crèche facility.

Furthermore, a rigorous survey conducted in Falta SEZ, revealed that about 60% of the workforce in the SEZ were women, and many of the local inhabitants observed that the reason behind such a large number of female workers was that they were easier to exploit (Ray P.S. 2009) [16]. Wages for female workers were uniformly around Rupees 10 less than that for male workers. The survey further reported that sexual exploitation of women workers by supervisors was widespread. Women workers tolerate sexual harassment in order to retain their jobs and many even prepared and took food from their home for the supervisors.

The case of Tirupur, the largest export centre for knit wear, shows increased feminisation of work. The expansion of exports after 1985 gave way to subcontracting and informalisation of labor and hence miserable working conditions of women who constitute about 60% of the workforce (Padma 2004)[17]. Similarly the situation of women in Peenya industrial estate in Bangalore was found to be equally terrible. This garment based industry is export oriented and women constituted over 80% of the total workforce. Inadequate number of toilets, absence of crèche and rest rooms add to the misery over and above the average 10-12 hours of work and minimal remuneration.

The horrifying death of 22 year old S Ambika, a permanent employee of Nokia Telecom SEZ in Sriperumbadur, Tamil Nadu, on 31st October 2010 revealed the atrocious working conditions of the zone which ironically claimed to have 'world class' safety systems designed keeping in mind 'worker's safety'[18]. In an attempt to release the jammed conveyor belt, Ambika's head got stuck and neck got crushed in the loader machine. It was reported that out of 25 such assembly line machines, 8 machines regularly got stuck at least 20 times a shift due to malfunctioning of the sensors; and in order to meet the production targets, workers cannot wait for the technicians.

The above evidences depict the hash, spiteful and unpleasant conditions of women workers in SEZs. In additions to the drawbacks and exploitation attached to the tag of weaker sex, women workers in these zones also face economic disparity, mental trauma and a number of insecurities. Some argue that SEZs have at least aided the jobless and can be instrumental in empowering women; but such arguments simply lose their worth in the face of such appalling and atrocious working conditions.

## Conclusion

India is the presently the second largest growing economy of the world. The era of 1990s has been a turning point and since then India has witnessed an overall growth in macro indicators like GDP, capital formation and exports.

Despite the growth, its benefits have definitely not trickled down to the grass root level, which is evident from the number of poor and unemployed in the country. The poor in turn form the vulnerable section of the society and respective women, in particular, are most vulnerable.

In order to develop in the true sense and to be able to sustain it in the long run, it is imperative to create an environment conducive to social integration of population, particularly those who are prone to risks and deprivation. Sustainable economic development cannot be achieved by mere attainment of economic goals. Rather, social goals should be pursued along with. This is where the importance of social protection is felt and it in turn has a crucial role of making growth more inclusive. Even though social security is not a new concept in India but its scope and vision has been ever expanding.

At present, SEZs are of crucial importance to boost manufacturing growth on one hand and create tremendous employment opportunities and regional development on the other. After examining the conditions of India's SEZs, it seems right to assert that they are only theoretically governed by the labor laws and workers do not benefit from these laws in reality. Unhealthy and unsafe working conditions and unreasonably low wages mark the working conditions of women workers in SEZs. Plausible and urgent action at the grass-root level and related macro policies need to be devised to emancipate women workers in SEZs from the wretched conditions, build skills and systems of security, and enhance their bargaining power. There should be no wage differentials with respect to their male counterparts and safe working environment along with health insurance benefits are imperative. Basic amenities of toilets, accommodation, crèche etc. should be adequately provided. Awareness and proper implementation of Vishakha Guidelines against Sexual Harassment at the Workplace is of utmost importance. Since women constitute a substantial share of employment in SEZs, it can, hence, be recommended that the government, along with adopting social protection policy covering the entire economy, should aim to adopt social protection measures targeting women workers in SEZs which in turn will help achieve the overall developmental objectives, directly and via its spill over effects.

**Reference**

1. Planning Commission, Government of India. "*Percentage and Number of Poor Estimated by Expert Group 1993 and Expert Group 2009*". Available at: http://planningcommission.nic.in/data/datatable/1705/final_38.pdf
2. Ibid
3. Planning Commission, Government of India. "*Unemployment Rates in various NSS rounds (CDS basis)*". Available at: http://planningcommission.nic.in/data/datatable/1705/final_48.pdf
4. Garcia A.B. and Gruat J.V. (November 2003). "*Social Protection: A Life cycle continuum investment for social justice, poverty reduction and sustainable development*", Version 1.0, International Labor Organisation, Geneva. Available at: http://www.ilo.org/public/english/protection/download/lifecycl/lifecycle.pdf
5. Sülzer R. (May 2008). Social Security in India – A System in the Making. In The Social and Ecological Market Economy – A Model for Asian Development? Published by: Deutsche Gesellschaft für, gtz. Available at: http://www2.gtz.de/wbf/4tDx9kw63gma/Asia_Social_and_ Ecological_ Market_ Economy_Reader-05_2008.pdf

6. Sakthivel S. and Joddar P., "Unorganized Sector Workforce in India: Trends, Patterns, and Social Security Coverage," Economic and Political Weekly (May 27, 2006)
7. Sülzer R. (May 2008). Social Security in India - A System in the Making. In The Social and Ecological Market Economy - A Model for Asian Development? Published by: Deutsche Gesellschaft für, gtz. Available at: http://www2.gtz.de/wbf/4tDx9kw63gma/Asia_Social_and_Ecological_Market_Economy_Reader-05_2008.pdf
8. Ibid
9. Ibid
10. Ibid
11. Aggarwal.A, "*Special Economic Zone: Revisiting the Policy Debate*", Economic and Political Weekly, November 4, 2006. Available at: http://sanhati.com/wp-content/uploads/2007/03/sezpolicy.pdf
12. Brijoy.C.R, "*Special Economic Zones: Profits at Any Cost*", October 22, 2007. Available at: Centre for Education and Documentation, http://www.doccentre.net/Tod/SEZs-Profits-At-Any-Cost.php
13. Lahiri.T, "*OECD Praises India's Economic Zone Policy*", *June* 14, 2011, The Wall Street Journal. Available at: http://blogs.wsj.com/indiarealtime/2011/06/14/oecd-praises-indias-economic-zone-policy/
14. Aggarwal.A (May 2007). "*Impact of Special Economic Zones on Employment, Poverty and Human Development*". Working paper No. 194, Indian Council for Research on International Economic Relations. Available at: http://www.icrier.org/page.asp?MenuID=24&SubCatId=175&SubSubCatId=285
15. Sinha.S, "*At What Cost, For Whose Benefit? Women Workers in SEZs*", Labor File Journal (Special Economic Zones: Their Impact on Labor), Vol 6, Nos 4-5, July - October 2008 (Arti- pages 25-27). Available at: http://www.laborfile.org/ArticleMore.aspx?id=1017
16. Ray.P.S," *Falta SEZ in West Bengal - A fact-finding report on workers and environmental impact*", November 26, 2009. Available at: http://sanhati.com/excerpted/1942/

17. Padma, "Women *Workers in India in the 21st Century – Unemployment and Underemployment*", February 2004, Communist Party of India (Marxist-Leninist) Liberation. Available at: http://www.cpiml.org/liberation/year_2004/febraury/WomenWorkers.htm

18. Menon N, "*Ambika's Death: Madhumita Dutta & Venkatachandrika Radhakrishnan*", KAFILA, January 21, 2011. Available at: http://kafila.org/2011/01/21/ambikas-death-madhumita-dutta-venkatachandrika-radhakrishnan

# 4

# Gender Inequalities and Human Right Violations of Women Workers in Unorganized Labor Sector in India

Unorganized labor sector, gender and human rights - all three have an intricate inter-relationship among themselves and deserve in-depth analysis of various facets and dimensions of such relationships. Unorganized labor sector is the unsung hero of Indian economy not only in providing employment; but also in boosting inclusive growth, reducing poverty and income inequalities, and promoting socio-economic well-being of millions of our citizens. Gender inequalities and discriminations are observed everywhere, but they assume alarming proportions especially in unorganized labor markets considering both the short-term and long-term consequences of such aberrations. The human rights of women workers in the unorganized sector need all the more protection since they are highly vulnerable to various kinds of discriminations and exploitations. This paper discusses about the unorganized labor market and the gender inequalities with special focus on the human right violations of women workers in unorganized sector in order to emphasize to both the policy makers and implementers the urgent need to address such issues on a priority basis.

## Unorganised Labor Sector

Unorganised labor is defined as those workers who have not been able to organize themselves in pursuit of their common interest due to certain constraints like casual nature of employment, ignorance and illiteracy, small and scattered size of establishments etc. (Krishnan, 2010). As per the Unorganized Workers Social Security Act 2008, an unorganized worker means "a home-based worker, self-employed worker or a wage worker in the unorganized sector and includes a worker in the organized sector who is not covered by any of the Acts mentioned in Schedule-II of this Act".

The unorganized sector is characterized by the lack of labor law coverage, seasonal and temporary nature of occupations, high labor mobility, dispersed functioning of operations, low productivity, minimum access to basic amenities, lack of organizational support, low bargaining power, etc. all of which make the workers vulnerable to socio-economic hardships. The nature of work in the unorganized sector varies between regions and between the rural and urban areas. In the rural areas unorganized sector workers comprise of landless agricultural laborers, small and marginal farmers, share-croppers, persons engaged in animal husbandry, fishing, horticulture, bee-keeping ,toddy tapping, forestry, rural artisanry, etc; whereas in the urban areas they comprise of manual laborers in construction, carpentry, trade, transport, communication etc. and also includes street vendors, hawkers, head load workers, cobblers, tin smiths, garment makers etc. (GoI, 2011b).

As per the 66$^{th}$ round survey of NSSO (GoI, 2009-10), total number of persons in labor force in both rural and urban India in 2009-10 is 469.88 million while total workforce is 460.16 million[1]. The gender-wise break-up of Labor force and Workforce (Figure 1) shows that labor in India is mainly concentrated in rural areas .

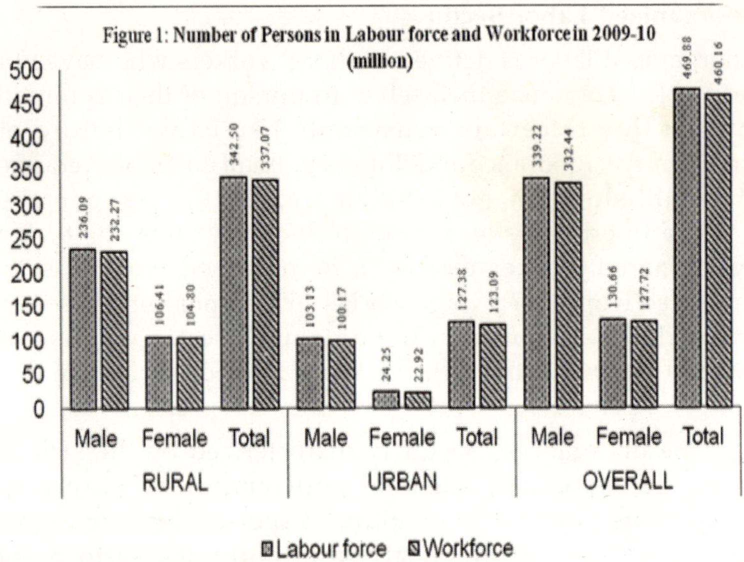


Source: Rangarajan, Padma and Seema, 2011 (2011)

**Figure 4.1: Number of persons in labor force and work force in 2009-10 (Millions)**

Numbers are less than one half to one fourth depending on the rural or urban area – both judged from labor force or from workforce point of view. In the period 2004-05 to 2009-10, there was an addition of 22 million males to the workforce accompanied by a decline of 21 million females from the workforce. While the male addition to the workforce was fairly even distributed between rural and urban areas, the decline in the female workforce was mainly concentrated in the rural areas. Of the 21 million declines in female workforce, more than 19 million was in rural areas. Did men pick up the jobs that females had vacated? That does appear to be the case (Table 1) as the decline in workforce was concentrated in agriculture (a sector known for supporting high levels of disguised unemployment), while the increase of workforce was spread to the secondary and tertiary sectors (Rangarajan, Padma and Seema, 2011).

**Table 4.1: Sectorial Disaggregation of Workforce**

| | Workforce (in million) | | | Shares (%) | | |
|---|---|---|---|---|---|---|
| | Primary | Secondary | Tertiary | Primary | Secondary | Tertiary |
| 2004-05 | 259.3 | 85.9 | 113.9 | 56.50 | 18.71 | 24.82 |
| 2009-10 | 238.2 | 100.7 | 120.8 | 51.76 | 21.89 | 26.25 |

Source: Rangarajan, Padma and Seema, 2011.

While official estimates suggest that the informal sector accounts for 93 per cent of total employment, other definition based on the National Sample Survey (1999-2000) suggests a figure somewhere between 86 and 89 per cent[2] (World Bank, 2010). Not only is this sector large, it is also the sector targeted by policy makers to absorb most of the additions to the country's workforce (Planning Commission, 2002). The composition of workers in unorganized sector shows that majority of them work in the agriculture sector, and then in the manufacturing & services sectors. The vast majority of new jobs created between 2004-05 and 2009-10 were in casual employment, mainly in construction (Planning Commission, 2011).

In order to take care of the social security and welfare of unorganized workers, two pronged strategy - legislative measures and implementation of welfare schemes and programmes - has been followed. In addition to the existing labor legislations[3], recently the Unorganized Workers' Social Security Act, 2008 has been enacted specifically to cater to the peculiar needs and concerns of the unorganized workers. The Act provides for the constitution of National and State Social Security Boards which shall recommend formulation of social security schemes viz. life and disability cover, health and maternity benefits, old age protection and any other benefits as may be determined by the Government for unorganized workers. Accordingly, a National Social Security Board has been constituted (GoI, 2011d). The various social sector schemes for unorganized workers include Indira Gandhi

National Old Age Pension Scheme, National Family Benefit Scheme, Janani Suraksha Yojana, Handloom Weavers Comprehensive Welfare Scheme, Handicraft Artisans Comprehensive Welfare Scheme, Pension to Master craft persons, National Scheme for Welfare of Fishermen and Training and Extension, Janshree Bima Yojana, Aam Aadmi Bima Yojana, Rashtriya Swasthya Bima Yojana etc. However, despite the presence of so many legislations, schemes and programmes the unorganised sector workers suffer from various kinds of problems, sufferings and challenges hampering their socio-economic development.

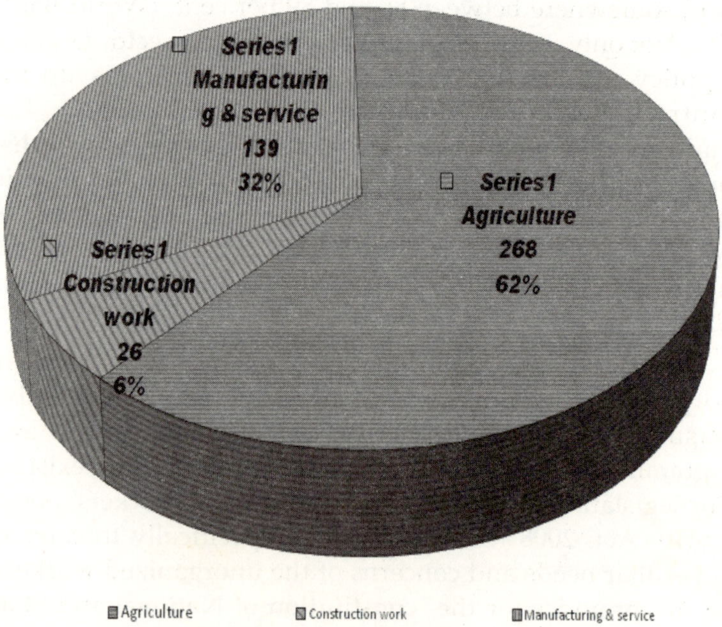


Source: GoI, 2011c, p.4

**Figure 4.2: Composition of workers in unorganized sector (Millions)**

## Gender Inequalities Among Labor

Jawaharlal Nehru once said "You can tell the condition of a nation by looking at the status of its women". 'Gender' refers to the social roles and relations between women and men (Bhasin, 2000). Women form an integral part of the Indian workforce. At overall level, the Labor Force Participation Rate (LFPR) is 359 of which LFPR of males and females is estimated to be 538 and 163 persons respectively. The sex ratio of the labor force at overall level is estimated to be 279. In the rural and urban sectors, the LFPR is estimated at 365 and 340 respectively. The sex ratio of the labor force in rural sector is 299 at overall level whereas for the urban sector the same is 222 (GoI, 2010, p.31). In the rural areas, women are mainly involved as cultivators and agricultural laborers. In the urban areas, almost 80 per cent of the women workers are working in the unorganized sectors such as household industries, petty trades and services, building and construction (GoI, 2011a). Gender division of labor leads to hierarchies and inequities because men and women's labor is not valued or rewarded equally.

Amartya Sen (2005) in his book 'The Argumentative Indian' mentions six types of gender inequalities - survival inequality, natality inequality, unequal facilities, ownership inequality, unequal sharing of household benefits and chores, domestic violence and physical victimization. Gender discrimination is one of the foremost kinds of discrimination prevalent in various modes and degrees across the world. Women constitute one-half of the world's population, perform two-third of its work hours, receive one-tenth of the world's income and own one-hundredth of the world's property. In developing countries, women have less job opportunities than in developed countries. A United Nations Report (1991) on women's work patterns states that women spend more time working than men in all developed and developing regions except Northern America and Australia[4]. It is now established that poor women have the least access to basic needs such as food, health and education. In the post-Independence era the women were mostly engaged in unskilled or semi-skilled occupations. But now due to spread of education, training, transport and communications women are working in different employment sectors (Sharma, 1999). Women have been victims of discrimination both in developed and under-developed countries. As the male is considered the bread winner of the family, the role of a female wage labor is regarded only as supplementary. Women are more dispensable than men since they are the last to be hired and the first to be fired in the labor market at the will and pleasure of the employers (Regina, 2001).

### Human Rights Violations of Women Workers in Unorganised Sector

Human rights are the birth rights of all the human beings and their protection and promotion is the first responsibility of the government. Inequality and discrimination in any form is a human right violation. The question that is frequently asked is whether women have different human rights. The answer is no. Though the human rights of women are no different from those of men, the forms and methods of their violation are different. Equal rights of men and women are mentioned in the UN Charter. The human rights of the unorganized sector women laborers are mainly as below -

- Right against torture and sexual harassment
- Right to be free from gender discrimination
- Right to equal pay for equal work
- Right to equal employment
- Right to primary health care and medical attention in case of illness
- Right to safe drinking water
- Right to good working atmosphere
- Right to association
- Right to participate in the cultural life of the community

- Right to rest and leisure
- Right to work and receive wages that contribute to an adequate standard of living
- Right against caste discrimination
- Right to freedom of religion
- Right to health
- Right to freedom of opinion and expression

The Constitution of India was drafted in such a way as to ensure that all workers, men and women were equally protected by law. The Directive Principles of State Policy are very clear about many of these rights. There are various provisions in the Constitution of India to protect and promote the interests of unorganised women workers including equal opportunity to all citizens in matters relating to employment.[5] However, violation against women on the basis of gender is one of the most pervasive human rights violations in the world today. The social, political, economic and civil rights of women workers especially at work, are abused at large. Despite the presence of various constitutional safeguards, legislations and welfare schemes, women workers are most vulnerable to the human right violations and discriminations of different kinds and orders. This is mostly because of the fact that their employment is temporary, enforcement of the laws is poor, and the inability of these women to fight for their rights (Elizabeth, 2011). It is necessary that the universal principles of human rights include women to bring about an equitable and just society, because without justice to women all other rights enshrined in the constitution are meaningless.

Many empirical studies have indicated that human rights of women workers are being violated. Women in the rural areas are many times forced to work for meager wages and without social security. Women have to work beyond working hours, even in advanced stages of pregnancy, and there is no leave facility. In some quarries in Orissa, women have to work at night and are found to have been sexually abused. Working conditions result in premature and stillbirths (Sengupta, 2011). Most of the employed in the unorganized sector face an array of uninsured risks that render them highly vulnerable to shocks. Table 2 showing the coverage of social insurance for the unorganized sectors clearly indicates that these workers are almost negligibly covered under the public and commercial social insurance schemes only except 23 per cent coverage under the Life Insurance (endowment). Though the figures of women workers have not been mentioned, it is obvious that the coverage of women workers of the unorganized sector would be miniscule. This all the more enhances the vulnerability of women in the unorganized sectors for exploitation and human right violations.

**Table 4.2: Coverage Rates of Social Insurance for Unorganized Sectors, 2004**

| Public Schemes | Percentage |
|---|---|
| EPF | 0.18 |
| Employees' Pension Scheme | 0.02 |
| Government Pension Scheme | 0.24 |
| Government Provident Fund | 0.21 |
| Contributory Provident Fund | 0.02 |
| Any Formal Pension Coverage | Less than 1 per cent |
| **Commercial Schemes** | |
| Life Insurance (endowment) | 23 |
| Personal Accident Insurance | 1.2 |
| Private Health Insurance | 0.5 |
| Non-life General Insurance | 1.4 |

Source: O'Keefe (2006)

Employees or workers are exploited by employers who violate laws sometimes with the help of bureaucracy (Sheth, 2004). The women in the unorganized sector face a lot of problems such as low wages, long and irregular hours of work, irregular payment of wages, non-availability of social security and welfare facilities, exploitative working conditions and sexual harassment at work place etc. (Gangrade and Joseph, 1983). Women tend to work longer hours than men and still earn less. Moreover, the work they do in their homes such as caring for children and the elderly does not get recognition in national and international accountings. Yet, women can be found to excel in every field/profession (Shafeeq, 2004). The time has come to take steps at individual, state and national/international levels to protect the human rights of women workers of unorganized sector.

**Recommendations**

The informal sector dominates India's labor markets. Given the current barriers for entry into the formal labor markets, the informal sector will remain huge in the medium term (World Bank, 2010). Violence against women is now recognized as a major issue of concern. Coverage of workers by formal social security and insurance programmes is extremely limited. It is time to address the issues and undertake policy reforms and institutional changes required for the emancipation and empowerment of rural female labor force. Empowerment should aim at changing the nature and direction of the power structures which marginalize the women laborers (Sengupta, 2011).

Labor market regulations are necessary to address important market failures and to protect workers. By providing protection against sudden and arbitrary job losses and poor working conditions, regulations can enhance the welfare and productivity of workers. However, India's labor regulations are unusually complex. "There are currently 47 central laws and 157 state regulations that directly affect labor markets. These are often inconsistent and, at times, overlapping. It is impossible for both firms and workers to be aware of their rights and obligations when rules and regulations are spread over numerous national and state-level Acts" (World Bank, 2010, p.13). The existing laws should be critically analyzed and suitable amendments be made. While compliance to the provisions of social security (where such provisions exist) must be ensured by improving the efficiency of the existing mechanisms or adopting alternative ones, a minimum measure of social security must be available on a statutory basis to the hitherto unprotected workers.

Gender should form an essential dimension in all aspects of labor market policy (GoI, 2008). Steps should be taken to ensure that women workers are treated on par with men workers with regard to duration of work, wages for overtime, adequate rest and satisfying social needs. There is a need to evolve a system that is gender sensitive, easy to approach, inexpensive, speedy and with minimum legal formalities (Jacob, 2004). All labor regulations must be subjected to gender equality test and those positively specifying equality and prohibition of discrimination should be strictly implemented (GoI, 2008). The labor laws are not very effective in providing protection, security, and benefits to workers due to weaknesses in the enforcement machinery. Regulatory reforms that address these barriers will increase employment and earnings of the poor in the informal sector. A key area of reforms would be strengthening labor inspections and labor law enforcement. Building a culture of compliance through mass media campaigns and education in business schools will help.

Welfare measures meant for women workers should be properly implemented. NGOs, Village Panchayats can be involved in speedy delivery of welfare measures. Alternative employment should be generated through establishing small scale and cottage industries, and organization of women workers into Self Help Groups. Also, labor education on various provisions of labor laws should be provided with Central Board for Workers Education playing a more pro-active role. The National/State Social Security Boards constituted under the Unorganized Workers Social Security Act, 2008 should play more active roles in providing protection to the workers. The Workers Facilitation Centers to be constituted as per the above Act should disseminate information on available social security schemes for unorganized workers. There should also be a thrust on the skill upgradation of the women workers.

**Concluding Remarks**

Unorganized or informal sector is the major employment provider and continues to be a thrust sector for socio-economic upliftment of millions of people and for inclusive growth of our country. Gender inequalities and discriminations are observed everywhere, but they assume alarming proportions especially in unorganized labor markets. The human rights of women workers in the unorganized sector need all the more protection since they are highly vulnerable to various kinds of discriminations and exploitations. This study shows that judging the human right violations by various components and parameters, the women workers of Kullu district of Himachal Pradesh suffer from such violations in more than 50 per cent of the cases. Even by using 4D Sensitivity Analysis to judge such violations, the degree of HR violations varies by 2-3 percentage points only which vindicates that human rights of majority of the women workers in the unorganized sector are being violated. The study highlights the need to critically analyze legal labor protective measures and provide suitable amendments to protect the rights of unorganized sector workers. Also, there is a need of creating awareness about the legal rights of women workers in unorganized sector. Regulatory reforms need to be complemented with effective and active labor market policies that can help such women workers become more productive, obtain more protection against unemployment, and enhance skills. Ultimately, it is imperative to work towards the goal of decent and remunerative work for all women and men in conditions of freedom, equity, security and human dignity to take India into higher levels of sustainable and inclusive growth. This is both a challenge as well as an opportunity. However, the challenges will have to be converted into opportunities to usher in a win-win situation for all.

## Notes

1 The 'labor force' consists of those persons who are seeking work. Those who find employment out of them are designated by the NSS as 'workforce' and the remaining are designated as unemployed'. Since the 'labor force' is the total of which the 'workforce' is a part, any changes in the former are bound to have an impact on the latter. This is an extremely important feature which must be kept in mind before drawing inferences about the workforce from the surveys (Rangarajan, Padma and Seema, 2011).

2 The NSS 55th round provided information on the affiliation of workers with different types of establishments, public and private, and the class of employment size to which they belonged. Information on UPSS workers was broken down into 'formal' and 'informal' categories on the basis of the following criteria: (i) all employees in public sector undertakings were considered to be in the formal sector; (ii) private sector wage workers working in units that had electricity and employed 10 or more workers, or units with no electricity but employing 20 or more workers, were considered to be in the formal sector; and (iii) self-employed workers with higher secondary or more education were considered to be in the formal sector.

3 like the Minimum Wages Act, 1948, the Workmen's Compensation Act, 1923, the Maternity Benefit Act, 1961, the Bonded Labor System (Abolition) Act, 1976, the Contract Labor (Regulation & Abolition) Act, 1970, the Inter-State Migrant Workmen (Regulation of Employment and Conditions of Service) Act, 1979, the Building and Other Construction Workers (Regulation of Employment & Conditions of Service) Act, 1996, B&OCW Cess Act 1996 etc. These legislations also provide for registration of workers as beneficiaries, provision of I-Cards, Welfare Boards, safety & health measures, conditions of service etc.

4 In Africa, Asia and the pacific women work an average 12-13 hours more than men per week.

5 The Principles contained in Part IV of the Constitution have been read into Article 21 of the Fundamental Rights in Part III to safeguard and guarantee the workers of their rights. Article 14 guarantees equality before law and equal protection of the law, while Article 15 prohibits discrimination on the grounds only of sex amongst other forms of discrimination. Article 15(3) provides for special provisions to be made for women and children. Article 16 prohibits discrimination in matters of employment. While Article 38 speaks of the promotion of welfare of all the people, Article 39(a) speaks specifically of right to an adequate means of livelihood for men and women equally. Article 39(d) addresses the issue of equal pay for equal work for both men and women and Article 39(e) particularly directs the state to ensure that its policy secures that the health and strength of workers, men and women and children are not abused and that the citizens are not forced by economic necessity to take to vocations unsuited to their age or strength. Article 41 adds strength to Article 39 (a) by stating that within the limits of its economic capacity and development the State should make effective provisions for securing the right to work amongst other things to its entire people. Article 42 takes into consideration the very specific context of pregnancy related discrimination in the context of

employment and therefore it directs the State to make provisions for securing not only just and humane conditions of work but also for Maternity Relief.

## References

Bhasin, Kamla (2000), *Understanding Gender*, Kali for Women, New Delhi.

Elizabeth, V.S. (2011), "Labor and Fundamental Human Rights: Is Discrimination Law Doing the Job it is supposed to do?", National Law School of India University, India, *http://www.ialsnet.org/meetings/labor/papers/Elizabeth-India.pdf*, accessed on 28 September 2011.

Gangrade, K.D. and Joseph Anthony Gathia (1983), *Women and child workers in unorganised sector: non-government organisation's perspectives,* Concept Publishing Company, University of Michigan.

GoI (2008), *Draft Employment Policy*, Ministry of Labor & Employment, Government of India, New Delhi.

_____ (2009-10), *Key Indicators of Employment and Unemployment in India*, Ministry of Statistics and Programme Implementation, July 2009-June 2010, NSS 66th round, Government of India, New Delhi.

_____ (2010), *Report on Employment & Unemployment Survey (2009-10)*, Ministry of Labor & Employment, Government of India, Labor Bureau, Chandigarh, October.

_____ (2011a), *Annual Report 2010-11*, Ministry of Labor & Employment, Government of India, New Delhi.

_____ (2011b), *General Overview*, Ministry of Labor & Employment, Government of India, New Delhi.

_____ (2011c), "Strategic Plan of Ministry of Labor & Employment for next five years", *http://www.labor.nic.in/main/ Strategic -Plan-Document%20.pdf*, accessed on 17 September 2011.

Jacob Lovely (2004), "Violence against Women; related laws and social justice", *Women's Link*, April-June, pp. 9-13.

Krishnan, S. (2010), "Human Rights Violations in Unorganised Sectors - Govt Initiatives - A Case Analysis", paper presented in the National level seminar held at GRI-Gandhigram, March, *http://karuvelamptty.blogspot.com/2011/01/human-rights-violations-in-unorganised.html*" accessed on 10 Sepember 2011.

O'Keefe, Philip (2006), "Strengthening Employment and Social Security for Unorganised Sector Workers in India", published in the Conference Papers of India: Meeting the Employment Challenge, *Conference on Labor and Employment Issues in India,* The Institute for Human Development, New Delhi, 27-9 July.

Planning Commission (2002), *Report of the Special Group on Targeting Ten Million Employment Opportunities Per Year over the Tenth Plan Period,* Planning Commission Reports on Labor and Employment, New Delhi, Academic Foundation.

_____ (2011), *Faster, Sustainable and More Inclusive Growth,* An Approach to the 12th Five Year Plan: Draft, Planning Commission, New Delhi, August.

Rangarajan, C., Padma Iyer Kaul and Seema (2011), "Where Is the Missing Labor Force?", *Economic & Political Weekly,* September 24, Vol. XLVI No 39, pp.68-72.

Regina, G.M. (2001), *Mainstreaming Gender Equity in the Collective Bargaining Process,* A Capacity Building Document used in the workshop on Integrating Gender in Collective Bargaining Training conducted for COTU-Kenya and FES Tom Mboya Labor College, Kisumu.

Sen, Amartya (2006), *The Argumentative Indian,* 2006, Penguin.

Sengupta, Prantika (2011), "Condition of Women Working In the Unorganised Sector", *http://www.legalserviceindia.com/article/l432-Condition-of-Women-Working-In-the-Unorganised-Sector.html,* accessed on 16 September 2011.

Shafeeq, Nikhat Yasmin (2004), "Gender and discrimination - a review of the issues", *Social Change,* March, Vol.34 (1), pp.126-131.

Sharma, Alakh, (1999), *Gender and Employment in India,* Vikas Publishers, Noida, Uttar Pradesh.

Sheth, N.R. (2004), Book Review, "Negotiated Change: Collective Bargaining, Liberalization and Restructuring in India", *Journal of Entrepreneurship,* Sage Publishers, September 13, pp. 205-207.

United Nations (1991). *The World's Women 1970-1990,* New York.

World Bank (2010), *India's Employment Challenge: Creating Jobs, Helping Workers,* Oxford University Press, New Delhi.

# 5

# Impact of MNREGA on the Rural Labor Market

## (A micro study)

**Abstract**

*This paper is based on sample of 320 beneficiary and 240 non-beneficiary households spread over 16 Gram Panchayats of four districts in UP. The study has aimed to examine the effectiveness of implementation of NREGA with regarding the condition of employment, job security, income security and changing characteristics of labor market and structure of wages in rural areas. The works initiated under NREGA in the sample districts were viz ponds, check dam and kachcha/pucca link roads. However the working condition at the worksites was very unsatisfactory. Except the facility of drinking water the other facilities which are to be made available according to NREGA provisions were hardly provided at any of the worksite. Even the facility of drinking water and first aid was only seen available by a little over 41 beneficiaries and 21 percent respondents respectively. Due to lacking any facility of looking after the children at the worksites a half of women were leaving their children at home and the children of another 7 percent women were being look after by their neighbors while remaining women were forced to bring their children with them at the worksite, which were look after by themselves along with working at the sites.*

*Workers got employment under NREGA during almost all the seasons but more during summer season. The proportions of working days of participants got employment under the NREGA were 9 percent. Still the non- NREGA activities in general and the activities providing self-employment opportunities were found contributing a significant role in creation of employment for both participants and non- participants. The benefit of creation of employment opportunities under the NREGA has mostly gone in favor of landless Laborers followed by marginal and small farmers than the other categories of farmers. However the proportion of working days under non- NREGA employment of different categories of farmers except large farmers among the participants were significantly higher than their non – participant counterparts*

*The contribution of NREGA in the total income of landless households was recorded as high as 22 percent followed by 19 percent in the households of marginal farmers and lowest at 12 percent in the households of larger category of farmers. But the average size of income derived from non – NREGA activities was found highest in the larger categories of farm households which consistently declined with declining the size of holdings of the households.*

*The impact of NREGA on the rural market is concerned, earlier the procedure for employing casual labor was well prevailing in all the districts and the payment of wages were very low and employment regularity was highly un-secure. Now these conditions were moderately prevalent. Since the wage rates have been increased and are paid regularly. Also, there has been a remarkable change in the form of employing farm servant in sample areas. Earlier, it was highly prevalent in 38 percent GPs, but it was currently prevalent in 19 percent GPs. In fact, a significant level of impact has been indicated in mode of wage payments after the introduction of NREGA. The system of employing contract migrant labor has either boost up or it is constant, after initiating NREGA in all the districts. The provision of providing credit to different types of labors is continued today while the proportion of GPs making cash payment of wages were declined but the system of payment of wages both cash was boosting up.*

*The fixation of high wage rates under NREGA has directly influenced the increasing trends of wages of both for agricultural and non- agricultural labors. But the wage rates of agricultural labors were lagging far behind to the non-agricultural labors. However, the wage rates of latter category of labors has been picking up more sharply than the case of former category of labors. Similarly, the wage rates of women were at much lower order than their male counterpart in both agricultural sector and non-agricultural sector. Also the wages of men has been increasing more sharply than the women in agriculture sector but the reversal was the situation in non- agriculture sector.*

**Introduction**

Rural economy in India has been characterized by a huge volume of surplus labor in the form of disguised as well as open unemployment. The labor force in this agrarian surplus economy has been largely depending on wages which they receive through undertaking unskilled, casual, and manual works in rural farm and non-farm sectors (Singh, 1994, Mathur 1993). Rural labor constitutes the most marginalized and disadvantageous section of our society despite the fact that agriculture is a major occupation of people in rural areas. Thus, the problems of rural labor are multi-dimensional and concerned with economic, social and political. These problems has given birth to many challenges before the society as they are facing various problems like unemployment, under-employment, low wage rate, low income, etc. resulting in chronic poverty. They also face problems like poor working conditions, malnutrition, under-consumption and exploitation. These problems are closely interwoven and have taken a shape of serious challenge before the economy as well as the society, which should be tackled is a cautious manner so that no imbalance could take place ( Gupta 2009).

The outcome of these emerged problems has caused a major challenge for policy makers and planners in view of the creation of additional employment opportunities for additionally increasing labor force in rural areas. To meet out these challenges, several wage employment and self-employment programmes for creating additional employment opportunities and workforce programmes that offered wage employment on public works on minimum wages were initiated beginning from the introduction of First Plan in India

(Chadha 1994). The objectives of these employment oriented programmes were essentially to create additional employment for rural labor force and income for rural households thus to accelerate the growth of rural economy directly through creation and utilization of rural productive assets. But due to one or other reasons these initiatives had been merely successful in achieving the desired goal in the past. The weaknesses of these wage employment programmes can be listed in terms of, (i) low programme coverage (ii) more than fifty percent beneficiaries were not from most needy group (iii) bureaucracy dominated planning and a little participation of community in planning (iv) work to women lower than stipulated norm of 30 percent (v) only 16 to 29 days employment provided to household (vi) assets created not durable and (vii) corruption, reports of false muster rolls, contractors persisted and payment often less than prescribed wages (Mehrotra, 2008).

This paper is out come of a study entitled "Management of NREGA: Issues and Challenges" carried out by the author at the Giri Institute of Development Studies

With the background of a little success achieved in providing employment security, improving the condition of employment and reasonable wages through introducing various wage employment schemes in the past the NREGA was enacted to reinforce the commitment towards livelihood security in rural areas on 7th September, 2005. The significance of NREGA is that it creates a right-based framework for wage employment programmes and makes the Government legally accountable for providing employment to those who ask for it. NREGA aims at enhancing the livelihood security of the households in rural areas by providing at least 100 days of guaranteed wage- employment in a year to every household whose adult members volunteer to do unskilled manual work. Earlier wage-employment programmes were allocation-based. NREGA is not supply driven but demand driven. The public delivery system has been made accountable. The choice of works suggested in the Act addresses causes of chronic poverty like drought, deforestation and soil erosion, so that the process of employment generation to be maintained on a sustainable basis.

The present paper attempts to examine at the effectiveness of NREGA in matters related to the condition of employment, employment and income security and changing characteristics of labor market and structure of wages in rural areas of Uttar Pradesh. The paper has been based on primary data obtained among a sample of 320 beneficiary and 240 non- beneficiary households spread over in 16 Gram Panchayats of four districts; two backward and two developed districts located in four different agro- climatic zones in Uttar Pradesh.

**Working conditions**

The rural population was engaged in undertaking NREGA works on the basis of both daily wage and piece rate. However, an overwhelming majority of 80 percent of respondents were engaged in digging and /or carrying earth followed by 19 percent in composite task and 10 percent in water supply. Even the proportion of respondents engaged in digging and /carrying of earth were accounted as high as 90 percent in Chitrakoot followed by 84 percent in Kheri Lakhimpur. Only around 2 percent respondents were performing skilled works.

**Facilities at work place**

Most of the essential facilities which should be made available at the worksites were largely lacking in almost all the districts except providing drinking water facility. As indicated by the fact that an overwhelming majority of over 58 percent respondents reported that there was not any type of facility available at the worksites where they worked in the past. The facility of crèche was seen by only less than one percent respondents in Hardoi only. The facility of drinking water was seen available by a little over 41 beneficiaries while the facility of first aid was seen available by 21 percent respondents at the worksites. In all, the proportion of

**Table 5.1: Working conditions of labor under NREGA**

| Type of work doing at present | Hardoi | Kheri Lakhimpur | Chandauli | Chitrakoot | Total | Total No. |
|---|---|---|---|---|---|---|
| No response | 7.50 | 0.00 | 0.00 | 5.00 | 3.13 | 10 |
| Digging and/or carrying earth | 67.50 | 83.75 | 78.75 | 90.00 | 80.00 | 256 |
| Breaking stones | 0.00 | 2.50 | 0.00 | 0.00 | 0.63 | 2 |
| Skilled work | 0.00 | 5.00 | 0.00 | 2.50 | 1.88 | 6 |
| Water supply | 18.75 | 13.75 | 0.00 | 11.25 | 10.94 | 35 |
| Composite task | 23.75 | 27.50 | 17.50 | 8.75 | 19.38 | 62 |
| Unclear | 3.75 | 0.00 | 0.00 | 0.00 | 0.94 | 3 |
| Total | 100.00 | 100.00 | 100.00 | 100.00 | 100.00 | 320 |

Source:- Based on field level investigation

respondents who had access to different facilities was relatively higher in Hardoi in comparison to remaining districts. Even the proportion of respondents who availed the facility of drinking water at the worksites was noted as high as 81 percent in the respective district. Also the proportion of respondents who were access to the facility of shed/floor sheet at the worksite were found over 47 percent in Hardoi as against none of respondents in both Chandauli and Chitrakoot and 16 percent respondents in Kheri Lakhimpur.

**Child Care Practices**

The study found that there were the children of below six years in only 4.38 percent of the women beneficiary households. Even there were no children in this age group in the sample households of Hardoi and Kheri Lakhimpur. The women beneficiaries were making the practices of keeping these children at more than one place depending upon the availability of type of facility available for the child care at the specific place. Due to lacking any facility of looking after the children at almost the worksites 50 percent of women were leaving their children at home and the children of another 7 percent women were being look after by their neighbors. Nearly 43 percent women were found sometimes bringing their children at worksites whether the facility of crèche is available or not at the worksite.

The facts were that in most of the cases the children of women beneficiaries were look after either by their siblings or by themselves along with working at the worksite. Only 7 percent of women respondents in Chitrakoot had reported that their children were look after by other people working at the worksite. The women beneficiaries reported that looking after the children along with engaging in undertaking work at the worksite happen to be very difficult but the prevailing poor economic condition of household force them to bring their child at the worksite. Even a majority of over 73 percent women reported that they feel anxious about their

**Table 5.2: Availability of Different Basic Facilities at the Workplace**

| Type of Facility Provided | Hardoi | Kheri Lakhimpur | Chandauli | Chitrakoot | Total | Total HH |
|---|---|---|---|---|---|---|
| First Aid | 67.95 | 13.75 | 0.00 | 3.75 | 21.07 | 67 |
| Drinking water | 80.52 | 31.25 | 16.25 | 38.75 | 41.32 | 131 |
| Crèche | 4.00 | 0.00 | 0.00 | 0.00 | 0.95 | 3 |
| Shade and floor sheet for workers | 47.37 | 16.25 | 0.00 | 0.00 | 15.51 | 49 |
| None of all | 10.00 | 68.00 | 83.75 | 61.25 | 58.44 | 187 |
| Total | 100.00 | 100.00 | 100.00 | 100.00 | 100.00 | 320 |

Source:- Based on field level investigation

child in keeping both at home and at the worksite. Enquiring regarding the reasons for feeling anxious a high majority of women were hesitated to reply in this context but a significant proportion of them were afraid of kidnapping the child or feel anxiety while the child start weeping when they are engaged in work at worksite

However, as a result of existing very cordial environment at the worksites among the beneficiaries of only one village working to gather at a single worksite a majority of women respondent reported they do not face any kind of difficulty even in breastfeeding at the worksite. The women beneficiaries were highly feeling the necessity of making the facility of child care at the worksite. As a very high majority of 79 percent women were highly interested to bring their child at the work side in case the concerned facility would be provided.

### Impact of NREGA on the Condition of Employment and Un-employment

The impact of employment created under NREGA has been examined through comparing the proportion of working day of participant and non-participant respondents in NREGA and other components of employment and as un-employment days. This analysis has been carried out at district level and in response to different categories of farmers.

**(i) Across the districts**: The members of only participant households were found participating in the works created under NREGA in all the districts. Even, as far as the impact of NREGA in creation of employment was concerned the study found that these participants were getting very negligible days of employment under the works created in NREGA during the whole year. Even a very high proportion of over one third of the working days of the NREGA participants remained under the situation of unemployment. However, irrespective of lacking participation of non–participants in employment created under NREGA the proportion of un -

**Table 5.3: Child Care Practices**

| Description | Hardoi | Kheri Lakhimpur | Chandauli | Chitrakoot | percentage | Total Respondents |
|---|---|---|---|---|---|---|
| No. of HH with children below 6 years | | | | | | |
| No response | 100.00 | 100.00 | 96.25 | 86.25 | 95.63 | 306 |
| Yes | 0.00 | 0.00 | 3.75 | 13.75 | 4.38 | 14 |
| Total | 100.00 | 100.00 | 100.00 | 100.00 | 100.00 | 320 |
| Places of Keeping the youngest child | | | | | | |
| No response | 0.00 | 0.00 | 0.00 | 0.00 | 0.00 | 0 |
| At the worksite | 0.00 | 0.00 | 33.33 | 45.45 | 42.86 | 6 |
| At home | 0.00 | 0.00 | 66.67 | 45.45 | 50.00 | 7 |
| With neighbor or relatives | 0.00 | 0.00 | 0.00 | 9.09 | 7.14 | 1 |
| Unclear | 0.00 | 0.00 | 0.00 | 0.00 | 7.14 | 1 |
| Total | 0.00 | 0.00 | 100.00 | 100.00 | 100.00 | 14 |

*Table 5.3 continued*

| Individual Looking after the child at the worksite | | | | | | |
|---|---|---|---|---|---|---|
| No response | 0.00 | 0.00 | 33.33 | 0.00 | 7.14 | 1 |
| Self | 0.00 | 0.00 | 66.67 | 72.73 | 71.43 | 10 |
| Siblings | 0.00 | 0.00 | 0.00 | 18.18 | 14.29 | 2 |
| Other | 0.00 | 0.00 | 0.00 | 9.09 | 7.14 | 1 |
| Total | 0.00 | 0.00 | 100.00 | 100.00 | 100.00 | 14 |
| **Bringing of child if child care facility available at work site** | | | | | | |
| No response | 0.00 | 0.00 | 0.00 | 27.27 | 21.43 | 3 |
| Yes | 0.00 | 0.00 | 100.00 | 72.73 | 78.57 | 11 |
| Total | 0.00 | 0.00 | 100.00 | 100.00 | 100.00 | 14 |

Source:- Based on field level investigation

employment days of non-participants were noted relatively less than the participants in almost the districts. This reflects the facts that the non-participants get sufficient days of employment by virtue of having large size of land and other productive assets which are lacked to non-participants.

Altogether, the proportion of working days of participants under the NREGA employment stood only 9 percent which ranged lowest of 5 percent in Hardoi to highest level of 11 percent in Chandauli. Still the non- NREGA activities in general and the activities providing self -employment opportunities were found contributing a significant role in creation of employment for both participants and non-participants. But the proportions of working days put under the self- employment were fairly much higher in case of latter groups of respondents than the former one.

**ii. Across the different category of Farmers:** In spite of the fact that a very little proportion of employment days were created under the NREGA that too only for participants during the whole agricultural season of 2007-08 its impact in providing employment has largely been recognized in favor of landless labors followed by marginal farmers and at lowest level for large farmers among the participants. In all, the non-NREGA wage employment and self-employment were playing a dominating role in providing employment to participants and non-participants respectively. However the proportion of working days put under non- NREGA employment of different categories of farmers among the participants were significantly higher than their counterpart among the non - participants. Reversal was the situation in matter related to the working days put under the self -employment in case of different categories of farmers among participants and non-participants during all the seasons. Also the proportion of un - employment days were found higher among all the category of farmers among participants than the non-participants, though same was not revealed during for landless labors and medium farmers.

**Table 5.4: Impact on Employment and Unemployment at Across the Districts**

| Proportion of Working Days | Participants | | | | | Non-Participants | | | | |
|---|---|---|---|---|---|---|---|---|---|---|
| | Hardoi | Kheri Lakhimpur | Chandauli | Chitra | Total Koot | Hardoi | Kheri Lakhimpur | Chandauli | Chitra Koot | Total |
| a) Under NREGS | 4.94 | 9.35 | 11.48 | 8.62 | 8.58 | 0.00 | 0.00 | 0.00 | 0.00 | 0.00 |
| b) Under Non-NREGS | 16.58 | 25.25 | 30.65 | 16.86 | 21.92 | 10.13 | 9.75 | 21.55 | 5.34 | 11.52 |
| c) Self-employment days | 45.60 | 35.31 | 26.50 | 36.49 | 36.01 | 59.67 | 62.25 | 55.96 | 61.25 | 59.86 |
| d) Un-employment days | 32.88 | 30.09 | 31.37 | 38.02 | 33.49 | 30.20 | 28.00 | 22.48 | 33.41 | 28.62 |
| h) Total days available for work | 100.00 | 100.00 | 100.00 | 100.00 | 100.00 | 100.00 | 100.00 | 100.00 | 100.00 | 100.00 |

Source:- Based on field level investigation

It further pointed out that the differences in employment days under NREGA were in favor of all categories of participant farmers except the larger farmers. This indicates that the benefit of employment created under NREGA has gone in favor of participant households owning small size of holdings than who owned larger holdings. However, the non -participant households were better placed than the participant households in getting employment as self-employment at their household level especially on their farm activities.

Even the differences in working days under NREGA for almost the categories of participant farmers except large farmers were accounted exceeding to the minimum of over 17 percent as compared to non -participants. But the concerned differences in favor of all categories of farmer participants under non- NREGA employment was higher than NREGA employment. On the other hand, almost the farm categories of non–participants had a significant level of edge over their participant counterpart in getting self-employment opportunities. The proportion of unemployment days were seen negatively related with the size of farm for both participants and non–participants.

## Impact on the Contribution of Income at Household Level

Similarly attempts have been made in the proceeding analysis about the level and extent of income being generated per participant and non- participant's households from undertaking NREGA works and its contribution in the total income of the households across the sample districts and among the different categories of farm households.

**i. Across the districts:** The contribution of NREGA was accounted 17 percent in the income of participant households during the whole agricultural year of 2007-08. But it varied highest from 20 percent in Chitrakoot followed by 18 percent in Kheri Lakhimpur to lowest at 12 percent in Hardoi. The non - NREGA employment were the only single sources of income of non- participant households which contribution in

**Table 5.5. Impact on Employment and Unemployment by Category of Farmers**

| Proportion of Working Days | Participants Households | | | | | Non-Participants Households | | | | | |
|---|---|---|---|---|---|---|---|---|---|---|---|
| | Landless | Marginal Farmer | Small Farmer | Medium Farmer | Large Farmer | Landless | Marginal Farmer | Small Farmer | Medium Farmer | Large Farmer | Total |
| a) Under NREGS | 11.93 | 7.12 | 6.46 | 6.96 | 3.97 | 0.00 | 0.00 | 0.00 | 0.00 | 0.00 | 0.00 |
| b) Under Non-NREGS | 35.01 | 16.98 | 12.70 | 12.25 | 9.40 | 8.46 | 11.49 | 3.56 | 20.45 | 19.29 | 11.52 |
| c) Self-employment days | 17.62 | 43.67 | 46.20 | 50.12 | 58.18 | 63.07 | 58.24 | 68.93 | 46.87 | 57.68 | 59.86 |
| d) Un-employment days | 35.44 | 32.23 | 34.64 | 30.67 | 28.45 | 28.47 | 30.27 | 27.51 | 32.68 | 23.03 | 28.62 |
| e) Total days available for work | 100.00 | 100.00 | 100.00 | 100.00 | 100.00 | 100.00 | 100.00 | 100.00 | 100.00 | 100.00 | 100.00 |

Source:- Based on field level investigation

their households was found much higher than the contribution of income generated together from NREGA and non - NREGA employment in the households of participants in almost the districts. It was therefore, the differences in the contribution of non - NREGA in favor of the households of participant were negative both in absolute term in two out of four districts and in aggregate terms at 80 percent against the participant households. Also the difference in contribution of non - NREGA employment was revealed in favor of non-participants though it was revealed positive in favor of participants in Chandauli and Chitrakoot.

**ii. Across the Different Category of Farm Households:** Further looking at the contribution of NREGA in the total income of different categories of farm households it was highest at 22 percent in the landless households followed by 19 percent in the households of marginal farmers and lowest at 12 percent in the households of larger category of farmers. In other words, the contribution of NREGA in the total income of different categories of farm households was negatively related with their size of land holdings. Obviously, the average size of income derived from non - NREGA activities was found highest in the larger categories of farm households which consistently declined with declining the size of holdings of the households. Also, the difference in the contribution of NREGA was highly positive in favor of all the category of participant's farm households over their non-participant counterpart of households during each of the agricultural seasons. In totality term the concerned differences reaches to the highest point of over 100 percent and 51 percent in favor of landless and marginal farm households respectively over their respective non-participant farm category of households. But the concerned differences were in negative terms in the contribution of non-NREGA to the total income of other category of participant households.

**Table 5.6: Contribution of NREGA in Total Income at District Level**

| Per HH Income By Source (Rs) | Participant | | | | | Non-Participant | | | | |
|---|---|---|---|---|---|---|---|---|---|---|
| | Hardoi | Kheri Lakhimpur | Chandauli | Chitrakoot | Total | Hardoi | Kheri Lakhimpur | Chandauli | Chitrakoot | Total |
| NREGS Income | 2574 | 4441 | 3890 | 6132 | 4259 | 0 | 0 | 0 | 0 | 0 |
| Non-NREGS Income | 18783 | 19850 | 21351 | 24511 | 21124 | 27186 | 31763 | 61939 | 42798 | 40922 |
| Total Income | 21356 | 24291 | 25241 | 30643 | 25383 | 27186 | 31763 | 61939 | 42798 | 40922 |
| Proportion of NREGS Income in Total Income | 12 | 18 | 15 | 20 | 17 | 0 | 0 | 0 | 0 | 0 |

Source:- Based on field level investigation

## Effect of NREGA on Rural Labor Market

Exploitation of labor in various forms had been a traditional concept in rural areas. The large land lords, money lenders and other influential people in villages have been exploiting rural labor in matters of offering very low wages in comparison to work undertaken, utilizing them for unlimited hours, maintaining ill and unwanted behavior in all aspects and so on. A prominent practice to hire labor has been in the form of casual labor, annual farm servant, contract labor and exchange of labor in the rural areas of sample districts. In this light the study has attempted to examine the outcome of the implementation of NREGA in changing the practices of hiring different form of labor and the structure of wages in rural areas.( Annexure- I)

### *a. Casual Labor*

The procedure for employing casual labor was highly prevalent in 44 percent villages while it was only moderately prevalent in same proportion of villages but still it was highly prevalent in 38 percent villages. A very favorable impact of NREGA has been witnessed in payments of wages. As a very high proportion of 50 percent casual labors were paid weekly and irregularly but now a highest proportion of 69 percent them receive wages regularly on daily basis. However, there has been no change in making advance payment of wages to the casual labor as only in 6 percent villages such procedure has been continuing before and after NRGEA. But the facility of providing credit to labors was well prevailing in all the GPs before the introduction of NREGA. A little impact has been revealed in the form of payment of wages. As in 75 percent GPs the wages were already being paid in cash. Now this proportion of GPs has gone up to 81 percent. A significant impact of NRGEA has seen in providing secure employment on regular basis.

### *b. Annual Farm Servants*

The form of employing farm servant was highly prevalent in 38 percent GPs, except in Chandauli but it was currently highly prevalent in 19 percent GP, though it has been moderately prevalent in 44 percent GPs. It indicates a greater change has been perceived in employing farm servant in the sample area. In fact, a significant level of impact has been indicated in the mode of wage payments. Earlier the payment of wages was made on weekly basis in half of the GPs but after implementation of NREGA the wages were paid on daily basis in a highest proportion of 44 percent GPs. However, no changes were revealed in providing credit to the farm servant. As, such system was already prevalent in all the GPs. At least some impact in the form of wage payment has been noted especially in Chitrakoot and in some extent in Kheri Lakhimpur while no impact was revealed in this regard in remaining two districts where payment of wages together in cash and kind was highly prevalent. Before the initiation of NREGA employment was insecure in all the GPs. Even today the employment of farm servant was reported not secured in almost the GPs but it reported secured in Hardoi only.

### *c. Contract Labor*

The impact of NREGA in hiring out of labor on contract was highly visible in Chandauli and Chitrakoot while it was moderately prevalent in Hardoi since earlier. However, the study did not find any impact of the NREGA on the system of wage payment as wages were largely paid on weekly basis even today. Similar was the case in matter related to the impact of NREGA on the system of advance payment, offering credit when it was required, form of wage payment and regularity of employment of the contract labor in all the districts. Since in a highest proportion of GPs the wage payments were made weekly, payment of wages in advance was well prevalent, credit was provided when it was required and employment was provided for a whole year.

### *d. Contract Migrant Labor*

There had been a negative impact of initiating NREGA in the pace and system of employing contract migrant labor especially in Hardoi where it was highly prevalent earlier but it remained constant in Kheri Lakhimpur and it started highly prevailing in Chitrakoot after initiating NREGA. Mode of wage payment has changed from its payment once in two days to daily basis in a highest proportion of GPs. However, there was no change in payment of wages in advance as concerned system was already well prevalent in 69 percent GPs. Even the facility of offering credit was already in practice in all the GPs. The wages were earlier being paid in cash in a highest proportion of 63 percent GPs but the proportion of such GPs has now increased to 88 percent. A significant impact of initiating NREGA was well depicted in ensuring the regularity in employment of contract migrant labor, particularly in Hardoi.

### *e. Exchange of Labor*

The system of the exchange of labor was moderately or less prevalent in only 31 percent GPs before the introduction of NREGA while after initiating NREGA the concerned system was prevalent in 37 percent GPs. But the system of wage payment has turned down from daily basis to weekly basis while the system of advance payment was gaining importance after initiating NREGA. The provision of providing credit to them was already in existence and was continued today while the proportion of GPs making cash payment of wages were declined but the system of payment of wages both cash and kind was boosting up. Under this system the labor were getting employments on a very irregular basis before the implementation of NREGA.

## Impact of NREGA on Rural Wages Structure

There has been a significant increase in the wage structure in both agriculture and non – agriculture sector among the sample districts after the introduction of NREGA. But it would be

**Table 5.7. Effect on the Wage Rates of Agricultural Labor**

| Particulars | Hardoi | Kheri Lakhimpur | Chandauli | Chitrakoot | Total |
|---|---|---|---|---|---|
| (a) Wage Rates for Agricultural Labors (Rs) | | | | | |
| (1) Present | | | | | |
| Total (Average) | 66 | 52 | 75 | 85 | 68 |
| Men | 71 | 59 | 77 | 88 | 74 |
| Women | 60 | 44 | 73 | 82 | 61 |
| (2) Before | | | | | |
| Total (Average) | 47 | 48 | 59 | 49 | 49 |
| Men (Actual) | 49 | 53 | 60 | 51 | 53 |
| Women (Actual) | 44 | 43 | 58 | 49 | 44 |
| (3) % Change | | | | | |
| Total | 40.42 | 8.33 | 27.12 | 70.00 | 38.78 |
| Men | 42.86 | 11.32 | 28.33 | 72.54 | 39.62 |
| Women | 36.36 | 2.33 | 25.86 | 67.35 | 38.64 |

Source:- Based on field level investigation

rather unrealistic to derive a conclusion about which elements have been determining the raising wage rates in both the sectors. One most important assumption is however, that relatively higher wage rates fixed in NREGA has indirectly influenced the increasing trends of wage rates for both agriculture and non- agriculture labors. However, it is clear from the analysis that the wage rates for non- agricultural labors has been lagging far behind to the agricultural labors. At the same time the wage rates of latter category of laborers has been increasing more sharply than the case of former category of labors. Similarly, the wage rates of women were at much lower order than their male counterpart in both agricultural sector and non-agricultural sector. At the same time, the wages of men has been increasing at the rate of nearly 40 percent as against 39 percent for women in agriculture sector. However, the differences in increasing trend of wages for men and women were largely varying across the districts. But the overall wage rates for both men and women has been increasing at a highest level in backward districts like Chitrakoot and at a lowest level in the developed districts as Kheri Lakhimpur Even the wage rates of both men and women non- agricultural labors has been indicated increased at highest level during the last one year. But the trend in this regard has been largely favoring to women than the men. At the same time, the wage rates of women were relatively less as compared to men in this sector in Hardoi and Chitrakoot but there were no differences in the wage rates of men and women in other two districts. On the whole the wage rates of women has been increasing at the rate of 26 percent as against 25 percent for men in non- agriculture sector.

**Table 5.8. Effect on the Wage Rates of Non-Agricultural Labors**

| Particulars | Hardoi | Kheri Lakhimpur | Chandauli | Chitrakoot | Total |
|---|---|---|---|---|---|
| (a) Wage Rates for Non-Agricultural Labors (Rs) | | | | | |
| (1) Present | | | | | |
| Total (%) | 53 | 33 | 90 | 87 | 64 |
| Men (Actual) | 65 | 33 | 90 | 90 | 69 |
| Women (Actual) | 40 | 33 | 90 | 83 | 58 |
| (2) Before | | | | | |
| Total (%) | 45 | 25 | 83 | 57 | 51 |
| Men (Actual) | 50 | 25 | 83 | 62 | 55 |
| Women (Actual) | 40 | 25 | 83 | 51 | 46 |
| (3) % Change | | | | | |
| Total | 17.78 | 32.00 | 8.43 | 52.63 | 25.49 |
| Men | 30.00 | 32.00 | 8.43 | 45.16 | 25.45 |
| Women | 0.00 | 32.00 | 8.43 | 62.75 | 26.09 |

Source:- Based on field level investigation

## Conclusions

The works initiated under NREGA in the sample districts were as ponds, check dam and kachcha/pucca link roads. However the working condition at the worksites was very unsatisfactory. Excepting the facility of drinking water the other facilities which are to be made available according to NREGA provisions were hardly provided at any of the worksite. Even the only facility of drinking water and first aid was seen available by a little over 41 beneficiaries and 21 percent respondents respectively. Due to lacking any facility of looking after the children at the worksites a half of women were leaving their children at home and the children of another 7 percent women were being look after by their neighbors while remaining women were forced to bring their children with them at the worksite, which were look after by themselves along with working at the sites.

The impact of NREGA in providing employment has been at least at some extent during all the seasons, especially during summer. The proportions of working days of participants under the NREGA employment were 9 percent. Still the non-NREGA activities in general and the activities providing self-employment opportunities were found contributing a significant role in creation of employment for both participants and non- participants. The benefit of creation of employment opportunities under the NREGA has mostly gone in favor of landless Laborers followed by marginal and small farmers than the other categories of farmers. However the proportion of working days under non- NREGA employment of different categories of farmers except large farmers among the participants were significantly higher than their non - participant counterparts. Again the contribution of NREGA in the total income of landless households was recorded as high as 22 percent followed by 19 percent in the households of marginal farmers and lowest at 12 percent in the households of larger category of farmers. But the average size of income derived from non - NREGA activities was found highest in the larger categories of farm households which consistently declined with declining the size of holdings of the households

The impact of NREGA in the rural market was concerned, earlier the procedure for employing casual labor was well prevailing in all the districts and the payment of wages were very low and employment regularity was highly un-secure. Now these conditions were moderately prevalent. Since the wage rates have been increased and are paid regularly. Also, there has been a remarkable change in the form of employing farm servant in sample areas. Earlier, it was highly prevalent in 38 percent GPs, but it was currently prevalent in 19 percent GP. In fact, a significant level of impact has been indicated in mode of wage payments after the introduction of NREGA. The system of employing contract migrant labor has either boost up or it is constant, after initiating NREGA in all the districts. The provision of providing credit to different types of labors is continued today while the proportion of GPs making cash payment of wages were declined but the system of payment of wages both cash was boosting up

The fixation of high wage rates in NREGA has directly influenced the increasing trends of wages of both for agricultural and non- agricultural labors. But the wage rates of agricultural labors continued to lagging far behind to the non-agricultural labors. However, the wage rates of latter category of labors has been picking up more sharply than the case of former category of labors. Similarly the wage rates of women were at much lower order than their male counterpart in both agricultural sector and non-agricultural sector. Also the wages of men has been increasing more sharply than the women in agriculture sector but the reversal was the situation in non- agriculture sector.

## References

Chadha G.K. (1994); Employment for Rural Households in India; Past Trends and Future Choices, in Mohanty B. (ed) Employment Perspectives in Rural India, APH Publishing Co. New Delhi.

Gupta M.S (2009); Rural Labor Problems and Prospects; Serial Publications. New Delhi

Kumar A. (1993), Rural Non - Farm Employment; A State and Dynamic Study of Inter State Variations, Indian Journal of Labor Economics, Vol. 36, No.3.

Mathur A. and Pani PK (1993); The Character of Rural Industrialisation and Its Employment Impact in India; Indian Journal of Labor Economics. Vol. 36, No.3

Mehrotra Santosh (2008) NREGA Two years On; Where Do We Go From Here?, Economic and Political Weekly , February 2,

Mehta G.S. (20040, Non –Farm Economy and Rural Development, Giri Institute of Development Studies, Lucknow Singh AK (1994), Changes in the Structure of Rural Workforce in U.P.; A Temporal and Regional Study, in Visaria P and Basant R (eds) Non-Agricultural Employment in India, Sage Publications New Delhi.

Singh AK (1994), Changes in the Structure of Rural Workforce in U.P.; A Temporal and Regional Study, in Visaria P and Basant R (eds) Non- Agricultural Employment in India, Sage Publications New Delhi.

Singh A.K. (1997), Agriculture Growth, Employment and Poverty in U.P. — Some Recent Trends, in Chadha G.K. AND Sharma AN (eds) Growth, Employment and Poverty; Change and Continuity in Rural India, Vikas Publishing House, New Delhi.

## Annexure- 1

**Impact of the NREGA on the condition and form of labor use**

| Description | Hardoi | | Kheri Lakhimpur | | Chandauli | | Chitrakoot | | Total | |
|---|---|---|---|---|---|---|---|---|---|---|
| | Before NREGA | After NREGA | Before NREGA | After NREGA | Before NREGA | After NREGA | Before NREGA | After NREGA | Before NREGA | After NREGA |
| A. CASUAL LABOR | | | | | | | | | | |
| I .Existence | | | | | | | | | | |
| Highly Prevalent | 4 (100.00) | - (0.00) | 3(75.00) | - | - | 2(50.00) | - | 4 (100.00) | 7 (43.75) | 6 (37.50) |
| Moderately Prevalent | - | 1(25.00) | - | 4(100.00) | 2(50.00) | 2(50.00) | - | - | 2(12.50) | 7(43.75) |
| Less PrevalenT | - | 3(75.00) | 1(25.00) | - | 2(50.00) | - | 4(100.00) | - | 7(43.75) | 3(18.75) |
| ii. Mode of the Payment of Wages | | | | | | | | | | |
| (i) Daily | 1(25.00) | 4 | 1(25.00) | 3(75.00) | - | 4(100.00) | - | - | 2(12.50) | 11(68.75) |
| (ii) Once in two days | - | - | 3(18.75 | - | - | - | - | - | 3(18.75) | - |
| (iii) Weekly | 3(75.00) | - | - | 1(25.00) | 4(100.00) | - | 1(25.00) | 1(25.00) | 8(50.00) | 2(12.50) |
| (iv) Fortnightly | - | - | - | - | - | - | 3(75.00) | 3(75.00) | 3(18.75) | 3(18.75) |
| iii. Practices of Advance Payment | | | | | | | | | | |
| (i) Yes | - | - | 1(25.00) | 1(25.00) | - | - | - | - | 1(25.00) | 1(25.00) |
| (ii) No | 4(100.00) | 4(100.00) | 3(75.00) | 3(75.00) | 4(100.00) | 4(100.00) | 4(100.00) | 4(100.00) | 15(75.00) | 15(75.00) |

*Annexure 1 continued*

| | | | | | | | | | | |
|---|---|---|---|---|---|---|---|---|---|---|
| **iv. Providing Credit as required** | | | | | | | | | | |
| (i) Yes | 4(100.00) | 4(100.00) | 4(100.00) | 4(100.00) | 4(100.00) | 4(100.00) | 4(100.00) | 4(100.00) | 16(100.00) | 16(100.00) |
| **v. Form of Wage Payment** | | | | | | | | | | |
| (i) Cash | 4(100.00) | 4(100.00) | 3(75.00) | 3(75.00) | 3(75.00) | 4(100.00) | 2(50.00) | 2(50.00) | 12(75.00) | 13(81.25) |
| (ii) Kind | - | - | - | - | - | - | - | - | - | - |
| (iii) Both | - | - | 1(25.00) | 1(25.00) | 1(25.00) | - | 2(50.00) | 2(50.00) | 4(25.00) | 3(18.75) |
| **vi. Regularity of Employment** | | | | | | | | | | |
| (i) Whole Year | - | 1(25.00) | - | - | 1(25.00) | 1(25.00) | - | - | 1(25.00) | 2(12.50) |
| (ii) Seasonal | 4(100.00) | - | 4(100.00) | 4(100.00) | 3(75.00) | 3(75.00) | 4(100.00) | 4(100.00) | 15(75.00) | 11(68.75) |
| (iii) Irregular | - | 3(75.00) | - | - | - | - | - | - | - | 3(18.75) |
| **B. ANNUAL FARM SERVANTS** | | | | | | | | | | |
| **I. Existing** | | | | | | | | | | |
| Highly Prevalent | 3(75.00) | | 2(50.00) | | | | 1(25.00) | 3(75.00) | 6(37.50) | 3(18.75) |
| Moderately Prevalent | 1(25.00) | 3(75.00) | 2(50.00) | 2(50.00) | 2(50.00) | 2(50.00) | - | - | 5(31.25) | 7(43.75) |
| Less Prevalent | - | 1(25.00) | - | 2(50.00) | 2(50.00) | 2(50.00) | 3(75.00) | 1(25.00) | 5(31.25) | 6(37.50) |
| **ii. Mode of the payment of Wages** | | | | | | | | | | |
| (i) Daily | - | 1(25.00) | 1(25.00) | 4(100.00) | - | 2(50.00) | - | - | 1(6.25) | 7(43.75) |
| (ii) Once in two days | 1(25.00) | 3(75.00) | - | - | - | - | - | - | 1(6.25) | 3(18.75) |
| (iii) Weekly | - | - | 3(75.00) | - | 4(100.00) | 2(50.00) | 1(25.00) | 1(25.00) | 8(50.00) | 3(18.75) |
| (iv) Fortnightly | 3(75.00) | - | - | - | - | - | 3(75.00) | 3(75.00) | 6(37.50) | 3(18.75) |

*Annexure 1 continued*

| | | | | | | | | | | |
|---|---|---|---|---|---|---|---|---|---|---|
| iii. Advance Payment | | | | | | | | | | |
| (i) Yes | - | - | 1(25.00) | 1(25.00) | - | - | - | - | 1(25.00) | 1(25.00) |
| (ii) No | 4(100.00) | 4(100.00) | 3(75.00) | 3(75.00) | 4(100.00) | 4(100.00) | 4(100.00) | 4(100.00) | 15(75.00) | 15(75.00) |
| iv. Providing Credit as required | | | | | | | | | | |
| (i) Yes | 4(100.00) | 4(100.00) | 4(100.00) | 4(100.00) | 4(100.00) | 4(100.00) | 4(100.00) | 4(100.00) | 16(100.00) | 16(100.00) |
| v. Form of Wage Payment | | | | | | | | | | |
| (i) Cash | 4(100.00) | 4(100.00) | 1(25.00) | 2(50.00) | - | 2(50.00) | - | - | 5(31.25) | 8(50.00) |
| (ii) Kind | - | - | 1(25.00) | - | - | - | - | - | 16.25) | - |
| (iii) Both | - | - | 2(50.00) | 2(50.00) | 4(100.00) | 2(50.00) | 4(100.00) | 4(100.00) | 10(62.50) | 8(50.00) |
| vi. Regularity of Employment | | | | | | | | | | |
| (i) Whole Year | - | | - | - | - | - | - | - | - | |
| (ii) Seasonal | 4(100.00) | | 4(100.00) | 4(100.00) | 4(100.00) | 4(100.00) | 4(100.00) | 4(100.00) | 16(100.00) | 12(75.00) |
| (iii) Irregular | - | 4(100.00) | - | - | - | - | - | - | - | 4(25.00) |
| C. Contract Labor | | | | | | | | | | |
| i. Existing | | | | | | | | | | |
| Highly Prevalent | 4(100.00) | 4(100.00) | - | - | - | 2(50.00) | - | 4(100.00) | 4(25.00) | 10(62.50) |
| Moderately Prevalent | - | - | 3(75.00) | 3(75.00) | - | - | - | - | 3(18.75) | 3(18.75) |
| Less Prevalent | - | - | 1(25.00) | 1(25.00) | 4(100.00) | 2(50.00) | 4(100.00) | - | 9(56.25) | 3(18.75) |

*Annexure 1 continued*

| | | | | | | | | | | |
|---|---|---|---|---|---|---|---|---|---|---|
| ii. Mode of the Payment of Wages | | | | | | | | | | |
| (i) Daily | - | - | 3(75.00) | 3(75.00) | - | - | - | - | 3(18.75) | 3(18.75) |
| (ii) Weekly | 4(100.00) | 4(100.00) | 1(25.00) | 1(25.00) | 4(100.00) | 4(100.00) | 4(100.00) | 4(100.00) | 13(81.25) | 13(81.25) |
| iii. System of Advance Payment | | | | | | | | | | |
| (i) Yes | 4(100.00) | 4(100.00) | 1(25.00) | 1(25.00) | 4(100.00) | 4(100.00) | 4(100.00) | 4(100.00) | 13(81.25) | 13(81.25) |
| (ii) No | - | - | 3(75.00) | 3(75.00) | - | - | - | - | 3(18.75) | 3(18.75) |
| iv. Providing Credit as required | | | | | | | | | | |
| (i) Yes | 4(100.00) | 4(100.00) | 4(100.00) | 4(100.00) | 4(100.00) | 4(100.00) | 4(100.00) | 4(100.00) | 16(100.00) | 16(100.00) |
| v. Form of Wage Payment | | | | | | | | | | |
| (i) Cash | 4(100.00) | 4(100.00) | 4(100.00) | 4(100.00) | 4(100.00) | 4(100.00) | - | - | 12(75.00) | 12(75.00) |
| (ii) Kind | - | - | - | - | - | - | - | - | - | - |
| (iii) Both | - | - | - | - | - | - | 4(100.00) | 4(100.00) | 4(25.00) | 4(25.00) |
| vi. Regularity of Employment | | | | | | | | | | |
| (i) Seasonal | 4(100.00) | 4(100.00) | 2(50.00) | 2(50.00) | 4(100.00) | 4(100.00) | 4(100.00) | 4(100.00) | 14(87.50) | 14(87.50) |
| (ii) Irregular | - | - | 2(50.00) | 2(50.00) | - | - | - | - | 2(12.50) | 2(12.50) |
| D. CONTRACT MIGRANT LABOR | | | | | | | | | | |
| i. Existing | | | | | | | | | | |
| Highly Prevalent | 4(100.00) | - | 2(50.00) | 2(50.00) | - | - | - | 2(50.00) | 6(37.50) | 4(25.00) |
| Moderately Prevalent | - | 4(100.00) | - | 1(25.00) | 2(50.00) | - | 2(50.00) | - | 4(25.00) | 5(31.25) |
| Less Prevalent | - | - | 2(50.00) | 1(25.00) | 2(50.00) | 4(100.00) | 2(50.00) | 2(50.00) | 6(37.50) | 7(43.75) |

*Annexure 1 continued*

| | | | | | | | | | | |
|---|---|---|---|---|---|---|---|---|---|---|
| **ii. Mode of the payment of Wages** | | | | | | | | | | |
| (i) Daily | - | 4(100.00) | 2(50.00) | 2(50.00) | 2(50.00) | 2(50.00) | - | - | 4(25.00) | 8(50.00) |
| (ii) Once in two days | 4(100.00) | - | - | - | - | - | - | - | 4(25.00) | - |
| (iii) Weekly | - | - | - | - | 2(50.00) | 2(50.00) | 4(100.00) | 4(100.00) | 6(37.50) | 6(37.50) |
| (iv) Fortnightly | - | - | 2(50.00) | 2(50.00) | - | - | - | - | 2(12.50) | 2(12.50) |
| **iii. Advance Payment** | | | | | | | | | | |
| (i) Yes | 3(75.00) | 3(75.00) | 2(50.00) | 2(50.00) | 4(100.00) | 4(100.00) | 2(50.00) | 2(50.00) | 11(68.75) | 11(68.75) |
| (ii) No | 1(25.00) | 1(25.00) | 2(50.00) | 2(50.00) | - | - | 2(50.00) | 2(50.00) | 5(31.25) | 5(31.25) |
| **iv. Providing Credit as required** | | | | | | | | | | |
| (i) Yes | 4(100.00) | 4(100.00) | 4(100.00) | 4(100.00) | 4(100.00) | 4(100.00) | 4(100.00) | 4(100.00) | 16(100.00) | 16(100.00) |
| **v. Form of Wage Payment** | | | | | | | | | | |
| (i) Cash | 1(25.00) | 4(100.00) | 3(75.00) | 4(100.00) | 4(100.00) | 4(100.00) | 2(50.00) | 2(50.00) | 10(62.50) | 14(87.50) |
| (ii) Kind | - | - | - | - | - | - | - | - | - | - |
| (iii) Both | 3(75.00) | - | 1(25.00) | - | - | - | 2(50.00) | 2(50.00) | 6(37.50) | 2(12.50) |
| **vi. Regularity of Employment** | | | | | | | | | | |
| (i) Whole Year | - | 3(75.00) | - | - | 2(50.00) | 2(50.00) | 2(50.00) | 2(50.00) | 4(25.00) | 7(43.75) |
| (ii) Seasonal | 4(100.00) | - | 4(100.00) | 4(100.00) | 2(50.00) | 2(50.00) | 2(50.00) | 2(50.00) | 12(75.00) | 8(50.00) |
| (iii) Irregular | - | 1(75.00) | - | - | - | - | - | - | - | 1(6.25) |

*Annexure 1 continued*

| | | | | | | | | | | |
|---|---|---|---|---|---|---|---|---|---|---|
| **E. Exchange Labor** | | | | | | | | | | |
| i. Existing | | | | | | | | | | |
| Highly Prevalent | - | - | - | - | - | - | - | - | - | - |
| Moderately Prevalent | - | - | 1(25.00) | 1(25.00) | - | - | 4(100.00) | 2(50.00) | 5(31.25) | 3(18.75) |
| Less Prevalent | - | - | - | 1(25.00) | - | - | - | 2(50.00) | - | 3(18.75) |
| No | 4(100.00) | 4(100.00) | 3(75.00) | 2(50.00) | 4(100.00) | 4(100.00) | - | - | 11(68.75) | 10(62.50) |
| ii.Wages Paid | | | | | | | | | | |
| (i) Daily | 2(50.00) | 1(25.00) | 3(75.00) | 2(50.00) | - | - | - | - | 5(31.25) | 3(18.75) |
| (ii) Once in two days | - | - | - | - | 2(50.00) | 2(50.00) | - | - | 2(12.50) | 2(12.50) |
| (iii) Weekly | 2(50.00) | 3(75.00) | - | 1(25.00) | - | - | - | - | 2(12.50) | 4(25.00) |
| (iv) Fortnightly | - | - | 1(25.00) | 1(25.00) | 2(50.00) | 2(50.00) | 4(100.00) | 4(100.00) | 7(43.75) | 7(43.75) |
| (v) Half Yearly | - | - | - | - | - | - | - | - | - | - |
| (vi) Annual | - | - | - | - | - | - | - | - | - | - |
| iii. Advance Payment | | | | | | | | | | |
| (i) Yes | 1(25.00) | 2(50.00) | 2(50.00) | 2(50.00) | - | - | 2(50.00) | 2(50.00) | 5(31.25) | 6(37.50) |
| (ii) No | 3(75.00) | 2(50.00) | 2(50.00) | 2(50.00) | 4(100.00) | 4(100.00) | 2(50.00) | 2(50.00) | 11(68.75) | 10(62.50) |
| iv. Providing Credit as required | | | | | | | | | | |
| (i) Yes | 4(100.00) | 4(100.00) | 4(100.00) | 4(100.00) | 4(100.00) | 4(100.00) | 4(100.00) | 4(100.00) | 16(100.00) | 16(100.00) |
| (ii) No | - | - | - | - | - | - | - | - | - | - |

*Annexure 1 continued*

| | | | | | | | | | | |
|---|---|---|---|---|---|---|---|---|---|---|
| v. Form of Wage Payment | | | | | | | | | | |
| (i) Cash | 1(25.00) | 2(50.00) | 3 | 1(25.00) | - | - | 1(25.00) | 1(25.00) | 5(31.25) | 4(25.00) |
| (ii) Kind | - | - | - | - | - | - | - | - | - | - |
| (iii) Both | 3(75.00) | 2(50.00) | 1(25.00) | 3(75.00) | 4(100.00) | 4(100.00) | 3(75.00) | 3(75.00) | 11(68.75) | 12(75.00) |
| vi. Regularity of Employment | | | | | | | | | | |
| (i) Whole Year | - | - | - | - | - | - | - | - | - | - |
| (ii) Seasonal | 3(75.00) | 4(100.00) | 1(25.00) | 2(50.00) | 4(100.00) | 4(100.00) | 4(100.00) | 4(100.00) | 12(75.00) | 14(87.50) |
| (iii) Irregular | 1(25.00) | - | 3(75.00) | 2(50.00) | - | - | - | - | 4(25.00) | 2(12.50) |

Source:- Based on field level investigation

# 6

# Impact of Urbanisation on Informal Labor Migration in India

## Introduction

The recent thoughts on why the people migrate from one area to other areas within a state or across the states have reiterated multiple reasons. Some of the reasons are related to regional variations in providing basic services. By and large, unequal development in a region, distress on unemployment, marginalization, low wage rates, socio-economic exploitation, poverty, inequalities in getting basic services like education, housing, power, etc. are forcing both -rural skilled as well as unskilled work force to migrate (Lewis, 1954; Fei and Ranis, 1961; Ahluwalia, 1978).

Push and pull factors equally make out-migration possible. It seems out-migration' in India occurs depending upon socio-economic conditions of out-migrants[1] and state of services available and provided to common man. Out-migration phenomenon is basically multi-dimensional in nature, which does not give a single reason. It is very difficult to curb in a policy framework. As it has been found that most developed regions or states have attracted the work force, which needs regular employment, higher wage rate, exploitation free labor market, etc. Generally, on-going economic activities in a developed region persuade job seekers to migrate. Such activities provide employment opportunity to local work force as well as other migrants, who reside in other backward regions. In general, reasonably developed states or regions have normally a high degree of absorption capacity of surplus labor force, which is a unique characteristic of backward regions. Out-migration from low productivity region to high productivity region occurs because of comparative higher wage rate, regular employment opportunities, less exploitation, timely payment, collective bargaining power, and unique work culture[2]. Out-migration especially in backward regions corrects labor market disequilibrium and disparity in wage rate in both places- destination of migration and place of origin.

BIMAROU states[3] and Jharkhand[4] struggle to improve particularly socio-economic indicators and livelihood sources of the poor people, but they are still lagging behind in them as compared with national averages. As a result, majority of migrants moved from a group of these states. Agricultural economy in these states continues to be stagnant with negative growth rate because of poverty, primitive traditional cultivation practices, lack of basic facilities- irrigation facility, power, low quality seeds, and lack of training and extension services. Alternative sources of income like industrial development, including village and cottage industries, and service sector are undeveloped have widened a gap between the poor and non-poor. Especially, higher incidence of poverty and lack of employment opportunities have restricted the overall progress of vulnerable sections of the society that adversely affected their livelihood. Poverty Index, Human Development Index and Quality of Life Index remained below national average.

Various developmental schemes failed to make effective impact on improvement of the socio-economic condition of the poor people, despite huge budgetary allocation of the Central Government under central financial assistance programmes[5]. Still, nature and severity of problems differ in all working labor force[6] and rural educated middle class, resulting change in migration streams, which are chosen by them with specific purposes. Further, though the government has guaranteed 100 days employment under National Employment Guarantee Scheme[7], introduced in 2006, the Act itself becomes a ground of criticism for indulging corruption, while registering in it and providing job cards and unemployment allowances. In fact, the Act only covers unskilled work force, which also unable to get 100 days employment, neglect skilled workers, who are more migratory.

The Inter-state Migrant Workmen (Regulation of Employment and Conditions of Service) Act, 1979 ensures labor's rights and facilities[8]. However its provisions have remained unimplemented all these years.

### Rural Poverty, Backwardness And Migration

Rural economy mainly depends on the agricultural sector, which is itself low productivity area with high percentage of disguised employment sector. About 57 per cent of rural able population and about 98 per cent labor force works in the informal sector are engaged in this sector (Census of India, 2011, and various NSSO rounds). However, problems are more serious in the most backward states and some regions in within state. Such regions are unable to provide employment opportunities and social safety net to needy population. Such weaknesses affect livelihood and general well-being of the rural poor labor class results in high rate of chronic poverty, low literacy rate, high drop-outs rates, low Human Development Index (HDI) and low quality of life Index. Migration, urbanization, and regional disparity are strongly interrelated (Kundu and Gupta, 1996).

As estimated by the Planning Commission, based on the estimation (2004-05), poverty rates in BIMARUO states remained much higher than national average. Such group of states supply majority of work force. For example, poverty concentrating states-[9] Orissa, Bihar, Chhattisgarh, Jharkhand, Uttarakhand, Madhya Pradesh and Uttar Pradesh supply major work force to labor supply shortage states and territories- Maharashtra, Delhi, Haryana, Andhra Pradesh, Tamil Nadu, etc. Poverty requires more than economic reform and intervention (Dre'ze and Sen, 1995; World Bank, 1997; PROBE Team, 1999; Swaminathan and Rawal, 1999). Even the country has made strong efforts to reduce poverty, Sen (2001) did not find any reduction in poverty; instead, it might even have risen. Enormous amount of economic disparity, low growth rate and high rate of poverty are main driving forces (Datta and Ravallion, 2002).

The lowest literacy rate[10] in Bihar, followed by Jharkhand, Uttar Pradesh, Rajasthan, Andhra Pradesh, Orissa, Madhya Pradesh and Chhattisgarh indicate their educational backwardness, having even lower literacy rates, though improving in recent years than national average in 2011. In 2011, Bihar continues as the lowest literacy state (63.82), followed by Rajasthan (67.06 per cent), Jharkhand (67.63 per cent), Uttar Pradesh (69.72), Madhya Pradesh (70.63 per cent), Chhattisgarh (71.04), Orissa (73.45 per cent), etc. The India State Hunger Index[11] shows that Madhya Pradesh remains most vulnerable state in the country, which has the highest index score even than national average. The hunger index in Jharkhand, Bihar, Chhattisgarh, Gujarat, and Orissa are also scored alarming figures.

Even Human Development Index (HDI) is low in backward states. For example, Bihar has 0.367, which is the lowest in the country. Some other states, which are followed by Bihar states, are: Uttar Pradesh (0.388), Madhya Pradesh (0.394), Orissa (0.404), and Rajasthan (0.424).

Gupta Committee (2002) as well as other studies (de Hann, Datta and Ravallion, and others) also pointed out lack of basic services, which need to be provided on priority, especially good education, health care, transport, telecom, power, and water are out of reach in many areas of poor states mentioned above. Such economic disparities further aggravate perceptions of difference between sub-national, linguistic and communal groups, fostering ethnicity and communalism. Migration by single man is acceptable to society and other members of family stay at places of origin *(de Haan, 1994 and 2002*). Unbalanced development can have negative implications (Deshingkar and Start, 2003). Even having higher economic growth rate, it does not mean that the state hasn't poverty and poor population at all. The Gujarat state records more than 9 per cent growth rate after 1990, poverty in 36 villages, located in the northeast part of the state, changed hardly at all. 'Growth alone is hardly sufficient to achieve poverty reduction on any significant scale (Krishna *et al.*, (2005). Until recent years i.e. beginning of the 11th Five Year Plan (2007-2012), inclusive growth concept was not so popular, but now inclusive growth needs to be translated into better living conditions and job opportunities, especially for those below the poverty line (Bhalla and Hazell, 2003: 3481-3482). For example, migration from Bihar takes place mainly due to structural imbalance in the state's economy[12]. Bhide and Mehta (2010) pointed out that growth was not a significant factor in influencing entry into poverty.

Migration is a very complex phenomenon determined by various reasons and aspects that generally link to socio-economic condition of the poor people. The Law of Migration[13] noted that migrants proceeding long distances generally go by preference to one of the great centres of commerce or industry. The natives of towns are less migratory than those of the rural parts of the country. Regional unequal development causes disparity, and inequality, where surplus 'agricultural laborers' tend to find wage differences (Lewis, 1954). Todaro rightly observes four aspects of migration and reasons, which are: relative benefits and costs-mostly financial, but also psychological; expected wages differential; probability of job; urban-rural expected income differentials (Todaro, 1977). Researchers vividly describe "migration" as a movement of people for permanent or prolonged settlement (Gregory, 1928: 38-42; Weinberg, 1961; Caplow, 1975); Brown and Neuberger, 1977: 13). Lee points out that the decision of migration and process of migration are influenced by four factors: associated with the area of origin, the area of destination, intervening factors and personal factors (Lee, 1966).

But in the case of India, out-migration is a reaction against socio-economic distresses and dissatisfaction continues to exist in the society. It normally takes into account a calculation on cost and benefit of out-migration at particular point of time and place. More specifically, it is a stage of winning (satisfaction) over dissatisfaction. Migrants derive happiness, strength, and future security. Though the reasons are similar in most of the cases, satisfaction level at both places usually influences the decision on out-migration. Precisely, it is the result of "benefit" over "cost", i.e., "satisfaction" over "dissatisfaction". In other words, Migration is a process of "dissatisfaction" with the present state of "socio-economic weaknesses" around a person's locality and neighborhoods or in village, where push factors allow work force to react negatively on the available "resources and opportunities" at the point of 'migration origin' and positively on the "resources and opportunities" available at the point of 'destination of migration'.

## Migration Trends

The Census of India, 2001 collects data on migration with two parameters- migrants by the place of birth[14] and migrants by the place of last residence[15]. About 31 per cent (307 million persons) is classified under migration by the place of birth, which is slightly higher than of 1991. Out of them, about 14 per cent migrants were inter-state migrants during 1991-2001. Out of total 98.3 million persons migrated and classified under second category- place of last residence, majority i.e. 81 per cent persons were intra-state migrants, while about 21 per cent persons were inter-state migrants. In inter-state migration, rural to urban migration stream reported the highest percentage (38 per cent), followed by urban to urban stream (26.7 per cent), rural to rural areas (26.6 per cent) and urban to rural areas (6.3 per cent). During the decade, the urban population growth rate is recorded 30.3 per cent. Migrated persons added 6.6 per cent to total growth rate in urban population growth rate. (See Table-6.1)

**Table-6.1: Migrants By Place of Last Residence Indicating Migration Streams (Duration 0-9 Years) in India in 2001**

| Migration Streams | Intra-state (%) | | | Inter-state (%) | | |
|---|---|---|---|---|---|---|
| | Males | Females | Persons | Males | Females | Persons |
| Rural to Rural | 41.6 | 68.6 | 60.5 | 20.7 | 32.7 | 26.6 |
| Rural to Urban | 27.1 | 13.6 | 17.6 | 44.7 | 30.9 | 37.9 |
| Urban to Rural | 8.6 | 5.6 | 6.5 | 6.1 | 6.4 | 6.3 |
| Urban to Urban | 18.3 | 9.7 | 12.3 | 25.9 | 27.5 | 26.7 |
| Unclassified | 4.4 | 2.6 | 3.1 | 2.6 | 2.5 | 2.6 |

Note: Figures in parentheses are percentages.
Source: Abstract on Data Highlights - MIGRATION TABLES - D1, D2 & D3, Census of India, 2001.

The highest percentage of 'out-migration' was reported in rural-rural migration stream for intra-state, as compared with inter-state migration. About 61 per cent migrants moved from rural area to rural area within state, while 26 per cent migrants moved in other states. It happens mostly within state because of family relation like marriages, availability of employment opportunities and higher wage rates.

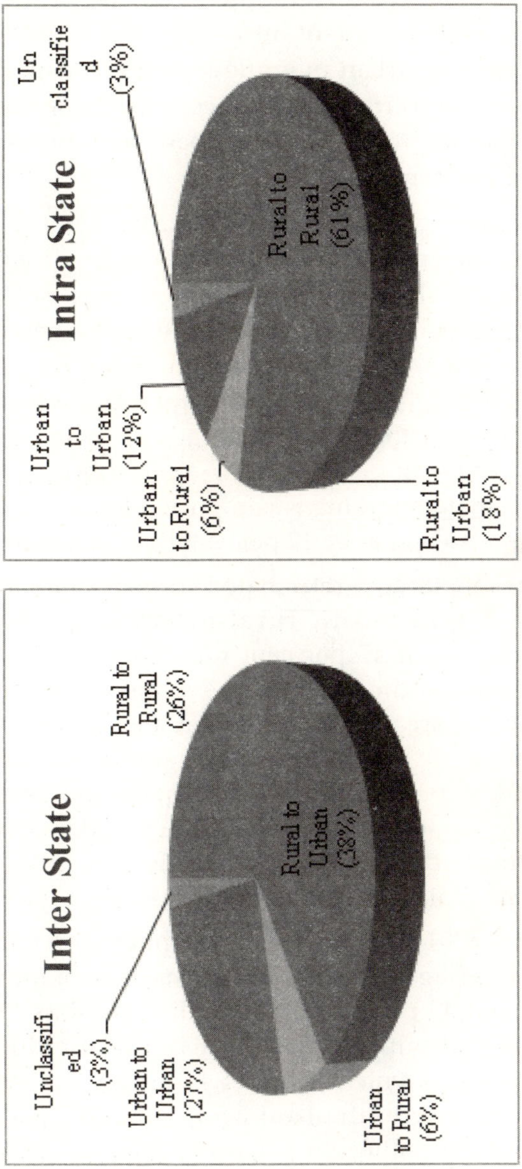


**Figure 6.1: Inter State Migration streams**

In regard to inter-state migration, the highest percentage was reported in rural-urban migration stream, which accounts for 38 per cent, while in case of intra-state, it accounts about 18 per cent. Urban to urban migration stream constitutes 27 per cent, while rural to rural stream accounts 26 per cent. In case of intra-state migration, urban-urban migration stream accounts for 12 per cent.

While comparing male-female migration intensity, the female out-migration records the highest percentage than male migration in 2001 in all types of migration streams. But, rural-rural migration in within state is comparatively higher among all migration streams. In percentage term, about 69 per cent female migrated from rural area to rural area, which was higher by 27 per cent than the percentage of male migrants (42 per cent). Even in case of inter-state migration, the percentage of female migrants was reported for about 33 per cent, which was also higher by 12 per cent than male migrants.

Male migrants largely dominated in intra-state as well as inter-state migration in rural-urban migration. In percentage term, about 45 per cent male migrated in other states and 27 per cent in within state, while corresponding female percentages are about 31 per cent and about 13.6 per cent respectively. The Urban to rural migration consistently continue with low percentage for both male and female in intra-state and inter-state migration. In case of urban to urban migration, female dominancy is prevalent in inter-state migration, while male dominancy in intra-state.

The Census, 2001 recorded reasons of migration into six[16]. Among them, marriage was reported by majority of migrants, constituting about 43 per cent (43. 1 million persons). It was followed by moved with household about 20.6 million (21 per cent), work/employment about14.4 million persons (14.7 per cent), moved after birth about 6.5 million (6.7 per cent), education about 2.9 million (3 per cent), business about 1.1 million persons (1.2 per cent) etc. But, the observation finds that female remained more migratory than male. Out of total

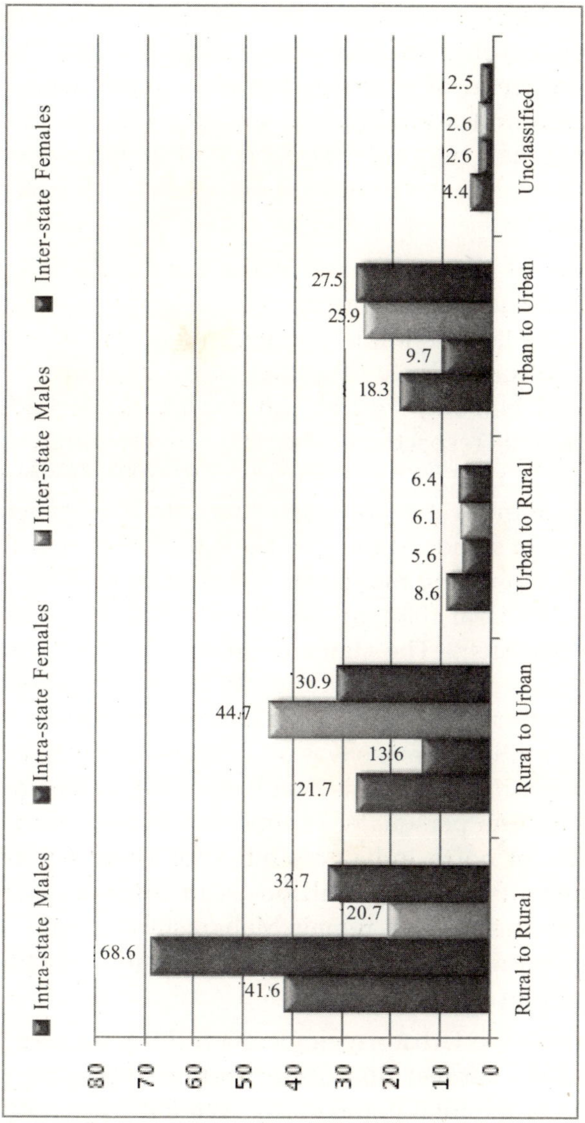


**Figure 6.2: Migration streams and male female migration intensity**

migrants, about 65.4 million are females (about 67 per cent) by last residence among them, about 64.37 per cent migrated due to marriage, while out of total 32.8 million male migrants, 37.50 per cent migrated for work/ employment'. There is an increasing trend of marriage between male, who works in urban area and a girl lives in town or village. It happens because of male migrant's family collection in town or village as well as cultural, ethnic, religious, and socio-economical homogeneity.

Some of the states are in the list of 'most favoured destination' of in-migration. For example, Maharashtra received the largest number of migrants (7.9 million persons) by place of birth, including inter-states migrants and other countries. Delhi and West Bengal stood in the second and the third positions respectively. But, trends were different in 1991 as it sharply rose in 2001. During 1991-2001, the number of migrants in India (excluding J&K) rose by 32.9 per cent, while Maharashtra stands at the first position in net migration (2.3 million persons) and the state is followed by Delhi (1.7 million persons), Gujarat (0.68 million persons) and Haryana (0.67 million persons). The states like Uttar Pradesh, Jharkhand and Bihar registered high intensity of 'out-migration. Uttar Pradesh reported 4.1 million persons as 'out-migrants', while about 1.4 million persons was in–migrants. Similarly, in Bihar about 2.8 million persons were reported as out-migrants' while 1 million persons were reported as in-migrants. These two states of north India accounted for about 6.9 million as 'out-migrants' and 2.4 million as in-migrants. The most favourable destinations remain Maharashtra[17], Delhi[18], Gujarat and Haryana as these states provide employment opportunities.

Among the Urban Agglomeration (UA), Greater Mumbai received the largest number of in-migrants (15.1 per cent migrants of the total population). About 4.3 per cent persons migrated from other parts of the state, whereas 9.6 per cent persons have migrated from other states. On the other hand, Delhi UA received 2.1 million persons and about 2 million persons have migrated from other states. These two cities are followed by Bangalore, Hyderabad, Chennai and Kolkata. (See Table 6.2).

The migrants from UP, Jharkhand, and Bihar initially migrate without families. But, they regularly remit money through bank or post to the family members- wife, and parents, who live at original home. After settling down at destinations, sometimes, they bring their families-wife and children at migration destination.

Even some states and union territories are highly urbanized. For example, Delhi has highly urbanized territory in India, followed by Chandigarh, and Pondicherry. The other states like Tamil Nadu, Goa, and Mizoram reached to having about 50 per cent urbanized population. Maharashtra will join other states in coming decades. On the other hand, Himachal Pradesh, Bihar, Sikkim, Assam, and Orissa have comparatively higher percentage of rural population, ranging from 90 per cent to 85 per cent rural population. However, out-migration is prevalent in these states.

### Decadal Population Growth Rate

The Census data shows that urban population grew at a faster rate than rural population growth rate because of in-migration in cities. The highest decadal growth rate was measured 46.14 for urban area in 1981. Since then, it started downward. Rural population decadal growth rate consistently declined as low as 12.2 per cent in 2011 that virtually closed to the decadal growth rate of 1941. The urban population is consistently increasing and rural population consistently decreasing. There are two reasons for downward spiral. One is out-migration for various purposes, including of education, distress migration, marriage, employment, business, etc. The second is that the sharp decline in the growth rate in rural areas. If this trend continues, it is bound to happen that more than 50 per cent population of the country would live in urban area in

**Table-6.2: Number of in-Migrants by Last Residence (Duration 0-9 Years) into Important Urban Agglomerations: 2001 Census**

| Name of the UA Census 2001 | Population | In-migrants | | | Total In-migrants | In- migrants to total population( per cent) |
|---|---|---|---|---|---|---|
| | | From within the state | From other states | From other countries | | |
| INDIA (Urban) | 28,61,19,689 | 2,49,74,372 | 1,11,57,574 | 3,48,060 | 3,64,80,006 | 12.7 |
| Greater Mumbai UA | 1,64,34,386 | 8,92,706 | 15,71,181 | 25,665 | 24,89,552 | 15.1 |
| Delhi UA | 1,28,77,470 | 77,663 | 19,88,314 | 46,386 | 21,12,363 | 16.4 |
| Chennai UA | 65,60,242 | 3,34,972 | 94,964 | 5,684 | 4,35,620 | 6.6 |
| Kolkata UA | 1,32,05,697 | 4,70,601 | 2,97,279 | 54,509 | 8,22,389 | 6.2 |
| Hyderabad UA | 57,42,036 | 4,07,861 | 88,216 | 2,406 | 4,98,483 | 8.7 |
| Bangalore UA | 57,01,446 | 4,01,932 | 3,53,156 | 6,397 | 7,61,485 | 13.4 |

Source: Table D3 UA City, Census of India 2001.

1940's. As a result, the percentage of aged population would be more in rural area because of out-migration of young population and on the other hand, urban area will have more young working population than in rural area.

**Findings of Primary Survey**

The field study was conducted in Pune city of Maharashtra with about 100 sample households, who were migrants. The findings are discussed in following paragraphs. Most of workers/ laborers have travelled from the states like Uttar Pradesh (UP), Bihar, Madhya Pradesh (MP), Jharkhand, Chhattisgarh and West Bengal. The workers migrated from UP have their origin, particularly in Allahabad, Jaunpur , Balrampur, Sultanpur, Azamgarh, Chitrakoot and Kushinagar districts. They are belonging to SC, ST, OBC and Muslim categories. Those migrated from West Champaran, and Muzaffarpur districts of Bihar are belonging to ST category, while migrants from Jharkhand migrate from Godda and Dhanbad districts are belonging to SC and ST categories. Those, who have migrated from Raipur district, Chhattisgarh state, are belonging to SC and ST categories. Mostly workers belong to weaker sections of the society, and poor persons are migrants.

Migrants are engaged in about eleven types of activities, mostly in unskilled and semi-skilled activities. Majority of them (65 per cent) are engaged in building construction related activities such as tiling works, window glass fitters, painters, carpenters and security guards. Remaining migrants are engaged in self-operated small shops, small and medium scale industries like tailoring work, selling *bhepuri, pan shops, floor* mill, and oil Packaging. The study has found that the workers from U.P., Chhattisgarh, Jharkhand, and Bihar states work in the industries.

It has observed that few migrant workers (23.75 per cent) have completed primary schooling. However, they all are

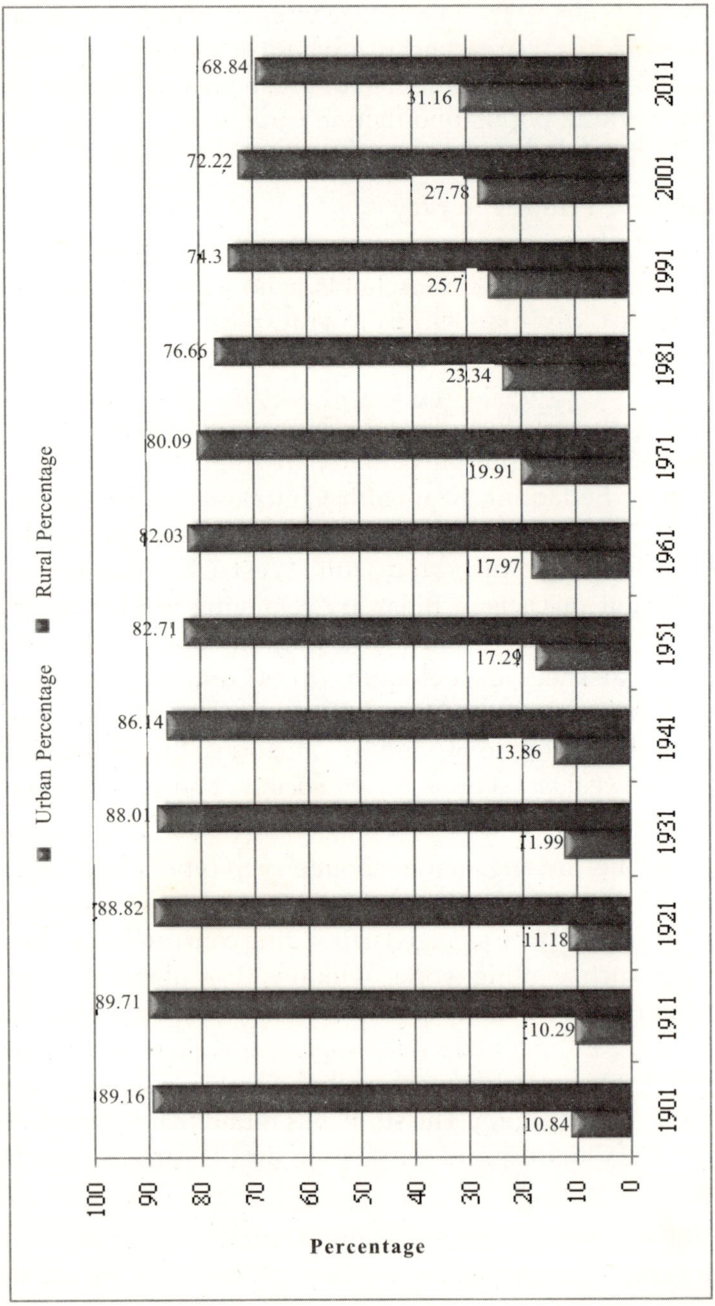


**Figure 6.3: Decadal Population growth rate**

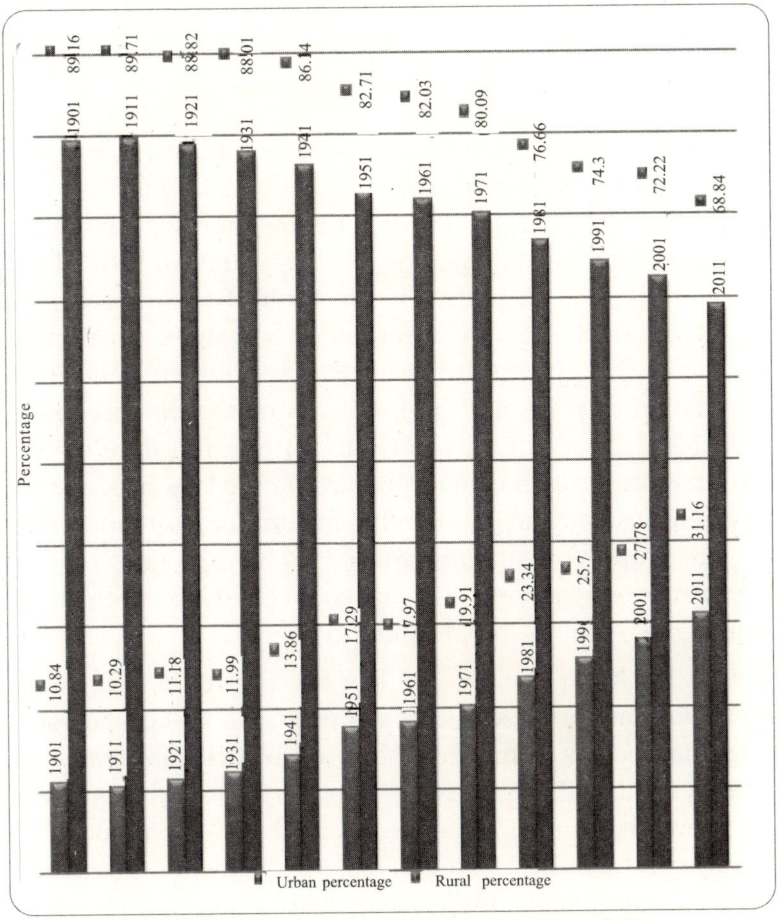


**Figure 6.4 : Urban Rural Percentage of Population**

drop-outs at middle school level. About 39 per cent workers are drop-out at primary schooling level. Among all the sample migrants, about 37.50 per cent are illiterate. None of them has completed middle school level study.

The migrants have stated multiple reasons for out-migration as push and pull factors. They migrate because of their vulnerable socio-economic conditions, lack of availability of employment opportunities, low wage rates and poor basic amenities at their home place. More specifically poverty and socio-economic exploitation at village level push the prospective migrants out. In such regions, surplus labor force always look forward for getting job opportunities, particularly in labor shortage regions. The decision of out-migration is usually taken after getting information on wage rates, regular employment opportunities, and connectivity to migration destination by road, and rail. The migrants from UP, Bihar, Jharkhand, and M.P., even though illiterate, they collect information through contacts regarding the jobs, wage rates, payment system, and job stability. In addition, full time work, regular employment, comparative high wage rate, regular payment, saving potentiality, and connectivity to the city have emerged as 'pull factors' to Pune city.

In backward states, it is very difficult in getting employment for 15 days in a month. As discussed, out-migration occurs in most of the cases in backward states for employment and higher wage rates. Prior to out-migration, only few migrants (8.75 per cent) could get employment for 16 days at the most. However, majority of them (75 per cent) have got employment for 8 days only in a month. Uncertainty over getting regular employment with reasonable wage rate has disappointed able work force. True, sustainable income can reduce poverty, but in reality, people struggle for getting regular work. The state governments in backward areas fail to frame a development strategy so that workers can be retained. There is a positive linkage between poverty and out-migration. When workers migrate to Pune, they are paid wages higher than what they get in the local areas. About 94 per cent migrants have reported that they usually get full time regular works (24 days in a month) and satisfactory higher wage rate as compared with the rates prevalent at hometown. Regular work and higher wage rate have increased monthly total income by three/ four times in a single month. Within a few days of their working in the city, they have remitted money to other family members in their home town. Some migrants (6.25 per cent) have worked even for about 28 days in a month. However, the minimum safety measures have not been provided to them at work places. Moreover, Inter-State Migrants Act, 1979 has not made any breakthrough in favor of them. In fact, it is non-operative in informal sector.

The wage rates are important for migration. Usually, the wage rates at migration destination higher than these are given in the hometown. In states like Bihar, UP, MP, Jharkhand, West Bengal, and Orissa, the wage rates are low, ranging from Rs.70 to Rs.110 a day, whereas in Pune, they are not less than Rs 131 a day with free boarding and lodging. The migrants are normally paid Rs.200-250 a day, which is higher than what they get in home places. Further, sometimes, the contractors pay railways fare to them from the hometown to Pune and back once in a year. After meeting all their they are able to save money.

The migrants always receive several benefits in many ways. As stated above, getting regular employment and higher wage rate[19] increase the total monthly income, changing their social as well as economic life. Their consumptions expenditure increases. Still, they save and remit money to family members, repay old loan, renovate an old house or construct a new house, purchase new clothes, etc. They also spend on other commitments like farm renovation marriage ceremonies, etc.

A majority of migrants (86.25 per cent) reported that they spend some of the income for raising social status at hometown. They expressed their satisfaction over income and employment at migrated place and dissatisfaction over amenities available at their villages.

The study has found that the migrants make systematic plan for spending their income. Some of them live together in a group and share expenses on rent and food. This reduces the total monthly personal expenditure and increases the saving. Sometimes the contractors also provide shelter and food near work. They normally pay wages at the rates decided by both the parties. In such cases, the expenditure on rent and food is zero. They regularly remit the money to family members, who live at the hometown. They spend about 20 to 30 per cent of monthly income on "consumption" at work place, about 40 to 50 per cent of income is remitted to families, and about 25 to 30 per cent income is saved for future expenses at hometown.

## Conclusions

A person usually migrates if he/she does not get regular employment and comparative reasonable higher wage rate. The present dilemma of the primary agriculture and allied sector fails to generate adequate employment for the marginal farmers and landless workers. Poverty has been a major reason of out-migration. The socio-economic conditions are still vulnerable. Educational attainment, dropout rates, illiteracy and unemployment are still high among migrants.

Prospective migrants usually collect information on employment potentiality, wage rates, payment system and availability of transport facilities through labor contractors, relatives, media, etc. Those, who migrate, do mainly menial works like - construction work, driving, domestic work help, and security jobs.

Some of them are self-employed. They receive higher and regular remuneration. They spend their earnings renovation of old houses or construction of new houses, improvement of agriculture farms, marriages, etc. raising social and economic status (clothes, food, etc. at hometown) and so on. They live at migrated places in a better condition.

The decision of migration is not only an "economic decision" but "social" too. Social and economic discriminations are still common in the backward regions of states. it is advisable that the government should take protective measures and villages through regional planning and development so that local work force will be retained at its own town. States like Bihar, Uttar Pradesh, Orissa, Jharkhand, Madhya Pradesh, etc. are lacking in planning and effective implementation of policies, despite huge budgetary allocations from the central government. Poverty certainly prevails owing to mismanagement and corruption also.

### Footnotes

1 Unique work culture means once migrants select the nature of works, they mostly continue as long as they able to do.

2 BIMARU states are Bihar, Madhya Pradesh, Rajasthan, Orissa and Uttar Pradesh.

3 The state is created by the Bihar reorganization Act on November 15,2000 as the 28th state of the Indian Union.

4 Some states do not utilise financial assistance properly and sometimes, corrupt officials do not spend on schemes.

5 The government does not provide good health facilities for olds and pension.

6 The National Employment Guarantee Act (NREGA) is renamed as Mahatma Gandhi National Employment Guarantee Act (MNREGA) from 2$^{nd}$ October 2009 on the occasion of 50 years of completion of Panchayati raj (golden Jubilee) in India.

7 Timely payment, suitable residential accommodation, medical facilities, protective clothing at the sites of work as well as off sites etc for migrants. In case of accident or causalities, the act also makes mandatory to the contractors for notifying such incidents to specified Authorities and kin. Additionally, it ensures smooth dispute redressal mechanism at work place as well as in origin of states, if disputes between contractors, and laborers.

[8] Poverty rate in respective states- Orissa (46.4 per cent), Bihar (41.4 per cent), Chhattisgarh (40.9 per cent), Jharkhand (40.3 per cent), Uttaranchal (39.6 per cent), Madhya Pradesh (38.3 per cent), and Uttar Pradesh (32.8 per cent). Tendulkar committee estimated have high rate of poverty in these states.

[9] Literacy rate in 2001 in Bihar (47 per cent), followed by Jharkhand (53.56 per cent), Uttar Pradesh (56.27 per cent), Rajasthan (60.41 per cent), Andhra Pradesh (60.47 per cent), Orissa (63.08 per cent), Madhya Pradesh (63.74 per cent) and Chhattisgarh (64.66 per cent)

[10] Please refer INDIA STATE HUNGER INDEX, Comparisons of Hunger Across States by Purnima Menon, Anil Deolalikar, and Anjor Bhaskar, Washington, D.C., Bonn, and Riverside, February 2009

[11] IIPA study in 2009.

[12] Entitle 'The Law of Migration' by E. G. Ravenstein, *Journal of the Statistical Society of London*. Vol. 48.No.2. (Tun., 1885). pp. 167-235, published by: Blackwell Publishing for the Royal Statistical Society, Stable URL: http://www.jstor.orglstable/2979181.

[13] Migrants by place ofbirth are those who are enumerated at a village/town at the time of census other than their place of birth.

[14] A person is considered as migrant by place of last residence, if the place in which he is enumerated during the census is other than his place of immediate last residence. By capturing the latest of the migrations in cases where persons have migrated more than once, this concept would give a better picture of current migration scenario.

[15] There are six main categories of migration- Work/Employment, Business, Education, Marriage, Moved after birth, and Moved with household.

[16] The state is the most favorite migration destination for work force in the country particularly from Uttar Pradesh, Jharkhand, and Bihar.

[17] It is capital of India, second favorite destination for migration

[18] Comparative higher wage than migrants wage at home places.

## References

Brown, Alon. A and Neuberger, Egon (1977), ed.: *Internal Migration*, Academic Press, N. York.

Caplow, Theodore (1975), *The Sociology of Work, Minneapolis*, The University of Minnesota Press p.11.

Datt, G. and M. Ravallion (1998), Why Have Some Indian States Done Better Than Others at Reducing Rural Poverty? *Economica*, 65, 17-38.

Deshingkar, Priyanka and Daniel Start (2003), *Seasonal Migration for Livelihoods in India: Coping, Accumulation and Exclusion*, ODI, London.

Dev, Mahendra S, C Ravi (2007), Poverty and Inequality: All-India and States, 1983-2005, *Economic and Political Weekly*, February 10, 2007, p 509-21.

GoI (2001d), *Census of India 2001*, Ministry of Home Affairs, Government of India, New Delhi.

GoI (2001), Census of India 2001- Data Highlights, MIGRATION TABLES (D1, D1 (Appendix), D2 and D3 Tables).

Gregory, J.W (1928), Human Migration and Future, Seeley, Service & Co. ltd. London , *World Bank Economic Review*, 10, pp. 1-25.

Guruswamy, Mohan and Ronald Joseph Abraham(2006), Redefining Poverty - A New Poverty Line for a New India, *Economic and Political Weekly*, June 24, 2006. Pp 2534-41.

Harris , John R. and Michael P. Todaro (1970), Migration, Unemployment and Development: A Two Sector Analysis." *American Economic Review* 60 (1): 126-142.

Himanshu (2007), Recent Trends in Poverty and Inequality: Some Preliminary Results, *Economic and Political Weekly*, February 10, 2007, pp 497-508.

IBRD (2000), *India Country Study on Reducing Poverty, Accelerating Development*, OUP, Delhi.

Kozel, Valerie and Parker Barbara, (2001) *Poverty in Rural India: The Contribution of Qualitative Research in Poverty* Draft Paper.

Kurian, N.J., (2000), Widening Regional Disparities in India: Some Indicators, *Economic and Political Weekly*, February 12, 2000.

Lee, E. S. (1966), A theory of migration. Demography, 3:7-57.

Mehta, Aasha Kapur and Amita Shah (2001), *Chronic Poverty in India: Overview Study*, CPRC Working Paper 7, Chronic Poverty Research Centre, (ISBN Number: 1-904049-06-0).

Patnaik, Utsa (2006), *Poverty And Neo-Liberalism In India*, Rao Bahadur Kale Memorial Lecture delivered at Gokhale Institute of Politics and Economics, Pune, February 03.

Radhakrishna, R., K. Hanumantha Rao, C. Ravi and B. Sambi Reddy (2007), *Estimation and determination of chronic poverty in India: an alternative approach,* CPRC Working Paper 90, August. This paper was presented at the CPRC Workshop on Concepts and Methods for Analysing Poverty Dynamics and Chronic Poverty, 23 to 25 October 2006, University of Manchester, UK. See http://www.chronicpoverty.org/news events/ConceptsWorkshop-Oct2006.htm .

Radhakrishna, R., Rao, K.H., Ravi, C. and Reddy, B.S. (2006), *Chronic poverty and malnutrition in India: incidence and determinants.* In Mehta, A.K. and Shepherd, A. (eds), Chronic Poverty and Development Policy. New Delhi: Sage Publications.

Sivaraman, B (2006), Contours of the Deepening Agrarian Crisis, Liberation, January.

Sundaram, K. and Suresh D. Tendulkar (2003), Poverty Among Social and Economic Groups In India in the Nineteen Nineties, Working Paper No. 118, September, website: http://www.cdedse.org.

Thorat, Sukhadeo And Motilal Mahamallik (2005), Persistent Poverty – Why Do Scheduled Castes And Scheduled Tribes Stay Chronically Poor, *Paper Presented At* Cprc-Iipa Seminar On 'Chronic Poverty: Emerging Policy Options And Issues" 29th And 30th, September, 2005, Indian Institute Of Public Administration, New Delhi.

Todaro, Michael P. (1969), A Model for Labor Migration and Urban Unemployment in Less Developed Countries, *The American Economic Review (AER)*, 59(1), 138 - 48.

Todaro, M. P. and J. Harris (1970): "Migration Unemployement and Developement : A Two Sectors Analysis," *American Economic Review*, 60 (1):126-42.

Todaro, Michael P (1977), *Economics for A Developing World,* Long man.

UNDP (2005), Human Development Report 2005, United Nations Development Programme, United Nations, New York.

Weinberg, A.A. (1975), Migration and Belonging, A study of Mental Health and Personal Adjustment in Israel 1961 Cited in Loszek A. Kosinski and R. Mansell Prothero (eds. People on the move: Studies on Internal Migration, London, Melhun and co. Ltd.)

# 7

# Problems of Domestic Female Workers

## (A Micro Study)

### Introduction

In a society where much of women's work is informalised and undervalued, domestic work remained unrecognized as a legitimate form of activity. It was thus 'invisible' even within the domain of unorganized work. Even today, it is no surprise that domestic workers are not addressed as a group of workers who need support from the state- in the form of regular and fair wages, holidays, safe conditions of work, pension benefits. They do not even find in the Unorganized Sector workers social Security Bill 2005.

### Statement of the Problem

The International Labor Organization has done well to include a draft convention on decent work for domestic workers in the 100$^{th}$ session of International Labor Conference held at Geneva in the month of June 2011. For centuries the domestic workers have lived along the margins of the international workforce. Well-documented reports by the ILO and other organizations point to the Universality of their Woes. Entirely informal in nature, domestic work, at its most anguished state, is nothing but a form of slavery; at its best, it is dogged by uncertainty. The most common failing by societies is the exploitation of this ubiquitous group of workers. Data available with the ILO suggest that domestic work ranges from four percent to 10 percent total employment in developing economics and between one percent and 2.5 percent in industrialized countries. As the ILO's 2010 report, 'Decent work for domestic workers', pointed out that this section of the workforce is undervalued and poorly regulated and a major part of it is overworked, underpaid and unprotected. An international convention backed by the ILO is an overdue move towards mainstreaming this long-neglected workforce.

In India, as in the rest of the world, there is no clarity on the number of domestic workers. National estimation varies from 4.5 million to more than 10 million. One estimate shows that there are 47,50,000 to 64,00,000 domestic workers in India. As elsewhere, they are drawn from the informal sector and comprise, largely, women and children. However, there are moves by the central and various state governments to put in place legal measures that have the potential to create a better future. That only a handful of states have set minimum wages for domestic workers is one clear indication that the country has a long way to go before it gives them statute - backed recognition and dignity. Two recommendation by the central government's task force merit urgent attention; the need to include domestic work in the union list of scheduled work for fixation and enforcement of minimum wages, and the extension of welfare measures, including health, maternity, and disability benefits and old age pension, to domestic workers. The current moves, in India and elsewhere, can only be described as a much - delayed attempt to do the minimum decent thing by this crucial segment of the workforce. The hope is that this will be the beginning of a coordinated process that addresses a global social injustice that has persisted for centuries and will continue unless there is political and social will to end it.

In this context an attempt is made to understand the determinants, and disparity of income and to project various problems faced by domestic workers.

## Objectives

The following are the objectives of this study

- To determine the differences in income earned by the Domestic Workers.
- To understand the influence of community on income.
- To study the problems faced at work place.

## Methodology

This paper is based on the primary data collected from the identified 130 sample by random sampling method from Theni town in Theni District of Tamil Nadu during the month of July 2011. These studies are related to only the women domestic workers and are categorized as Full-Time Domestic and Part-Time Domestic Workers for analysis purpose. The study is restricted only to the income earned, community and income, and problems faced by them at work place. Among the sample distributions, out of 130 respondents, 28 of them belong to Full-time workers and 102 of them come under Part - time workers categories.

**Table 7.1: Income Distribution of the Sample Respondents**

| Sl.No. | Monthly Income (Rs.) | Full Time (Residential) | | Part Time (Non-Residential) | |
|---|---|---|---|---|---|
| | | Frequency | percentage | Frequency | percentage |
| 1. | Below 500 | - | - | 9 | 8.82 |
| 2. | 500-1000 | 3 | 10.71 | 22 | 21.57 |
| 3. | 1000-1500 | 12 | 42.86 | 61 | 59.80 |
| 4. | 1500-2000 | 8 | 28.57 | 7 | 6.86 |
| 5. | Above 2000 | 5 | 17.86 | 3 | 2.94 |
| | Total | 28 | 100 | 102 | 100 |

Source : Based on field level investigation

Table No.7.1, gives the income distribution of the sample respondents. In the Full-time worker category majority of them fall in the income group between Rs.1000-Rs.1500. No one fall in the income group of below Rs.500.

In the Part-time worker category a majority of them come under the income group of Rs.1000-Rs.1500, only a few of them earn above Rs.2000.

The mean income for both full - time and part - time worker categories are Rs.1265 and Rs.1118 respectively. Compared to the workers in part-time category, workers in full-time category earn in an average a higher income.

With regard to the difference in income earned to mean deviation for full-time category are 0.75 and the part-time category it is 0.65. This indicates that the difference in income is more in the full-time category than the part-time worker category. In order to ensure the deviation the value standard deviation were obtained. This also clearly indicates that the deviation is high in the full-time category ( s = 455) compared to part-time category (s = 275).

**Table 7.2: Community wise distribution of domestic workers**

| Sl.No. | Community | Full Time (Residential) | | Part Time (Non-Residential) | |
|---|---|---|---|---|---|
| | | Frequency | percentage | Frequency | percentage |
| 1. | BC | 18 | 64.29 | 59 | 57.84 |
| 2. | MBC | 7 | 25.00 | 27 | 26.47 |
| 3. | SC | 3 | 10.71 | 16 | 15.69 |
| | Total | 28 | 100 | 102 | 100 |

Source : Based on field level investigation

The table 7.2 shows that domestic workers belong to BC, MBC and SC categories. Workers are not found from other communities. Both in the Full-time and Part-time groups' majority of them belong to BC community followed by MBC. Only a few of them belong to SC community. This is because of the reason that still workers from SC category are not accepted in to the houses of other community people.

Community wise income distribution shows that in the BC category in Full-Time division majority of them belong to the income level of Rs.1000-Rs.1500. Four of them earn above

**Table 7.3: Income Distribution and Community**

| S.No | Monthly Income (Rs.) | Full Time | | | | | | Part Time | | | | | |
|---|---|---|---|---|---|---|---|---|---|---|---|---|---|
| | | BC | | MBC | | SC | | BC | | MBC | | SC | |
| | | Frequency | % | Frequency | % | Frequency | % | Frequency | % | Frequency | % | Frequency | % |
| 1. | Below 500 | - | - | - | - | - | - | - | - | 2 | 7.41 | 7 | 43.75 |
| 2. | 500-1000 | - | - | 1 | 14.28 | 2 | 66.67 | 7 | 11.86 | 10 | 37.03 | 5 | 31.25 |
| 3. | 1000-1500 | 9 | 50.00 | 2 | 28.57 | 1 | 33.33 | 47 | 79.66 | 10 | 37.03 | 4 | 25.00 |
| 4. | 1500-2000 | 5 | 27.78 | 3 | 42.86 | - | - | 3 | 5.08 | 4 | 14.81 | - | - |
| 5. | Above 2000 | 4 | 22.22 | 1 | 14.28 | - | - | 2 | 3.39 | 1 | 3.70 | - | - |
| | Total | 18 | 100 | 7 | 100 | 3 | 100 | 59 | 100 | 27 | 100 | 16 | 100 |

Source : Based on field level investigation

Rs.2000. In the MBC category 42.86 percent of the workers get income ranging from Rs.1500-Rs.2000. In the SC category 66.67 percent belong to the income range of Rs.500 - Rs.1000.

Comparatively workers of SC category are poorly paid than other community workers.

In the part-time worker category among BC community, like that of full-time workers, majority of them, 79.68 percentage, come under the income level Rs.1000-Rs.1500. With regard to workers in MBC category equal number belong to the income category of Rs.500-Rs.1000 and Rs.1000-Rs.1500. Majority of SC community workers belong to the income level of below Rs.500.

From the analysis it could be observed that community which the worker belongs, determine the amount of wage paid.

**Problems faced by Domestic Workers**

The Third objective of the article is to identify the problems faced by domestic workers in the work place. Depending largely on the native of the employer and the family members, work place of the domestic workers have an inherent potential to inflict emotional, physical or sexual injuries on the hapless women. Being at the employer's house and often being the sole worker in the household, puts the women in a particularly vulnerable position. Abuses could take oral, physical and sexual form, besides curtailment of basic human rights of the worker. This article relates to only three major problems, verbal abuse, physical abuse, and sexual abuse.

**Verbal Abuse**

Verbal abuse refers to inconsiderate and indiscriminate scolding of workers by employers as a way of exercising authority.

**Table 7.4: Frequency of Verbal Abuse experienced by the Respondents**

| Occurrence of Verbal Abuse | Full Time | | Part Time | | Total | |
|---|---|---|---|---|---|---|
| | Frequency | % | Frequency | % | Frequency | % |
| Never | 10 | 35.71 | 75 | 73.29 | 85 | 65.38 |
| Sometimes | +13 | 46.43 | 22 | 21.56 | 35 | 26.92 |
| Frequently | 5 | 17.86 | 5 | 4.90 | 10 | 7.69 |
| Total | 28 | 100 | 102 | 100 | 130 | 100 |

Source : Based on field level investigation

Some of the respondents opined that verbal abuse is almost day-to-day affair and is somehow to be tolerated by them. However, full-time workers are frequently abused than part timers (Table 7.4). Since domestic workers work under constant monitoring of the employers' family members, there is a tendency on their part to verbally abuse the worker's. Worker's lack of skill, physical inability to work or conflicting instructions from the employers could lead to the occurrence of mistakes at work, which would open the way for scolding, such scolding is resorted to just to humiliate or for keeping the workers under control.

## Physical Abuse

Physical Abuse might include any form of inflicting pain on another person, which might result out of a variety of offensive behavior ranging from mild pinching, knuckling and stroking to more serious and heinous forms such as canning and throwing objects at the persons. Irrespective of its form or degree, corporal ill-treatment is an explicit form of aggression shown by some employers towards their workers, especially when the latter realize the desperation of the former to stay in the present occupation.

On the whole 76.15 percent of the housemaids have said that they never experienced any form of physical abuse. Only 7.69 percent of the respondents have reported that they had the experience of physical abuse very often and are to be condemned by all means.

**Table 7.5: Physical Abuse by Residential Status**

| Physical Abuse | Full Time | | Part Time | | Total | |
|---|---|---|---|---|---|---|
| | Frequency | % | Frequency | % | Frequency | % |
| Never | 16 | 57.14 | 83 | 81.37 | 99 | 76.15 |
| Sometimes | 7 | 25.00 | 14 | 13.72 | 21 | 16.15 |
| Frequently | 5 | 17.86 | 5 | 4.90 | 10 | 7.69 |
| Total | 28 | 100 | 102 | 100 | 130 | 100 |

Source : Based on field level investigation

Physical abuses is found to be more in the case of full-timers than the part-timers.

**Sexual Abuse**

Women entering remaining in domestic work endure hardships in order to earn a life of dignity and a moral way of earning their livelihood. When even this is subjected to threat by decadent advances by their employers, the resulting experience is likely to be extremely traumatic. In reality, domestic service is said to be a field that is prone to numerous forms of sexual abuses, due to the nature of relationship involved, the time periods during which the worker stays at the employers' homes and the anonymity conditions associated with the work place.

From the analysis depicted in Table 7.6, it might be seen that 24.6 percent of the domestic workers have reported to have experienced harassment in the form of sexual abuse. Irrespective of the category of the workers, Sexual abuse is to be experienced by the domestic workers.

**Table 7.6: Forms Of Sexual Abuse Experienced By Respondents**

| Forms of Sexual Abuse | Full Time | | Part Time | | Total | |
|---|---|---|---|---|---|---|
| | Frequency | % | Frequency | % | Frequency | % |
| Never | 21 | 75.00 | 77 | 75.49 | 98 | 75.38 |
| Sometimes | 5 | 17.85 | 19 | 18.62 | 24 | 18.46 |
| Frequently | 2 | 7.15 | 6 | 5.88 | 8 | 6.15 |
| Total | 28 | 100 | 102 | 100 | 130 | 100 |

Source : Based on field level investigation

## Conclusion

Female domestic work has continued to remain at a theoretical discourse, and at a peripheral level. Although domestic labor is treated as one category, it is a fact that there are several sub-categories, one such categorisation being residential and non-residential workers. The governments have a long way to regularize and protect this section of workers in the unorganized category.

## Reference

Hamid Areeba (2006); Domestic Workers, EPW, April1, PP,1235-1237.

Bhatt, Ek (1989); Shramshakti: Report of the National Commission on Self – employed women and women in the Informal Sector.

Thina Malar (Tamil Daily) : Madurai Edition, October, 2011.

Main Streaming Domestic Workers, The Hindu, Friday, March 18, 2011.

# 8

# Determinants of Self Employability of Female Informal Entrepreneurs

## (A Field Level Investigation)

**Abstract**

*Overall economic development of a country and its sustainability depend on the society which is based on socio-economic equality, equal opportunities of work and entitlement to wealth and property. Equality of the society is expected to have the context of economic, social and gender. In fact the sustainability of development is a function of the above mentioned priorities. Women from around 50 per cent of the part of world population in general and that of India in particular. Both in formal and informal way the role of women in economic activity is not less than their male counterpart. In India the contribution of informal sector to country's GDP is around 92 per cent and women work force in informal sector outnumber the men folk. Feminization of workforce and self-employment activities amongst women are the predominant outcomes of post reforms economic policy. Women's participation in agriculture cultivation is also significant. On an average, more than 65 per cent of agricultural work is performed by women. Their changing role and proactive participation in labor market has changed the reporting face of the Census – 2001. This is most evident in highly patriarchal society of northern parts of India like that of Punjab. Sectors like Textile, Electronics, Finance, BPOs, and Hospitality in urban and Agriculture, Animal husbandry, Dairy and Poultry in rural parts have an increasing dependence on women workforce. The number of women in self-employment is continuously increasing. Education, financial abilities of families, banking facilities and state policies towards small scale industries after the 1980s have increased the number of self employed women in urban areas. Electronics, automobiles, food processing and textiles can be identified as the suitable areas of female self-employment opportunities. Female participation in socio-economic and political life of Maharashtra has also a long precedence. Women studies in academics in the world and India has traveled a long with making the beginning from 1967 in the west and from 1974 in India. In India the studies on different aspects of women were catapulted after the report, 'Towards Equality', which was tabled in the Parliament in March 1974. After that many studies which were undertaken on women by social scientists have highlighted different socio-economic aspects of women as an economic agent. Important among them have been the studies in Economics. In recent times women studies have covered economic aspects from different angles, both in rural and urban areas. During the period of post reforms the share of women in every economic activity has increased. About 80 per cent of the female workers are engaged in agriculture, leaving around 5 per cent in household industries and near about 15 per cent in other type of the works. In urban metropolitan areas the picture even is different. Women have found their place in regular salaried and self-employment due to the education and awareness of families about the facilities available and their rights along with other factors facilitating their employability.*

The present paper attempting to study the determinants of self-employability of female informal entrepreneurs is based on the primary data that have been obtained from the field level investigation of 150 women entrepreneurs from Pune district of Maharashtra , where the concentration women entrepreneurial activity of various kinds is more.

**Introduction**

Increasing women participation in the Indian workforce either through self-employment or through their participation in formal and informal sector has changed the reporting face of the census of 2001 and the overall picture of economic activity of value generation. The gender composition of informal sector suggests that more than 199 million (32.2 percent) women are engaged in such employment (Satpathy, 2004).In other words, there are around 48 women in informal sector employment per one hundred men. The informal nonagricultural sector of India alone provides employment to about 2602 million women.

In manufacturing and commodity services there are nearly 44 and 46 women per hundred men. Recent research paradigm has shown that most of the women employed in manufacturing take the form of sub-contract home based works. In India, apart from agriculture, the important nonagricultural segments in terms of concentration of female informal workers are trade, manufacturing, commodity services and self-employment. Another important dimension of in-formalization of labor market in developing countries is its feminization (Charms, 2002). India is no exception to it as more than 96% of all female workers work in informal employment compared to 91.5% to such male workforce (1999-2000) together producing more than 60 per cent of country's G.D.P. (NCEUS, 2009).

An analysis of the patriarchal society of India clearly establishes that the female workers face severe disadvantages compared to male workers in terms of their educational attainments and entry in the self-employment. Traditionally there has been very little number of women in self-employment. But in the recent times women participation in workforce both through employment and self-employment is going up in a highly patriarchal society of Punjab (Census 2001). There are many factors contributing which determine the self-employment of women in recent times. Those factors are particularly the education, family background, social status, availability of bank funds, technology, aspiration, family support ...etc.

## Data and Methodology

The entire analysis that making up the present paper attempts to analyze the relative significance of the factors that determining the self-employability of women is mainly based on the primary data obtained through the personal interviews of 150 self-employed women from the segment of small entrepreneurs from Pune district of Maharashtra. It was attempted to bring out the determining factors and their relative significance of women self-employment with the help of the statistical analysis on the basis of the data pertaining to variables. The initial analysis of the paper also pretends to focus on the relative national level picture through the NSSO data ranging between 38th (1983) and 61st (2005) rounds.

## National Scenario (Pre and Post Reforms)

**Table 8.1: Type of Employment of Usually Working Urban Women (1983 - 2005)**

| Year | UPS | | | UPSS | | |
|---|---|---|---|---|---|---|
| | SE | Regular | Casual | SE | Regular | Casual |
| 1983 | 37.3 | 31.8 | 30.9 | 45.8 | 25.8 | 28.4 |
| 1987-88 | 39.3 | 34.2 | 26.5 | 47.1 | 27.5 | 25.4 |
| 1993-94 | 37.2 | 35.5 | 27.3 | 45.8 | 28.4 | 25.8 |
| 1999-00 | 38.4 | 38.5 | 23.1 | 45.3 | 33.3 | 21.4 |
| 2004-05 | 40.4 | 42.2 | 17.4 | 47.7 | 35.6 | 16.7 |

NSSO, Various Rounds

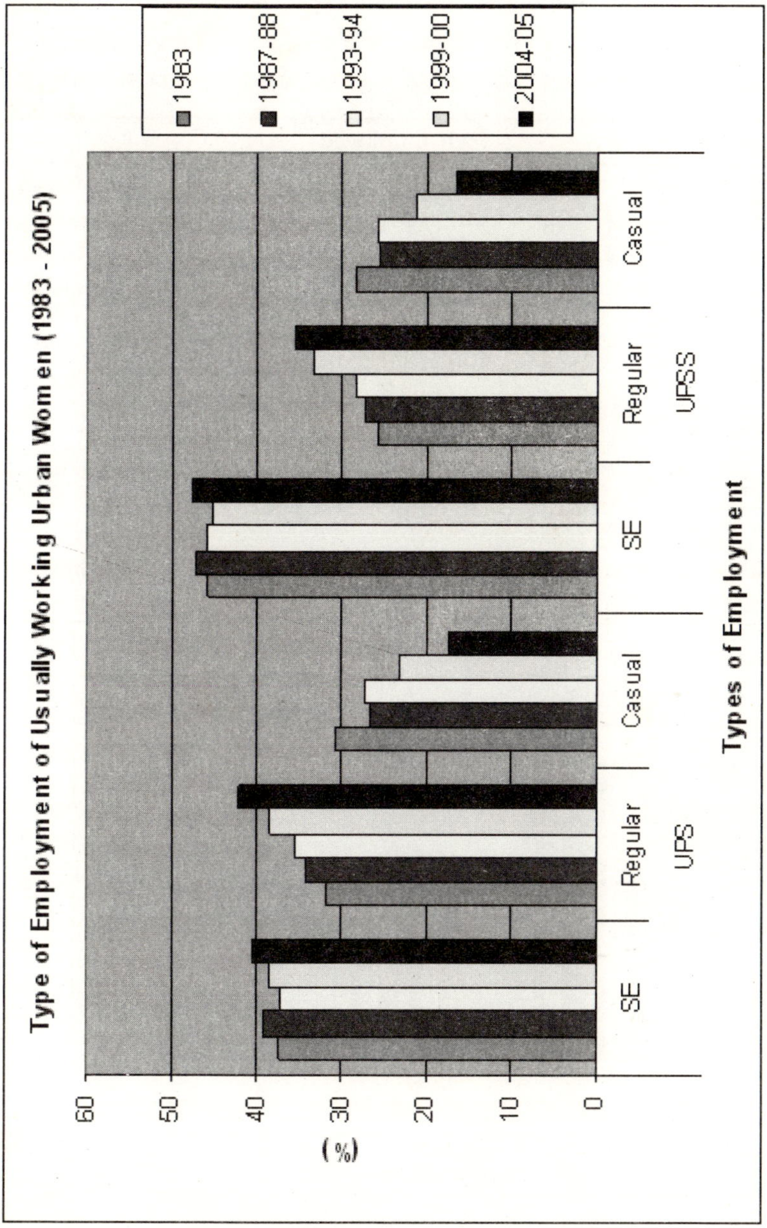


**Figure 8.1: Type of employment of usually working urban women (1985-2005)**

**Table 8.2: Urban Female Workers by type of Activity in the Manufacturing Sector (1983 - 2005).**

| Rounds<br>Year | 38th<br>1983 | 43rd<br>1987-88 | 50th<br>1993-94 | 55th<br>1999-00 | 61st<br>2004-05 |
|---|---|---|---|---|---|
| | | Self Employed | | | |
| UPS | 37.3 | 39.3 | 37.2 | 38.4 | 63.4 |
| UPSS | 45.8 | 47.1 | 45.8 | 45.3 | 69.9 |
| | | Regular & Salaried | | | |
| UPS | 31.8 | 34.2 | 35.5 | 38.5 | 24.8 |
| UPSS | 25.8 | 27.5 | 28.4 | 33.3 | 18.5 |
| | | Casual | | | |
| Ups | 30.9 | 26.5 | 27.3 | 23.1 | 11.9 |
| UPSS | 28.4 | 25.4 | 25.8 | 21.4 | 11.6 |

Source:-NSSO, Various Rounds

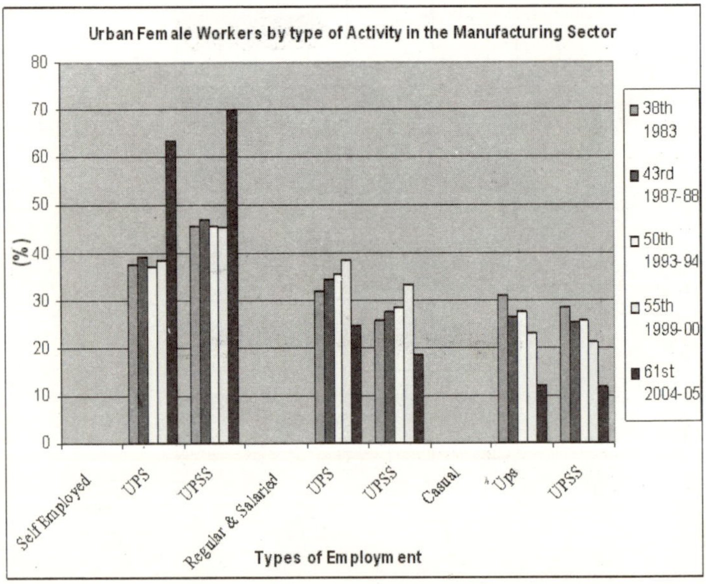


**Figure 8.2: Urban female workers by type of activity in the manufacturing sector**

**Table 8.3: Urban Female Workers by Type of Activity in Trade (1983 - 2005)**

| Round<br>Year | 38th<br>1983 | 50th<br>1993-94 | 61st<br>2004-05 |
|---|---|---|---|
| | Self Employed | | |
| UPS | 89.1 | 84.2 | 79.7 |
| UPSS | 90.4 | 85.7 | 80.9 |
| | Regular & Salaried | | |
| UPS | 5 | 8.9 | 13.9 |
| UPSS | 4.2 | 7.9 | 12.3 |
| | Casual | | |
| UPS | 5.9 | 6.9 | 6.4 |
| UPSS | 5.4 | 6.4 | 6.9 |

NSSO, Various Rounds, (Based on Table 3.3 Given Above)

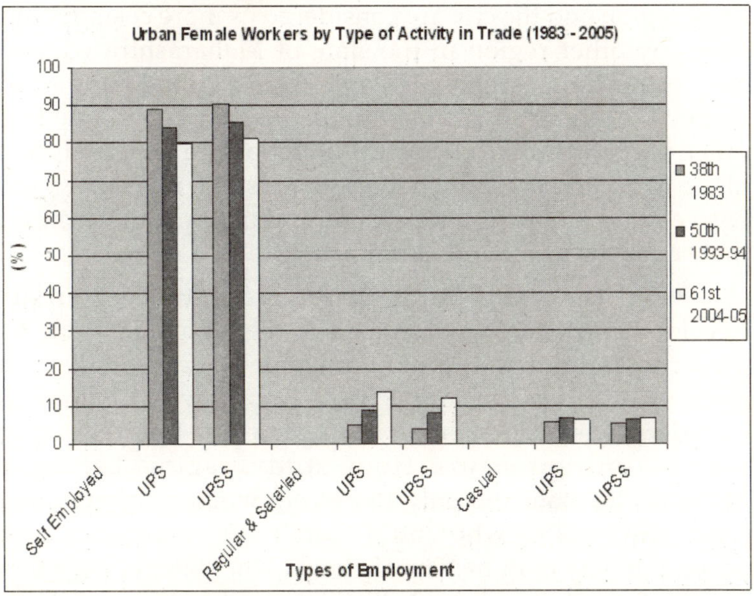


**Figure 8.3: Urban female workers by type of activity in trade (1983-2005)**

Employment opportunities at national level that have been available for the urban women have been under the categories of self-employed and regular employed which have undergone a continuous rise during the period between 1983 to 2004-05, the period comprises both the pre and post reforms era. Looking at the urban female workers by type of activity in the manufacturing sector for the same period the information on the self-employment reveals that there has been more thrust on the same during the second generation of the economic reforms. Whereas self-employment of women in trade has increased much faster than the manufacturing sector. This is mainly because the active participation of urban women through, 'at home economic activity' of productive in nature which can be accrued to the Information Technology revolution that took place during the 1990s and the 2000s.

## Discussion

### Place of Origin of Self Employed Women

Pune region and the city are considered as more cosmopolitan than any other region in the state of Maharashtra which is due to the composition of people from various parts of the country. There are a sizable number of people in Pune from other parts of India other than Maharashtra. An analysis is made to ascertain as to whether there is any relevance to the native state amongst women entrepreneurs in determining their entry in to the industrial activity.

From the view point of female entrepreneurship development, which is presented in the adjoining Table No. 8.4 it comes out that it is more convenient for the native state women to enter the arena of self-employment than the outsiders. Therefore more than 80 percent (84 percent) of the women entrepreneurs from study region belong to Maharashtra state and only 16 percent women entrepreneurs from other states who could start their small scale units around the city of Pune. They belong to the states of Rajasthan, Kerala, Karnataka, Gujarat, Bihar, Uttar Pradesh and Delhi. The historic adaptive multilingual nature of the people of

**Table 8.4: Place of Origin of Self Employed Women**

| Sr. no. | Native State | Total No of women Entrepreneurs | Percentage |
|---|---|---|---|
| 1 | Maharashtra | 126 | 84.00 |
| 2 | Bihar | 001 | 00.67 |
| 3 | A. P. | 002 | 01.33 |
| 4 | M.P. | 002 | 01.33 |
| 5 | Rajasthan | 008 | 05.33 |
| 6 | Gujarat | 002 | 01.33 |
| 7 | Karnataka | 003 | 02.00 |
| 8 | Tamil Nadu | 001 | 00.67 |
| 9 | Kerala | 003 | 02.00 |
| 10 | Uttar Pradesh | 001 | 00.67 |
| 11 | Delhi | 001 | 00.67 |
| 12 | Total | 150 | 100.00 |

Source – Based on Field Investigation

Maharashtra in general and that of Pune region in particular makes it convenient for many to opt for the way of livelihood of their choice in the area.

The breakup of the traditional joint family system both in urban and the rural parts of Maharashtra has opened up many challenges including to that of the farmers' families in the state. Even the nucleated structure of farm families in rural parts of the state has been considerably responsible for high number of farmer's suicides in the country (Talule, 2011). The reason being the sole responsibility of the risk comes on a single person. Hence the traditional joint family structure has to be regarded as the significant aspect of the support of the family. 53.33 percent (80 out of 150) of the studied women entrepreneurs hailed from Joint families and 46.67 percent of them from Nuclear family structure. The traditional joint family structure is more convenient in sharing the responsibility and also can be significant for financial contribution. Among Mechanical Engineering industrial units 60.32 percent of women entrepreneurs are from joint family structure whereas in Chemical industries 83.33 percent of women entrepreneurs who are in the business are from joint

**Table 8.5: Relationship Between Family Structure and Type of Industry**

| Sr.No. | Family Structure | Mechanical Engineering | Chemical Industry | Electronic Industry | Plastic Industry | Food Industry | Ready-made Garments | Total |
|---|---|---|---|---|---|---|---|---|
| 1 | Joint | 38(60.32) | 05(83.33) | 12(44.44) | 04(30.77) | 08(50.00) | 13(52.00) | 80(53.33) |
| 2 | Nuclear | 25(39.68) | 01(16.67) | 15(55.56) | 09(69.23) | 08(50.00) | 12(48.00) | 70(46.67) |
| 3 | Total | 63(100) | 06(100) | 27(100) | 13(100) | 16(100) | 25(100) | 150(100) |

Source – Based on Field Investigation

families and for the garment industrial units 52 percent of women entrepreneurs belong to the same kind of the family structure.

In case of the electronic industrial units relatively the higher proportion of (55.56 percent) women entrepreneurs are in the field from nuclear families and remaining from joint family structure. Same kind of the situation prevails for the plastic industries where the higher proportion of (69.23 percent) women entrepreneurs are from nuclear family and relatively less number of them are from joint family structure. Similar kind of the observation can be noted for food sector also where the proportion is almost same for both the categories of family structure where the concerned women entrepreneurs hail from. The family structure can be noted as a significant determinant of women self-employability for getting in to the entrepreneurial activity for the kind of an industry where the more amount of capital and manual support is required. These areas can be noted as the engineering and chemical industries.

**Table 8.6: Education Level of Self Employed Women**

| Sr. No | Educational Level of Women Entrepreneurs | Total No of Women Entrepreneurs | Percent |
|---|---|---|---|
| 1 | Below Matriculation | 06 | 04.00 |
| 2 | Matriculation | 20 | 13.33 |
| 3 | Higher Secondary | 14 | 09.33 |
| 4 | Graduate | 55 | 36.67 |
| 5 | Post Graduate | 14 | 09.33 |
| 6 | A) Total of Non-Technically Educated | 109 | 72.66 |
| 7 | B) Technically Qualified | 41 | 27.34 |
| 8 | Total of A + B | 150 | 100.00 |

Source - Based on Field Investigation

At national and individual household level investment in education always have a probability of significantly high degree of returns . Education plays an important role in the inculcation of certain drives and ambitions amongst the young ones. Also the education is an important aspect of human resource capacity building in economic activities as well as coping with social problems (Sidhu, Singh & Bhullar 2011). The surveyed women entrepreneurs when classified into different groups according to their educational attainments and their technical qualifications it revealed that the level of education and the probability of getting in to a self-employment are positively correlated. The information reveals that more than one third of (36.67 percent) women entrepreneurs (55 out of 150) are general graduates and exhibit the higher degree of entrepreneurial ambition. 13.33 percent of the women entrepreneurs have just completed their matriculation. Interestingly 4 percent of the women entrepreneurs' educational attainment is below S.S.C. where as 27.34 percent women entrepreneurs are technically qualified (Technical Graduates, Post Graduates and Diploma holders). The data in the same Table 4.3 depict that among 150 women entrepreneurs only 27.34 percent women entrepreneurs were technically qualified and 72.66 percent women entrepreneurs were non-technical educated. Perhaps the more number of non-technical women are in the entrepreneurial activity just either to get benefits of state policy entitled for women empowerment such as priority in allotment of the piece of land in industrial area or the finance at the concessional rate and subsidy that the male member of the family cannot avail. Even in few cases the entire credit of success goes to the female concerned but in majority of the cases the credit goes to the male member of the family where the concerned woman is just on the record.

**Education Base of the Family Members**

Young girls in the family are encouraged for obtaining skills and education where parents at the earlier stage of their life have a greater role to play. It is true that the female work participation rate in case of the economically better off families is always lower than the poor families those who need more earning members for the family. But in some cases even the economically sound families encourage their women / girls to educate well, to acquire better skills and either to support the family business or make them to start their own enterprise. After the marriage husband of a concerned lady has even a greater role than parents to promote or encourage a woman in the economic activity.

**Table 8.7: Education Base of the Family Members**

| Sr.No. | Education Level | Husband | | Father | | Mother | |
|---|---|---|---|---|---|---|---|
| | | Total | % | Total | % | Total | % |
| 1 | Illiterate | -- | -- | 07 | 04.67 | 30 | 20.00 |
| 2 | Below Matriculation | 03 | 02.00 | 18 | 12.00 | 30 | 20.00 |
| 3 | Matriculation | 10 | 06.67 | 24 | 16.00 | 24 | 16.00 |
| 4 | Higher Secondary | 07 | 04.67 | 13 | 08.67 | 35 | 23.33 |
| 5 | Graduate | 53 | 35.33 | 70 | 46.66 | 29 | 19.33 |
| 6 | Post Graduate | 33 | 22.00 | 15 | 10.00 | 02 | 01.34 |
| 7 | Technical Education | 38 | 25.33 | 03 | 02.00 | – | – |
| 8 | Technical Training | 06 | 04.00 | – | – | – | – |
| 9 | Total | 150 | 100.00 | 150 | 100.00 | 150 | 100.00 |

Source - Based on Field Investigation

The progressive behavior either of the parents or a husband can be expected only when the family has a better educational and economic background. It was observed that the family background of all surveyed women entrepreneurs' has been well educated and in most cases their education attainment was of higher order such as graduates, post graduates and in good number (38) of cases the husbands were technically qualified. Therefore it clearly comes out that better the education attainment of the family higher is the probability of development of women from the family and this automatically becomes the significant determinant of their future quality of life.

## Previous Occupation of Self Employed Women

Traditionally in countries like India the inter-relationship between one's community and her / his occupation is a well-established social phenomenon. It is likely to some extent that women may be influenced either by the occupations or ideas of their parents or husbands. Women could also be influenced by the family environment; hence an enquiry into their occupations prior to starting an enterprise can lead towards understanding the relative degree of significance of such factor.

**Table 8.8: Previous Occupation of Self Employed Women**

| Sr. No | Occupation | Total No of women Entrepreneurs | Percentage |
|---|---|---|---|
| 1 | Housewife | 89 | 59.33 |
| 2 | Education | 18 | 12.00 |
| 3 | Employed | 31 | 20.67 |
| 4 | Family Business | 09 | 06.00 |
| 5 | Social Worker | 02 | 01.33 |
| 6 | Other | 01 | 00.67 |
| 7 | Total | 150 | 100.00 |

Source - Based on Field level Investigation

About 59.33 percent of women entrepreneurs (89 out of 150) were housewives during the earlier stage of their life, 12 percent have entered the activity immediately after completing their education who were immediate past students, 20.67 percent of them were employed in some other firms, 6 percent were engaged in own family business hence had the background and experience, where as 1.33 percent were social workers. Most of the women entrepreneurs were housewives, and at the latter stage they entered into the business which is very positive change in case of such women. Women are not only engaged in managing traditional household responsibilities but they entered into the manufacturing sector and continuing successfully which has led towards the inclusive growth of the family as well as that of the society.

**Ambitions of female entrepreneurs**

Ambition from within or aspirations acquired motivate human being also it activates and broadens their vision and make the life meaningful and successful. Ambition is a psychological index of one's own resourcefulness. It has been realized that entrepreneurship is to be developed from a very young age. What is more it electrifies one's actions. What matters most is what economic aspirations men/women have and what do they do to realize them. It goes without saying that ambitions differ from individual to individual according to one's ability and temperament. They also differ from family to family, depending upon the circumstances and background particularly the economic background in which they are placed and priorities which they set for themselves. Sometimes, personal aspirations may come in the way of achieving national aspirations. It should however, be realized that ambitions or aspirations which are unfulfilled and passed on to the next generations are likely to be pursued with greater efforts and vigor. Therefore ambitions which can nourish the achievement and motivation bring about economic growth and development. When inquired into the childhood aspiration and ambitions of women entrepreneurs, the reasons which prompted them to become entrepreneurs as motivational factors and which factor facilitated the process of their entrepreneurship most it was understood that the enlisted ambitions in the table no. 4.6 have had their impact in deciding the economic motivation of concerned women in future.

Entrepreneurship is not an accidental outcome but the outcome of a longstanding ambition and aspiration nourished over a period of time. In many cases, entrepreneurship takes a long time to unfold itself. The interval between conceiving an idea and materializing the same may range from a few years to few decades. The women entrepreneurs under the present study have ranked their different ambitions in the order of importance according to their preference of choice. It showed the different ambitions. They include, becoming rich, to fulfill desire of self, to gain social prestige, to be an independent career woman, to utilize skills and knowledge, etc. There could be several such other ambitions too. The ambitions indicated by the women entrepreneurs were rated by weighted score, according, three points to the ambition ranked first, two to the ambition ranked second and one point to the ambition ranked third.

The ambition to be an independent career woman was ranked first (weighted score of 29.11 percent) of all the specified ambitions. Nearly 72 percent of the women entrepreneurs have marked this ambition as one of their three ambitions, 34 it ranked second and 14 of them ranked third. The ambition to full fill desire of self / husband's / father's was ranked second (21 percent) and to become rich has been ranked third (17.38 percent). The ambition to utilize skills and knowledge and to gain social prestige ranked fourth (15.33 percent) and fifth (12.78 percent) respectively. The category of any other was ranked sixth (4.44 percent).Ambitions such as liking towards to be an independent career woman, to full fill desire of self / husband's / fathers are more suggestive to getting big rather than getting rich. In the weighted score percentage near about 50 percent women entrepreneurs had mentioned these two ambitions. Though the ambition to making money is the prime in the minds of most of the entrepreneurs, its rating is only 17.33 percent. It is clear from the data in the adjoining table (under title 4.6) that the aggregate pull of ambition other than to become rich was much greater. This does not at all mean to become rich is not an important factor on the contrary it is the leading ambition but is closely linked with other ambitions too.

Family members' encouragement can be identified as the major factor influencing to start the enterprise by a woman entrepreneur. In case of the present study 90 out of 150 (60 percent) women entrepreneurs were influenced by the family encouragement. If seen community wise, 28 Brahmin women entrepreneurs out of 52 (53.85 percent), 25 Maratha out of 39 (64.10 percent), 9 O.B.C. out of 13 (69.23 percent), 7 S.C. / S.T, out of 15 (66.67 percent), the only Christian, 10 Jain /

**Table 8.9: Ambitions of female entrepreneurs**

| Sr.No. | Ambition | Entrepreneur's Ranking | | | Weighted Score | Rating Percent | Rank |
|---|---|---|---|---|---|---|---|
| | | One | Two | Three | | | |
| 1 | To Become Rich | 17 | 29 | 47 | 156 | 17.33 | 3 |
| 2 | To Fulfill Self / Husband's / Father's Desire | 31 | 34 | 28 | 189 | 21.00 | 2 |
| 3 | To Gain Social Prestige | 10 | 23 | 39 | 115 | 12.78 | 5 |
| 4 | To be an Independent Career Woman | 60 | 34 | 14 | 262 | 29.11 | 1 |
| 5 | To Utilize Skill and knowledge | 23 | 27 | 15 | 138 | 15.33 | 4 |
| 6 | Not Specific | 09 | 03 | 07 | 40 | 04.44 | 6 |
| 7 | Total | 150 | 150 | 150 | 900 | 100.00 | |

Source – Based on Field level Investigation

**Table 8.10: Community Background and Influencing Factors**

| Sr.No. | Community(Caste) | Influencing Factors | | | | | | | Total |
|---|---|---|---|---|---|---|---|---|---|
| | | Success Stories | Previous Experience | Previous Employment In the Same Line | Family Existing Unit | Own Skills | Family Encourag-ement | Other / Not Specific | |
| 1 | BrahminRC | 03<br>(05.77<br>(60.00 | – | 02<br>(03.85<br>(40.00 | 11<br>(21.15)<br>(35.48) | 06<br>(11.53<br>(60.00 | 28<br>(53.85<br>(31.11 | 02<br>(03.85<br>(25.00 | 52<br>(100.0<br>(34.67 |
| 2 | MarathaRC | – | 01<br>(02.56)<br>(100.00) | 02<br>(05.13<br>(40.00 | 06<br>(15.39)<br>(19.35) | 01<br>(02.56<br>(10.00 | 25<br>(64.10<br>(27.78 | 04<br>(10.26<br>(50.00 | 39<br>(100.0<br>(26.00 |
| 3 | O.B.C.RC | 01<br>(07.69<br>(20.00 | – | – | 03<br>(23.08)<br>(09.68) | – | 09<br>(69.23<br>(10.00 | – | 13<br>(100.0<br>(08.67 |
| 4 | S.C./S.TRC | 01<br>(07.13<br>(20.00 | – | – | 02<br>(14.29)<br>(06.45) | 02<br>(14.29<br>(20.00 | 07<br>(50.00<br>(07.78 | 02<br>(14.29<br>(25.00 | 14<br>(100.0<br>(09.33 |

*Table 8.10 continued*

*Table 8.10 continued*

| | | | | | | | | | |
|---|---|---|---|---|---|---|---|---|---|
| 5 | MuslimRC | – | – | – | – | – | 02<br>(100.0<br>(02.22 | – | 02<br>(100.0<br>(01.33 |
| 6 | Jain/MarwadiRC | – | – | – | 05<br>(33.33)<br>(16.14) | – | 10<br>(66.67<br>(11.11 | – | 15<br>(100.0<br>(10.00 |
| 7 | ChristianRC | – | – | – | – | – | 01<br>(100.00)<br>(01.11 | – | 01<br>(100.00)<br>(00.67 |
| 8 | OtherRC | – | – | 01<br>(07.14<br>(20.00 | 04<br>(28.58)<br>(12.90) | 01<br>(07.14<br>(10.00 | 08<br>(57.14<br>(08.89 | – | 14<br>(100.0<br>(09.33 |
| 9 | TotalRC | 05<br>(03.34<br>(100.0 | 01<br>(00.66)<br>(100.00) | 05<br>(03.34<br>(100) | 31<br>(20.67)<br>(100.00) | 10<br>(06.66<br>(100.0 | 90<br>(60.00<br>(100.0 | 08<br>(05.33<br>(100.0 | 150<br>(100.0<br>(100.0 |

Source – Based on Field level Investigation
R = Figures in parentheses indicate row percentage to total.
C = Figures in parentheses indicate column percentage to total.

Marwadi out of 15 (66.67), both the Muslim women and 8 from the other communities out of 14 (57.14 percent) were influenced by their own family encouragement. 31 women entrepreneurs out of 150 (20.67 percent) were exclusively influenced by their husband / father. Community wise picture brings out that 11 women entrepreneurs out of 52 (21.15 percent) from Brahmin community, 15.39 percent from Maratha community, 23.08 from OBC, 14.28 from S.C. / ST, 33.33 from Jain and 28.58 and percent women from other communities have been supported by their husband. In fact the success stories of other women entrepreneurs should be the influencing factor but only 5 women entrepreneurs out of 150 (3.34 percent) feel that they were prompted by this factor, among them 3 were from Brahmin and each one from OBC and SC/ST community.

Success stories influencing women entrepreneurs were quite revealing. It means that the proper dissemination of success stories of our industrial giants and pioneer entrepreneurs can create a positive image about entrepreneurship. The respective entrepreneurial development agencies could direct the information about the success stories to the targeted group for motivation. Previous experience has not been much influencing factor. Only one woman entrepreneur was found influenced by this factor. Previous employment in the same line was also an influencing factor for the women from traditionally prosperous communities such as Brahmins and Marathas (Predominantly the agriculturist and relatively hard working community of the state) and for other communities the proportion was 3.34 percent. 8 Women entrepreneurs out of 150 were influenced by several factors together where their families had a greater role in deciding their economic activism and the progress.

Economic determinants such as the success stories of hard work, earlier experience in the same line of economic activity either through family or through previous employment, family history, own skills, etc. are often found even in case of the success of established industrial houses. Near about 50 percent

**Table 8.11: Economic Factors for Women Entrepreneurship**

| Sr.No. | Annual Family Income (Rs. / Lakh) | Influencing Factors | | | | | | | Total |
|---|---|---|---|---|---|---|---|---|---|
| | | Success Stories | Previous Experience | Previous Employment | Family Existing In same line | Acquaint Skill Unit | Family Encoura-gement | Other/Not Specific | |
| 1 | Below 1 LakhRC | – | – | 01<br>(50.00<br>(20.00 | 01<br>(50.00<br>(03.23 | – | – | – | 02<br>(100.0<br>(01.33 |
| 2 | 1 - 3 RC | 02<br>(09.52<br>(40.00 | – | – | 05<br>(23.81<br>(16.13 | 05<br>(23.81<br>(50.00 | 07<br>(33.33<br>(07.78 | 02<br>(09.52)<br>(25.00) | 21<br>(100.0<br>(14.00 |
| 3 | 3 - 6 RC | 03<br>(04.41<br>(60.00 | 01<br>(01.47)<br>(100.00) | 04<br>(05.88<br>(80.00 | 05<br>(07.35<br>(16.13 | 04<br>(05.88<br>(40.00 | 44<br>(64.71<br>(48.89 | 6<br>(08.82)<br>(75.00) | 68<br>(100.0<br>(45.33 |
| 4 | 6 - 10 RC | – | – | – | 17<br>(30.36<br>(54.84 | – | 39<br>(69.64<br>(43.33 | – | 56<br>(100.0<br>(37.33 |
| 5 | Above 10 RC | – | – | – | 02<br>(66.67<br>(06.45 | 01<br>(33.33<br>(10.00 | – | – | 03<br>(100.0<br>(02.00 |
| | TotalRC | 05<br>(03.33<br>(100.0 | 01<br>(00.66)<br>(100.00) | 05<br>(03.33<br>(100.0 | 31<br>(20.67<br>100.0 | 10<br>(06.67<br>(100.0 | 90<br>(60.00<br>(100.0 | 08<br>(05.33)<br>(100.00) | 150<br>(100.0<br>(100.0 |

Source - Based on Field Investigation
R = Figures in parentheses indicate Row percentage to total.
C = Figures in parentheses indicate Column percentage to total.

of women entrepreneurs whose annual income was below Rs.3 lakh were attracted by success stories of other entrepreneurs and previous employment in the same line where as about 50 percent were influenced by their family encouragement and husband's / father's existing unit. In case of higher income group (more than Rs. 3 lakh) about 108 women entrepreneurs out of 127 (85.50 percent) were influenced by family members' encouragement and existing industrial activity in the family rather than other factors whereas the women from lower income group category were more influenced by factors like success stories and earlier association of them in the same line but the women from better economic status were not influenced by these factors to the same extent but were influenced by inherited property and family encouragement. This, therefore, meant that the women of lower economic status took to the entrepreneurship with a positive hope of improving their economic status while women of the higher economic status sought entrepreneurship to fulfill certain higher motivational desires of their own or the family, but not for improving their own economic status. The preoccupation with money which is considered to be one of the characteristics of entrepreneurs was present among the women of higher economic status while this was not the case of women with relatively lower economic category.

About 26 percent of women entrepreneurs those who were willing to start their enterprise there was not any compelling reason behind it. Need to earn money was ranked second with an overall score of 18.89 percent. To utilize idle / leisure time on hand, happened to be the third compelling reason with a total score of 12 percent women entrepreneurs whereas to utilize available opportunities becomes the fourth most compelling reason with overall score of 11.67 percent. Fifth ranking goes to the use of technical skills which they have acquired either through education or through earlier employment (10.56 percent). Sixth compelling reason was force of own from within (88 percent) whereas to make use of idle funds ranked seventh (6 percent). Diversification of economic

**Table 8.12: Compelling Reasons for Starting the Enterprise**

| Sr. No. | Compelling Reasons | Entrepreneur's Ranking | | | Weighted Score | Rating (%) | Rank |
|---|---|---|---|---|---|---|---|
| | | One | Two | Three | | | |
| 1 | Need to Earn Money | 23 | 34 | 33 | 170 | 18.89 | 2 |
| 2 | Dissatisfaction With Job | 05 | 00 | 02 | 17 | 01.89 | 9 |
| 3 | Use of Technical Skill | 16 | 18 | 11 | 95 | 10.56 | 5 |
| 4 | Make Use of Idle Funds | 02 | 11 | 26 | 54 | 06.00 | 7 |
| 5 | Diversification of Economic Interests | 02 | 04 | 13 | 27 | 03.00 | 8 |
| 6 | Utilize Available Opportunities | 10 | 30 | 15 | 105 | 11.67 | 4 |
| 7 | Force of Family Members | 13 | 14 | 13 | 80 | 08.88 | 6 |
| 8 | Utilize Idle Time | 03 | 34 | 31 | 108 | 12.00 | 3 |
| 9 | No Compelling Reasons | 76 | 03 | 00 | 234 | 26.00 | 1 |
| 10 | No Specific Reason | 00 | 02 | 06 | 10 | 01.11 | 10 |
| 11 | Total | 150 | 150 | 150 | 900 | 100.00 | |

Source – Based on Field level Investigation

interest was rated comparatively less which comes out to be 3 percent only and dissatisfaction with the earlier employment was ranked last with total score of 1.89 percent.

### Technical Education

Possessing technical expertise through education could be a most prompting reason for starting an enterprise as one feels compulsory to utilize the skills one possesses.

In all 82 of surveyed women entrepreneurs out of 150 (54.67 percent) did not have any technical education, 21 women entrepreneurs completed certificate course, 16 were technical diploma holders, 30 were engineering graduates whereas only one woman entrepreneur was post graduate in engineering. It means that less than 50 percent of women entrepreneurs were technically qualified. The information clearly states that none of the woman entrepreneur who had technical education started her enterprise to use idle funds or for the diversification of economic interest. Among all the entrepreneurs possessing technical skills, the main reason for being compelled to start an enterprise was to utilize the technical skills. The entrepreneurs had reasons such as to utilize available opportunities, force of family members, dissatisfaction with the earlier employment and utilize idle time and need to earn money to start an enterprise but not to use of the idle funds. In the case of entrepreneurs with graduation and post-graduation in technical education, the reason for starting an enterprise was on no account due to the leisure time on hand. There were some women entrepreneurs who were determinant about acquiring technical skills braving all the difficulties and thus were interested in utilizing them completely and hence they did not start enterprises because they had leisure time on hand. These women entrepreneurs could be counted those with high achievement motivation who were keen on doing or becoming something in their life. So, for people who had acquired some form of technical education, the possibility of participation in

**Table 8.13: Technical Education Women Entrepreneurship**

| Sr.No. | EducationLevel | Compelling Reason | | | | | | | | | Total |
|---|---|---|---|---|---|---|---|---|---|---|---|
| | | Need to Earn Money | Dissatis-faction With Job | Use of Technical Skills | Use of Ideal Fund | Diversif-cation of Economic Interest | To Utilize Available Opportu-Nities | Force of Family | To Utilize Ideal Time | No Comp-elling Reason | |
| 1 | No Technical EducationRC | 17<br>(20.7<br>(73.9 | 03<br>(03.66<br>(60.00 | – | 02<br>(02.4<br>(100 | 02<br>(02.44<br>(100) | 08<br>(09.76)<br>(80.00) | 10<br>(12.20<br>(76.92 | 02<br>(02.4<br>(66.6 | 38<br>(46.3<br>(50.0 | 82<br>(100)<br>(54.6 |
| 2 | Certificate Course RC | 06<br>(28.5<br>(26.0 | – | 02<br>(09.5<br>(12.5 | – | – | 01<br>(04.76)<br>(10.00) | 02<br>(09.52<br>(15.38 | 01<br>(04.7<br>(33.3 | 09<br>(42.8<br>(11.8 | 21<br>(100)<br>(14.0 |
| 3 | Diploma RC | – | 02<br>(12.50<br>(40.00 | 03<br>(18.7<br>(18.7 | – | – | 01<br>(06.25)<br>(10.00) | 01<br>(06.25<br>(07.69 | – | 09<br>(56.2<br>(11.8 | 16<br>(100)<br>(10.6 |
| 4 | Graduate RC | – | – | 10<br>(33.33)<br>(62.5 | – | – | – | – | – | 20<br>(66.67)<br>(26.3 | 30<br>(100)<br>(20.00) |
| 5 | PostGraduateRC | – | – | 01<br>(100<br>(06.2 | – | – | – | – | – | – | 01<br>(100)<br>(00.6 |
| 6 | TotalRC | 23<br>(15.3<br>(100 | 05<br>(03.33<br>(100) | 16<br>(10.6<br>(10 | 02<br>(01.3<br>(100 | 02<br>(01.3<br>(100) | 10<br>(06.67)<br>(100) | 13<br>(08.67<br>(100) | 03<br>(02.0<br>(100 | 76<br>(50.6<br>(100 | 150<br>(100)<br>(100) |

Source - Based on Field Investigation
R = Figures in parentheses indicate row percentage to total.
C = Figures in parentheses indicate column percentage to total.

economic activity is supposed to be more than of women without technical education. Therefore it would be proper to suggest that it would be in the interest of the society and the economy to have more number of technically oriented useful courses catering to the requirements of rural and urban girls.

**Economic Status**

Poor person cannot expect or think to set up an industry worth few lakhs of rupees, neither does a rich person wish to set up a pan shop nor does he to intend become a hawker. This is because the choice of line of activity is considered on the bars of not only the skills available, but also on the earlier economic status of the family and its relationship with the choice of the line of activity.

Women entrepreneurs with family incomes of all types mostly preferred to select the line of activity based on easy to set up. The other two important categories were no difficulties in securing technical know-how and existing of family business. The lower income group (less than Rs. 3 lakh) considered it easy to set up as the main consideration (43.48 percent), followed by existing family business (17.39 percent) and help of family members (13.04 percent) as second and third reason. In case of the middle income group (Rs. 3 – 6 lakh) 26 women entrepreneurs out of 68 (38.24 percent) stated the main reason as easy to set up followed by the no difficulties in securing technical knowledge (27.94 percent). And for the remaining, existing family business (14.71 percent), help of family members (8.82 percent) and previous experience (5.88 percent) have been the motivating factors.

In case of the higher income group category (more than Rs. 6 lakh), the main reason for choice of the line of industrial activity was that there was no difficulty in securing technical knowledge (37.29 percent) and second reason that it was easy for them to set up ( 25.42 percent) and third the existence of family business (18.64 percent).

**Table 8.14: Economic Status Women Entrepreneurship**

| Sr.No. | Annual Family Income (Rs.) | Reasons For the Choice of the Line of Activity | | | | | | | | Total |
|---|---|---|---|---|---|---|---|---|---|---|
| | | Easy to Set up | Previous Experience | No Competition | Availability of Market | Availability of Help of Family | Related to Occupation | Existing Family Business | No Difficulties in Securing Technical Know-how | |
| 1 | Less than Rs 1 lakh RC | 01<br>(50.00)<br>(01.96) | – | – | – | – | – | 01<br>(50.00)<br>(04.00) | – | 02<br>(100)<br>(01.33) |
| 2 | 1 - 3 lakh RC | 09<br>(42.86)<br>(17.65) | 02<br>(09.52)<br>(22.22) | – | 02<br>(09.52)<br>(33.33) | 03<br>(14.29)<br>(25.00) | – | 03<br>(14.29)<br>(12.00) | 02<br>(09.52)<br>(04.65) | 21<br>(100)<br>(14.00) |
| 3 | 3 - 6 lakh RC | 26<br>(38.24)<br>(50.98) | 04<br>(05.88)<br>(44.44) | 01<br>(01.47)<br>(100) | 02<br>(02.94)<br>(33.33) | 06<br>(08.82)<br>(50.00) | – | 10<br>(14.71)<br>(40.00) | 19<br>(27.94)<br>(44.19) | 68<br>(100)<br>(45.33) |
| 4 | 6 - 10 lakh RC | 12<br>(21.43)<br>(23.53) | 03<br>(05.36)<br>(33.33) | – | 02<br>(03.57)<br>(33.33) | 03<br>(05.36)<br>(25.00) | 03<br>(05.36)<br>(100) | 11<br>(19.64)<br>(44.00) | 22<br>(39.29)<br>(51.16) | 56<br>(100)<br>(37.33) |
| 5 | Above 10 lakh RC | 03<br>(100)<br>(05.88) | – | – | – | – | – | – | – | 03<br>(100)<br>(02.00) |
| | Total RC | 51<br>(34.00)<br>(100) | 09<br>(06.00)<br>(100) | 01<br>(00.67)<br>(100) | 06<br>(04.00)<br>(100) | 12<br>(08.00)<br>(100) | 03<br>(02.00)<br>(100) | 25<br>(16.67)<br>(100) | 43<br>(28.67)<br>(100) | 150<br>(100)<br>(100) |

Source – Based on Field Investigation
R = Figures in parentheses indicate row percentage to total.
C = Figures in parentheses indicate column percentage to total.

### Source of Finance

Adequacy of the quantum, price and the timely availability of credit are the significant preconditions of starting and operating every business organization which also is the most vital aspect of entrepreneurial exhilaration and the success in turn depends upon the sources of finance. There are many obstacles to financing small industries, but traditionally the risk has always been rated high as an obstacle out of all the factors, every financing agency stresses more on the risk involved in financing the small units and hence devices a procedure which minimizes the risks, of course the risk element is present in every industrial financing, but comparatively more risk is associated with the small industrial finance. The risk involved in financing small concerned is special because a small firm always has a limited pool of management capabilities and business experience and owing to limitations of goodwill, they cannot pool the required funds and therefore are forced to depend more upon their own resources and on those of their relatives and friends. As the capacity of small-scale women entrepreneurs to raise funds by themselves is limited in quantum, they have to rely either on institutional or non-institutional sources for the same such as the family and well-wishers. Financial soundness of an entrepreneur is expected to stimulate the growth of entrepreneurship as financial strength creates a sense of security against fear of failure. Among women, financial strength may not be the major motivating factor because their economic activity is often considered as supplementary in nature. Hence the financial sources which would have stimulated these women would have a direct bearing on their financial soundness but the same has not been found.

21.33 percent of the women entrepreneurs (32 out of 150) from the study region of the state have entered the activity with the help of their own finances and 64 percent (96 out of 150) through their husband's financial ability. Hence around 85.33 percent of the women entrepreneurs (128 out of 150) have started the units with their own family money which is

**Table 8.15: Source of Finance Women Entrepreneurship**

| Sr.No. | Financial Sources | Mechanical Engineering Industry | Chemical Industry | Plastic Industry | Electronic Industry | Food Industry | Ready-Made Garments | Total | % |
|---|---|---|---|---|---|---|---|---|---|
| 1 | Own Capital | 07 | – | 02 | 10 | 07 | 06 | 32 | 21.33 |
| 2 | Husband | 46 | 05 | 08 | 15 | 09 | 13 | 96 | 64.00 |
| 3 | FinancialInstitutions | 03 | 01 | 02 | 01 | – | 03 | 10 | 06.67 |
| 4 | Friends & Relatives | 05 | – | 01 | 01 | – | 02 | 09 | 06.00 |
| 5 | Money Lenders | – | – | – | – | – | – | – | – |
| 6 | Other Sources | 02 | – | – | – | – | 01 | 03 | 02.00 |
| 7 | Total | 63 | 06 | 13 | 27 | 16 | 25 | 150 | 100.00 |

Source – Based on Field level Investigation

not possible for majority of such aspirants whereas Financial Institutions have provided the capital assistance to only about 6.67 percent of women entrepreneurs in the region from where we obtained present information. Informal sources such as friends and relatives also have a substantial influence in helping financially to establish the business (6 percent), whereas only 2 percent of the women entrepreneurs were resorted to other sources such as to dispose of salable assets which they refrained from revelation. But not even a single woman entrepreneur approached to any commercial private source of finance such as the money lender for obtaining the same. It means that the women those who take on to the activity of entrepreneurship are either have the financial strength and / or are simultaneously educated hence getting entrapped in to the private debt is totally ruled out which is unlike the case of state farming community. Due to the own private capital strength, 91.66 percent of women started their business with their family money and did not consider any other source which also can become the reason for their further financial strength and sustaining in to the market.

**Knowledge of Government Facilities and Incentives.**

One of the identified twenty seven targets to achieve inclusive growth strategy of the eleventh five year plan was the growth of industrial sector for the purpose of employment generation and bringing horizontal equality among the regions. For which it was decided that the government through its fiscal measures will actively involve its agencies in accelerating the process of industrialization with balanced industrial development of the country. Therefore the government brought out a number of schemes and incentives in favor of small-scale units keeping in view their contribution to the economy. The policies intended to stimulate the development of manufacturing sector through entrepreneurship consisted the provision for infrastructure and other incentives such as the tax concessions. The objective behind this was by providing infrastructural facilities and attractive incentives such as tax concession; the latent entrepreneurship of the society can be stimulated and made proactive in the country. But the disjuncture between the government policy and administrative set up and the attitude led towards corruption at the ground level and cornering of benefits by influential few. Hence despite the policy attempts of government and its developmental agencies the achievement of plan target became difficult. Therefore the expected results could not be obtained. For the development of the micro, small and medium enterprises and women entrepreneurship, both the central and state governments and affiliated developmental institutions have been providing a number of facilities as well as incentives like the training, finance and the technology up gradation. They include establishing new industrial estates, tax concessions as noted in foregoing, technical and business training, subsidies, bank credit, etc. Subsequent industrial policies of the state in Maharashtra also have made attempts in the direction but the moot problem of trickle down has kept the limitations as it is.

About 66.67 percent (100 out of 150) women entrepreneurs from the studied region of Pune district have an adequate knowledge of government facilities. Among them 47.00 percent women entrepreneurs are from Mechanical engineering industries, followed by women entrepreneurs from electronic industries (22.00 percent) and the women entrepreneurs from ready-made garment industries which constitute around 17.00 percent of the part of women entrepreneurs from the study region. Women entrepreneurs those who are in the segment of plastic industry have very little information regarding government incentives where as 33.33 percent women entrepreneurs (50 out of 150) do not have any information regarding government facilities and incentives that are made available in public domain from time to time . On the contrary their remarks about the special package, facilities and schemes that are available had been very sharp and they reacted that the same offered by the government remains only on paper which does not materialize.

**Table 8.16: Knowledge of Facilities and Incentives available from government**

| Sr. No. | Knowledge of Government Facilities | Mechanical Engineering Industry | Chemical Industry | Plastic Industry | Electronic Industry | Food Industry | Ready-Made Garment Industry | Total |
|---|---|---|---|---|---|---|---|---|
| 1 | Yes RC | 47<br>(47.00)<br>(74.60) | 05<br>(05.00)<br>(83.33) | 02<br>(02.00)<br>(15.38) | 22<br>(22.00)<br>(81.48) | 07<br>(07.00)<br>(43.75) | 17<br>(17.00)<br>(68.00) | 100<br>(100)<br>(66.67) |
| 2 | No RC | 16<br>(32.00)<br>(25.40) | 01<br>(02.00)<br>(16.67) | 11<br>(22.00<br>(84.62 | 05<br>(10.00)<br>(18.52) | 09<br>(18.00<br>(56.25 | 08<br>(16.00)<br>(32.00) | 50<br>(100)<br>(33.3 |
| 3 | TotalRC | 63<br>(42.00)<br>(100) | 06<br>(04.00)<br>(100) | 13<br>(08.67<br>(100) | 27<br>(18.00)<br>(100) | 16<br>(10.67<br>(100) | 25<br>(16.67)<br>(100) | 150<br>(100)<br>(100) |

Source – Based on Field Investigation
R = Figures in parentheses indicate row percentage to total.
C = Figures in parentheses indicate column percentage to total.

In view of the need for such incentives and benefits that accrue to entrepreneurs and to the growth of entrepreneurship, it is obligatory that these schemes meant for small entrepreneurs need to be properly and systematically implemented so that they do reach those for whom they are meant for. In fact this type of a certainty is required for stimulation and strengthening of entrepreneurship.

**Concluding Remarks**

Economic development and its sustainability has become a major concern for developing countries like India. Some economies in the world like that of India, China and the economies of other East Asian countries are growing at a faster rate than ever before. The un-precedential growth rates of the Asian countries have even surpassed the western growth trajectory. The factor responsible for this kind of a faster growth has been the growth of non-farm sector of these economies. In India the manufacturing sector in last two decades has been growing at a much faster rate. The growth of the economy in recent times is determined by the entrepreneurial growth and the growth of the same depends both on the non-economic factors like tradition, customs, values , attitude, aspirations, education, technology and the economic factors such as availability of financial services, capital adequacy and the price of capital, factor productivity, labor and organizational capacity, etc. Growing in-formalization of manufacturing sector, feminization of labor market, female education , government priorities and changing family and social structure and values are finding roots towards the female self-employment and there by leading towards their entrepreneurial development. Women from around 50% of the part of the society and traditionally remained underutilized. But the changing social set up at least in the progressive states like Maharashtra has become reason for their self-employability. Utilization of entrepreneurial potential of women could be vital for the development of nation as well as their own development and change in the status of women in a traditional patriarchal society. The status depends more upon the role, opportunities, rights of participation in economic activity and there by entitlement to income and assets. The task of integrating women in development requires simultaneous efforts to facilitate the improvement in their working conditions in formal and informal sector, as well as, for boosting their participation in entrepreneurial activity and success which will be instrumental in changing their socio-economic status and finally that will lead to the massive contribution of the unused potential of better half of the society of a rapidly growing economy like India.

## References

Satpathy Anoop (2004), Size, Composition, and Characteristics of Informal Sector In India, V.V. Giri National Labor Institute, Noida (UP)

Ghosh Ruma et. al. (Eds.) (2002), Hard Labor at Tender Age: Child Labor in Home Based Industries In the Wake Of Legislation, V.V.Girir National Labor Institute, Noida (UP)

(1993) Report of the XVth International Conference on Labor Statistics, ILO, Geneva

NSSO (1983 - 2005), Various Rounds Between 38th and 61st, GoI

Sengupta Arjun / Chairman (2009), National Commission on Enterprises in Unorganized Sector, Report, GoI, New Delhi

Census (2001), GoI, New Delhi

Talule D. (2001), Dimensions of Farmers Suicides, Working Paper, II – 2001, Institute of Management Studies Carrier Development and Research, Ahmednagar (University of Pune), Maharashtra.

# 9

# Climate Change & Informal Labor Migration in India

**Abstract**

*In many poor countries, climate change has aggravated the problem of water ,access to energy , food security, availability of infrastructure, loss of lives, and livestock, causes indebtedness hunger and mortality. People who have no adaptability and less immune to cope with climatic changes prone to distress displacement for survival elsewhere. Distress displacement is a situation characterized by high vulnerability and immediate needed assistance. Distress migrants are poor and generally in a week position to negotiate the terms of their displacement. In 2008 globally, about 20 million people were displaced as a result of sudden onset climate-related weather events, compared to 4.6 million internally displaced by conflict and violence (World Displacement Report, 2010). Environmental degradation may be the result of changes in average annual temperatures or rainfall levels, but it may equally be the result of deforestation or poor land management or a combination of these factors. Displacement is (and always has been) an important adaptive mechanism to deal with climate stress, but it is not the first adaptive response, households take when confronted by climate stress; rather it resorted to when other means of adaptation (such as selling livestock) are insufficient to meet their immediate needs and often when their communities or governments have proven incapable of giving assistance. Displaced rural- Urban migrants face a host of serious problems, including questionable labor practices, insufficient payment, precarious living conditions, and dealing with shanty settlements and harassment. Social protection programmes like employment programmes, cash transfers, and crisis related transfers, insurance relate transfers, climate monitoring transfers, climate monitoring and disaster risk management infrastructure, dissemination of timely qualitative early warning information is required. Government integrates adaptation into wider poverty reduction strategies and planning process. Ensure international co-operation on adaptation of climate change. Implement strictly polluter pay price by levying emission taxes to reduce negative externalities.*

## Introduction

Environmental stressors have induced people to migrate to new places since time immemorial. Environmental degradation undermine the capacity of development and poverty reduction efforts and reduce future development opportunities and compel government to spend current disaster management rather than development for poverty reduction. Rich biodiversity of flora and fauna will be destroyed; hence Indigenous communities will become displaced and vulnerable. Climate change can have disruptive social and economic effects, reduce access and productivity of resource and ultimately capability to earn will decline, which is the cause of chronic poverty. Climate change has the potential to create humanitarian disasters, ecological collapse and economic dislocation on a far greater scale than we see today (Human Development Report 2007-08).

Environmental insecurity is increasingly viewed as a current and future cause of hunger and poverty. Increasing drought, flooding, temperature and changing climatic patterns are most burning problems of the globe. A large proportion of the world's poor live in the rural areas of the developing world and faces a growing scarcity of land and water. Many of them are in ecologically fragile regions, such as arid and semi-arid zones, mountain areas and coastal areas are exposed to violent weather, and so on. It is the poor who are most exposed to environmental stress and resource poverty (Nitin

Desai 2007). India has been facing soil erosion problem causes loss of major crop production of about 72 Million tonnes every year and the per capita water availability has been declining (Hasim committee, World bank).In many parts of the world people feels that their environment is insecure and unable to satisfy their basic needs, which force them to displace.

Climate change refers to any change in climate over time, whether due to natural variability or as a result of human activity. United Nations Framework Convention on Climate Change (UNFCCC), which defines climate change as "change in climate which is attributed directly or indirectly to human activity that alters the composition of the global atmosphere and which is in addition to natural variability observed over comparable time periods " . Climate change may be the single factor that makes the future very different from the past; impeding the continuing progress in human development that history would lead us to expect (Human Development Report, 2010). In many poor countries, climate change has aggravated problem of water, access to energy, food security, and availability of infrastructure, loss of lives, livestock, consequently, indebtedness hunger, and mortality. People who have no adaptability and less immune to cope with changes prone to distress displacement for survival elsewhere. Climate change increase vulnerability of poor people by badly affecting their health, livelihoods and nullify developmental opportunities, which are vital for poverty reduction.

Poverty forces poor households and enterprises to exploit their immediate living and working environment often beyond its capacity to restore itself, and so destroys the basis for any future improvement in their own lives and those of their children International Labor Organisation, (ILO 2004). Land, water and air are the vital components of the physical environment surrounding the biosphere and provide the basic elements of the life support system. New technology in agriculture has given rise to resource degradation more particularly, land and water in resources fragile regions (Vyas

2004, Narendranath et al, 2005). Particularly, it is in these regions, that a considerable area has come under commercial crops like oil seeds, cotton, chilli, tobacco etc, in the post-Green Revolution period (Nadcarnim, 1996, Mujumdar, 2006). The indiscriminate and injudicious use of resources and agro-chemicals has been adversely affecting the soil, water and environment. The resultant externalities are resource depletion, bad soil condition, contamination of soil and water by chemicals, mono crop system, pest resistance etc.

## Methodology

This study is based on data which is collected from secondary sources like World development reports, Human development reports, Millennium development report, world migration report, newspapers, journals and internet sources.

## Organization of the study

This study is organized in to viii sections. section ii deals with review of literature, section iii explains the growing magnitude of displacement, section iv focused on the spillover effects of environmental insecurity, section v on displacement as an adaptation strategy, section vi describes the push and pull factors of displacement, section vii emphasized on international efforts to tackle climate disorders, and section viii ends with policy implications and conclusion

## Review of literature

Having briefly introduced the topic, objectives and research design it would be fruitful to acquaint ourselves of the findings of the existing studies undertaken by the researchers on the theme of our discussion. These studies are likely to through useful light on impact of climate change on distress migration of labor.

Dercon and Hoddinott (2004) felt that Floods and droughts will be more severe with climate change. Droughts have immediate harmful impacts on poverty rates and economic growth, but also long-lasting effects on lifetime earnings and health other extreme events, such as cyclones, are likely to increase in intensity and severity.

Erza,(2001) observed that labor displacement can form the basis of a sustainable livelihood in chronically degraded land, building resilience across households and communities, Indeed, families without labor migrants may suffer more during chronic or sudden onset disasters In that sense, it can be viewed as a positive adaptation strategy.

Climate change could have significant impacts on human displacement (IPCC 1990). Displacement will be one of the outcomes of the intensification of environmental stressors by climate change. (McLeman and Smit, 2006; Brown, 2007; Kniveton et al, 2008; Perch-Nielsen et al, 2008; Jäger et al, 2009; Barnett and Webber, 2009). Heavy precipitation, droughts, tropical cyclones, and sea level rise as potential sites of human out displacement (IPCC 2007). Climate change poses an enormous test for the international community – and the risks are extremely high.

Perch-Nielsen (2004) felt that displacement is affected by increasing flood frequencies, erosion, inundation and rising water tables. Whether or not people opt for displacement, is depended on their resilience to the environmental changes they are affected by, namely their ability to cope with environmental degradation. This is for a large part determined by the availability of alternative livelihoods (Martin 2010).

Income diversification through labor displacement can act as an adaptive response to environmental stressors. By earning a livelihood abroad, can reduce the vulnerability of individuals, households and communities to environmental risks, and increase their resilience (Barnett and Webber 2009; Lack 2010, Tacoli 2009). Adaptation thus involves both measures to reduce a population's vulnerability, so as to prevent them from having to migrate, and displacement itself as an adaptation strategy that allows people to reduce their vulnerability (Martin 2010b).

Displacement of one or more members of the household can help the rest of the family to increase their resilience to environmental disruptions (Barnett and Webber 2009). Displacement out of areas affected by recurring natural disasters, reduces the amount of individuals exposed to the disaster, and provides the area with an income stream that usually increases after a disaster has occurred ( Laczko and Collett 2005). Displacement might even help to slow down the process of environmental degradation, and allow those left behind to adapt their livelihood provision to changing ecosystem services (Acketoft 2008).

Where people rely heavily on rain-fed agriculture, circular displacement acts as an effective strategy to react to recurring droughts and changes in rain patterns (Tacoli 2009.) In order to facilitate international labor displacement, it is firstly necessary to remove some of the legal, financial and social barriers. Possible beneficiaries of a displacement programme need in the first place information on where to go, how to make a living, which rights and entitlements they have, etc. (Barnett and Webber 2009).

The most vulnerable persons could be enabled to leave their destructed environment, temporarily or permanently (Boncour 2009). Displacement might even help to slow down the process of environmental degradation, and allow those left behind to adapt their livelihood provision. Finally, remittances can help home communities to mitigate and/or adapt to environmental degradation (Acketoft 2008; Barnett and Webber 2009). A single climate event may stimulate a variety of possible displacement responses, as was seen following Hurricane Katrina (Fussell et al 2010).

The greatest amount of climate related displacement presently occurs at intra national or intra regional scales, and this is expected to continue to be the case in coming decades (Adamo and Izazola 2010, Massey et al 2010, Nelson 2010). In developing regions, where economic systems and livelihoods are closely tied to agriculture and natural resources, extreme climatic events and conditions are expected to accelerate already growing levels of rural to urban displacement (Hunter 2005, McLeman and Hunter 2010).

People at the lowest end of the socio economic spectrum - particularly landless laborers and tenant farmers - are the most mobile and most easily displaced (Massey et al 2010). Landowners, business operators and others at the upper end of the socioeconomic spectrum will also experience economic hardship, but are more likely to resist displacement because their household capital is tied to land and other assets that are not transportable (McLeman and Smit 2006).

Increased sea levels may also lead to salinazation of irrigation water, estuaries and freshwater systems. The many millions of people working in the agriculture sector will have to face change in the way crops are produced or even look for new pastures elsewhere. The agriculture sector is known for its growing job insecurity, low rates of pay, poor working conditions and growing levels of poverty. Climate change challenges will place an enormous burden on already affected workers.(ILO,2008).

**The Growing Magnitude of Displacement**

Distress displacement is a situation characterized by high vulnerability and need immediate assistance. Distress migrants are poor and generally in a week position to negotiate the terms of their displacement. The greatest single impact of climate change could be on human displacement—with millions of people displaced by shoreline erosion, coastal flooding and agricultural disruption. Since then, various analysts have tried to compile accurate projections of the future flows of climate migrants (sometimes called "climate refugees")—the most widely repeated prediction being 200 million by 2050 (IOM 2008). It would mean that by 2050 one in every 45 people in the world will have been displaced by climate change.

Climate change brings significant changes in displacement patterns throughout the developing world

(World Bank 2008). The United Nations High Commission for Refugees (UNHCR) reported an estimated 10.4 million refugees worldwide, and another 15.6 million involuntarily displaced within their own borders at the end of 2009 (UNHCR 2010). By 2050, the number of people forced to move primarily because of climate change will range between 200 million and 1 billion(Myers, 2005, Christian Aid, 2007).

In 2008 globally , about 20 million people were displaced as a result of sudden onset climate-related weather events, compared to 4.6 million internally displaced by conflict and violence (World Displacement Report , 2010) . Environmental degradation may be the result of changes in average annual temperatures or rainfall levels, but it may equally be the result of deforestation or poor land management - or a combination of these factors

### The Spillover Effects of Environmental Insecurity

#### *(a) Environmental Refugees*

International Organization for Migration (IOM, 2008) defined, "Environmental migrants are persons or groups of persons, who, for compelling reasons of sudden or progressive changes in the environment that adversely affect their lives or living conditions, are obliged to leave their habitual homes, or chose to do so, either temporarily or permanently, and who move either within their country or abroad". Climate related displacement tends to be framed in terms of "environmental refugees" (a term coined by El Hinnawi 1986), whereby people are involuntarily displaced in response to environmental conditions or events such as floods, droughts and so forth. Environmental displacement is a process by which exposed individuals or households may adapt to climatic exposures (McLeman and Smit 2006, Perch Nielsen et al 2008, Tacoli 2009, Bardsley and Hugo 2010).

### *(b) Threat to Common Property Resources*

Environmental assets, such as forest products, account for an average of twenty percent of household income in poor countries (Pearce 2005), so that environmental assets, and their protection, are certainly consistent with economic development . Common property resources constitute an important complementary source of income to the poor population in ecologically fragile, arid, mountainous and UN irrigated regions (Jodha 1986 : 95). The income earned by the rural poor from the sale of fuel wood, water for irrigation, fodder and other commercial grasses, berries and nuts and gum, forms a significant proportion of their earnings (Dasgupta 1998). If these environmental assets affect badly, causes displacement for safe living elsewhere.

### *(c) Threat to Food Security*

Food is the first among the Maslow hierarchical needs of human being. Food security means availability, accessibility and affordability of food to all people at all times. While the availability of food is a function of production of food grains, the accessibility to food relies on the states food policy coupled with the purchasing power of the consumers. The poor households are more vulnerable to food insecurity whenever there is a problem of production or distribution of food crops. The problem of food security cannot be viewed only in terms of procurement and distribution of food. It should also be seen in the context of production of food grains. Commercialization and mechanization of agriculture caused the reduction of demand for labor, so this tendency accelerated labor migration

A large section of people suffer from food and nutrition insecurity in India. The worst affected groups are landless or poor households in rural areas and people employed in ill paid occupations and casual laborers engaged in seasonal activities in the urban areas. The food insecure people are disproportionately large in some regions of the country , such as economically backward states with high incidence of poverty, tribal and remote areas, regions more prone to natural disasters etc. In fact the states of Utter Pradesh, Bihar, Jharkhand, Orissa, west Bengal, Chhattisgarh, parts of Madhya Pradesh, and Maharashtra account for largest number of food insecure people in the country.

### *(d) The Forced Displacement of Labor*

As climate change will have an enormous impact on employment and the labor market. The phenomenon of global warming, together with the loss of biodiversity, is increasingly causing large-scale displacement. Both slow-onset environmental degradation and sudden natural disasters threaten to force millions of people to leave their environment. International migration is increasingly recognized as a strategy to adapt to a changing environment. Environmental pressure as a fundamental cause of displacement has been generally downplayed until recently, when increased attention to the impacts of climate change has refueled the debate (Massey et al., 2007; Morrissey, 2009; Zolberg, 2001).

Developing countries—the least responsible for emissions of greenhouse gases—will be the most affected by climate change. Forced displacement hinders development in at least four ways; by increasing pressure on urban infrastructure and services, undermining economic growth, increasing the risk of conflict and leading to worse health, educational and social indicators among migrants themselves. Climate change could accelerate the brain drain as it is typically those with larger reserves of financial and social capital who are able to move away. Climate change will challenge the adaptive capacities of many different communities, and overwhelm some, by interacting with and exacerbating existing problems of food security, water scarcity and the scant protection afforded by marginal lands. At some point that land becomes no longer capable of sustaining livelihoods and people will be forced to migrate to areas that present better opportunities (International Organisation on Migration,2008).

### *(e) Agricultural Crisis and Displacement of Labor in India*

Agriculture sector by and large is dependent on uncertainty of monsoon and unprotected from the risks of crop failures despite expansion of significant network of irrigation. Rising cost of cultivation, embedded with insufficient infrastructure support and slowing down of employment and income, left farmers trapped in the syndrome of indebtedness and despair. Performance of agriculture remained at lower profile with a few exceptions, thanks to unpredictable monsoon and indifference of the government towards this sector. As a result, employment in rural sector grew at declining rate (Bhalla,2005). Agricultural economy of the country is facing diverse challenges. Growth rate of agriculture has decelerated over the last fifteen years. Employment growth is stagnant. Proportion of small and marginal holdings has been on the rise (RBI-2007).All these factors causing migration of labor from rural to urban areas.

The pessimistic trends in Indian agriculture that have persisted since the mid-1990s include ; declining profitability of agriculture , increasing risks , degradation of natural resources , steep fall in technological innovations in agriculture and collapsing agriculture extension. The neglect of agriculture in designing development programmes and ineffective implementation at the micro level fails to create adequate employment Opportunities. Public investment on agricultural research and extension was low at 0.49 percent of GDP(on average developing nations spend 0.7 percent and developed countries 2 to 3 percent). Institutional credit to agriculture sector is 10 to 11 percent, it is below the stipulated target of 18 percent. Half of the farmers are not access to institutional finance, India Development Report (2008).

### India's Inadequate Efforts to Tackle Displacement

India won a major battle at the global climate change meet at Bali with the 190 countries gathered there agreeing to set up an Adaptation Fund Board which will fund developing countries in securing themselves against risks from climate change like sea level rise and crop productivity declines, Drought,Floods, storms and rising sea levels are among the amplifying risks that the world faces, still miles to go walk ahead.

Constitutional guarantee of life is not limited to mere existence on the earth; it also includes healthy life. In view of various Constitutional Provisions and other Statutory Provisions contained in various laws relating to environment protection, the Supreme Court has held that the essential features of 'Sustainable Development' such as 'Precautionary Principle' and the 'Polluter Pays Principle' are part of the Environmental Law of the Country. In the Constitution of India it is clearly stated that it is the duty of the state to 'protect and improve the environment and to safeguard the forests and wildlife of the country'. It imposes a duty on every citizen 'to protect and improve the natural environment including forests, lakes, rivers, and wildlife'. Reference to the environment has also been made in the Directive Principles of State Policy as well as the Fundamental Rights. The Constitutional Provisions and Principles of Sustainable Development are backed by a number of laws - acts, rules.

The Ministry of Environment and Forests is the Government agency that implements the policies and programmes related to environmental concerns. The National Environment Policy, which was adopted in 2006, is a comprehensive strategy for ensuring environmental sustainability in the country. The legislations in the policy are broadly drawn from the Environment Protection Act, 1986, the Water (Prevention and Control of Pollution Act, 1974; the Water Cess Act, 1977; and the Air (Prevention and Control of Pollution) Act 1981. The legislations in the policy, related to the management of forests and biodiversity, are contained in the India Forest Act, 1927; the Forest (Conservation) Act, 1980; the Wild Life (Protection) Act, 1972, and the Biodiversity Act, 2002, among others.

### Displacement as an Adaptation Strategy

Displacement is (and always has been) an important adaptive mechanism to deal with climate stress, but it is not the first adaptive response households take when confronted by climate stress; rather it resorted to when other means of adaptation (such as selling livestock) are insufficient to meet their immediate needs and often when their communities or governments have proven incapable of giving assistance. The impact of climate change as a driver of future forced displacement depends on several factors: The quantity of future greenhouse gas emissions; the rate of future population growth and distribution; the meteorological evolution of climate change; the effectiveness of local and national adaptation strategies. (IOM,2008b)

Most displacement occurring from climate change is likely to be internal, with the affected populations seeking to find more habitable locations, with greater economic opportunities, within their own countries. A portion of such displacement will undoubtedly be international (The German Marshall fund of United States, 2010). Environmental displacement can take several forms, notably displacement - uprooting people, temporarily or permanently, from their origin communities; labor displacement - people moving to other places for work; household displacement - entire households moving to another location; and community resettlement - entire communities being resettled in another place.

According to the UN Human Development Report, international migration can contribute greatly to human welfare and development (UNDP 2009). Aside from a development strategy, displacement can also be regarded as an adaptation strategy for communities affected by environmental disasters. Climates changes are a significant cause of livelihood insecurity and it is one among the push factors for forced displacement of labor. Declines in the ability of households to be self-sustaining are related to climatic vagaries, long term declines in production (i.e. degradation), increasing population growth and land shortages. Where people are able to adapt, they might be able to remain in their environment. Where adaptation fails, people might be forced to leave their traditional habitat. However, there is now a growing recognition that displacement itself might be one of the possible strategies to adapt to a changing environment (Comcad,2011).

**The Push and Pull Factors of Displacement**

Robert McLeman of the University of Ottawa, stated that the drivers of forced displacement into two distinct groups. First, there are the climate drivers. These drivers are climate processes and climate events. Climate processes are slow onset changes such as sea-level rise, salinization of agricultural land, desertification, and growing water scarcity and food insecurity. Climate events, on the other hand, are sudden and dramatic hazards such as monsoon floods, glacial lake outburst floods, storms, hurricanes and typhoons. These force people off their land much more quickly and dramatically climate change might provide both "push" and "pull" for some population displacement.

For rural resource-based economies, the environment provides their livelihood and they must change the way that they interact with that environment. "The sustainable development approach via sustainable agriculture is based on sustainable use of resources-land, water, agricultural biodiversity, including that of plants and animals. The sustainable use of resources, among other things centers on decentralized ownership and control over natural resources-land, water, agricultural biodiversity and animals among agricultural communities in order to generate livelihood, provide food to all and conserve natural resources and maintaining balance in the ecosystem avoiding Reckless use of resources as far as possible.

### Globalization impact on displacement

Globalization is harmful and its intervention with agriculture is devastating both in-terms of disturbing ecological balance and consequent climatic change and increasing space of hunger, natural catastrophes and miseries for humanity and thus, heavy damage to natural and social capital at large. Poverty and a degraded environment are closely inter-related, especially where people depend for their livelihoods primarily on the natural resource base of their immediate environment. Restoring natural systems and improving natural resource management practices at the grassroots level are central to a strategy to eliminate poverty. The survival needs of the poor force them to continue to degrade an already degraded environment. Removal of poverty is therefore a prerequisite for the protection of the environment.

Ahluwalia ,M.S(2002) felt that the agriculture has suffered most notably from the decline in public investment in areas critical for agriculture growth during economic reforms, such as irrigation and drainage , soil conservation , and water management systems and rural roads. According to Gulati and Bathla (2001), public investment has declined more than offset by a rise in private investment in agriculture which accelerated after reforms. The direct benefit of subsidizing fertilizers and underpricing water and power goes mainly to fertilizer producers and high income farmers while leaving negative effect on the environment , production and even on income of small farmers.

Displacement is generally considered to be the intermediate stage which links environmental degradation and disasters to conflict (Homer Dixon, 1991 and 1994). As mass relocations are presumed to occur in response to degradation, conflict may erupt in receiving areas in response to competition, as environmental migrants may burden the economic and resource base of the receiving area and promoting contests over resources; ethnic tension, which may occur if migrants are from a different ethnic group; distrust between sending and receiving areas if the origin site perceives maltreatment of migrants; 'fault lines' which are pre-existing tensions following socioeconomic issues; or finally, 'auxiliary conditions' as developing economies are reliant on the environment for survival and if resources are scarce, environmental migrants may possibly join antagonizing groups or intensity the violence through any of the above conditions (Reuveny, 2000: 657-659). Percentage of people considering displacement was highest in drought areas (ranging from 10% to 31%) (Burton et al., 1993, and Perch-Nielsen, 2004: 81).

**Life cycle of climate-induced displacement**

Figure 1 reveals that, the life cycle of climate induced displacement will start if adaptation measure failed , it induces displacement, once displaced they may resettle at the destination or return back to the original habitation. Resettlement is possible by integration of the people with new environment and mitigation measures taken by the stake holders i.e. displaced people, Non-Governmental Organizations, employers, host country governments and the government of the country of their origin.

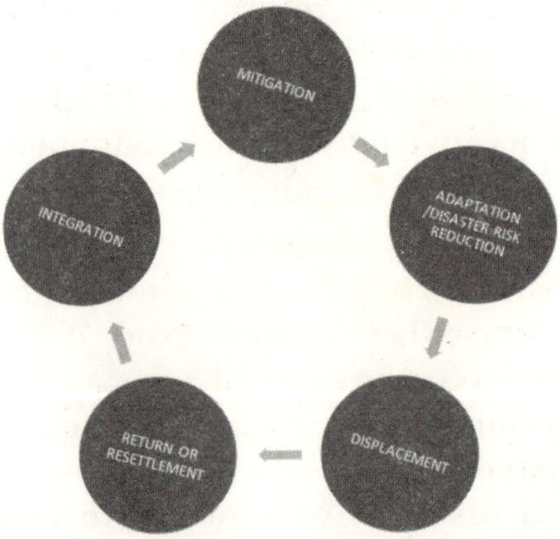


Source : The German Marshall fund of United States, (2010).

**Figure 9.1: Life cycle of climate-induced displacement**

**Poverty**

Poverty and environmental change have a direct causal relationship and can influence each other in some kind of cumulative causation process. Various studies conducted worldwide reveal that there is a two-way linkage between poverty and environmental degradation. Degradation of environment caused either by the poor or the rich but ultimately income of the poor will effect badly. Poor become poorer due to destruction of forest for fuel wood, infertility of land and contamination of water by the use of chemical fertilizer, pesticide, etc. Thus a vicious link is established between poverty and environmental degradation. Lele, S.M. (1991).

Environmental assets, such as forest products, account for an average of twenty percent of household income in poor countries (Pearce, 2005) so that environmental assets, and their protection, are certainly consistent with economic development. Common property resources constitute an important complementary source of income to the poor population in ecologically fragile, arid, mountainous and un irrigated regions (Jodha 1986: 95)The income earned by the rural poor from the sale of fuel wood, water for irrigation, fodder and other commercial grasses, berries and nuts and gum forms a significant proportion of their earnings (Das Gupta 1998).

There is link between the common property resources and the dynamics of poverty. Change in the quantity and quality and accessibility of these resources have influence on the rural poverty .Pressure on these resources affects sustainability of the livelihoods of the poor. Natural resources are the common property resources i.e. common pastures, forests, wastelands. Common property resources are those used by the community without any exclusive individual's ownership or access rights. According to Jodha (1986) "common property resources are community's natural resources where every member has access & usage facility with specified obligation without anybody having exclusive property rights over them." Environmental resources have been categorized into four types based on the relationship between the resources and resource user. They are (a)private property resources, (b)state property resources, (c)open access resources, (d)common property resources.

Poverty is the result of economic, political, environmental and social process that interacts with each other and frequently reinforces each other. Lesser assets , inaccessibility to markets, lesser accessible to common property resources and lesser job opportunities, jobs with low earnings, vulnerable to external and largely uncontrollable and unforeseen events-illness, violence, economic shocks, bad weather, natural disasters keep people in material poverty and weakens their bargaining power (WDR 2000-2001b)

An important part of the asset base of the poor comprises wealth from those natural resources to which they have access. The most important resource is the forest. Around 1 billion of the world's poor rely on forests for income or income supplements (United Nations Millennium Project, 2005)Poverty itself may make the poor agents of environmental destruction, which, in turn, makes poverty worse through ill health and low labor productivity. Environmental factors such as poor water quality, poor sanitation, and indoor air pollution, for example, are thought to account for almost 20 percent of adverse health outcomes in developing countries, compared to about 4 percent in developed countries (Looks, 2001).

According to the World Resource Institute (1990) nearly 500 million people in India depend upon Non Timber Forest Product (NTFP)for their livelihood. Poor do not possess any assets and do not have a regular source of income from wage employment often leads to excessive exploitation of these natural resources and can damage the environment. Investment by the government on common property resources will augment the flow of benefits to the village population in general and to the poor.

Poverty is often associated with degraded rural environments. Environmental degradation has many consequences, because a healthy natural environment sustains non- monetary economies and can be viewed as the "social security" of the rural populations. When the productive functions of healthy rural environments degrade, or when people lose access to those productive environments, movement to cities in search of alternative livelihoods can exacerbate urban poverty. Environmental degradation therefore undermines sustainable livelihoods and affects the rural poor by disproportionately affecting their health, livelihoods and security, and can aggravate poverty in already stressed urban environments. Displaced rural- Urban migrants face a host of serious problems, including questionable labor practices, insufficient payment, dangerous living conditions, and dealing with shanty settlements and harassment (Deskingkar, 2006; Surhke, 1993 and de Haan, 2000).

**International Efforts to Tackle Climate Disorders**

While historically, industrialized countries have been responsible for the bulk of emissions, developing and rapidly industrializing countries are becoming major emitters in aggregate, despite comparatively low emissions per capita (Disaster risk reduction(ILO 2008a) . Recklessness and over use of environmental resources to meet the unending greed, madly emission of CFCs by the advanced nations, deforestation, and irresponsible industrialization by both the developing and the developed nations are the reasons for environmental pollution. The on-going loss of biodiversity: decline of forest, freshwater, marine and soil resources: changing climate: loss of stratospheric ozone: and accumulation of toxic substances in soil, water, and living organisms, are all threats to the environmental goods and services upon which all human life depends for food, fodder, crop production, and innumerable other goods and services. It is usually the rural poor who are the first to suffer when these systems fail.

On the recommendation of the Economic and Social Council, the General Assembly of UN convened a conference on the "Human Environment" at Stockholm from 5 to 16 June in 1972. The Stockholm Declaration came out with guiding principles. Among them, the Principle 1: "Man has the fundamental right to freedom, equality and adequate conditions of life, in an environment of a quality that permits a life of dignity and well-being, and he bears a solemn responsibility to protect and improve the environment for present and future generations." The principle-2, "The natural resources of the earth, including the air, water, land, flora and fauna and especially representative samples of natural ecosystems, must be safeguarded for the benefit of present and future generations through careful planning or management, as appropriate" and the principle-3, "The capacity of the earth to produce vital renewable resources must be maintained and, wherever practicable, restored or improved."

UN Millennium summit (2000) in its Millennium declaration by the 189 nations , world summit on sustainable development agenda 21, UN Millennium summit 2005, UNDP, UNEP, World bank ,World Conservation Union (IUCN), International Institute for Environment and Development (IIED), the World Resources Institute, World Wildlife Fund (WWF), Swiss Re, and Harvard University recognized the linkage between environmental sustainability and poverty reduction i.e. better environment management is essential for poverty reduction. The World Summit on Sustainable Development ,emphasized the need for policy and institutional changes to improve governance, increase the assets of the poor, improve the quality of economic growth, and reform international and industrial country practices . Realizing the importance the member nations of UN mentioned environmental sustainability is one among the Millennium Development Goals.

United Nations adopted 8 Millennium Development Goals to achieve by 2015. Among the 8 goals , MDG7 meant for Ensuring environmental sustainability. The United Nations Framework Convention on Climate Change (UNFCCC) affirms that: "responses to climate change should be coordinated with social and economic development in an integrated manner with a view to avoiding adverse impacts on the latter." (UN 1992b). Principle 1 of the Rio De clarification on Environment and Development and Kyoto protocol states that "Human beings are at the centre of concerns for sustainable development. They are entitled to a healthy and productive life in harmony with nature". Human development involves the recognition of the need for active international efforts to preserve the quality of the environment where we live . Multilateral aid to finance adaptation has created viz.. (1) The least developed countries fund in 2001,(2) the special climate change fund in 2005, (3) the strategic priority on adaptation.

**Policy Measures**

The irreparable loss of environmental balance will also hamper efforts to meet other MDGs, especially those related to poverty, hunger and health, by increasing the vulnerability of the poor and reducing their options for development.(MDG report , 2010). Environmental degradation has real economic and social costs that undermine long-term local, national and global sustainability. Donnel Meadows stated some guidelines for restructuring world system towards sustainability. (1) Minimize the use of nonrenewable resources (2) prevent the use of renewable resources(3) use resources with maximum efficiency (4) Slow and eventually stop exponential growth of population (5) Monitor the condition of resources , the natural environment and the welfare of human beings.(6) improve response time for environmental stress.

Developing adaptation strategies Preparing evacuation plans Filling gaps in the legal and normative framework policies on internal displacement Establishing proactive resettlement policies Providing humanitarian assistance

Planning for return and resettlement More frequent and severe natural disasters are likely to trigger or accelerate displacement flows and could increase existing political tensions and instability (ILO, 2008).

**Economic development**

Economic development is necessary for the benefit of people and the nation at large but it makes no sense if it cannot be sustained for future generations and will be counter-productive for them. The most vulnerable and poorest populations and workers are often those that are the hardest hit by the effects of climate change. A rights-based approach in the form of International Labor Standards would offer protection that would shield affected workers from also suffering from structural changes to the labor market resulting from climate change.

**Adaptation**

Adaptation is a response to actual or expected climate stimuli or their effects which moderates harm or exploits beneficial opportunities (UNDP, 2007-08) to climate change refers to the collection of measures put in place to deal with and remedy its effects. These measures could be structural, managerial and political and they could be short- and/or long term. Adjustments can be both behavioural (human) and technical. The aim is to minimize the consequences of climate change. Adaptation measures could include: reduction of risks for flooding; alteration of crops or relocation; improvement of land management; the institutionalization of land reform, capacity building, financial incentives (subsidies taxes, etc.) (IPCC 2007a). Development interventions all over the world should focus on increasing the adaptive capacity of the poor to the impacts of climate change. Integrating climate change into national development and economic strategies can decrease the Poor's vulnerability, and better prepare governments to cope with its impacts.

**Mitigation**

All human interventions which reduce the sources of greenhouse gases or which embrace the sinks of greenhouse gases (UNDP, 2007-08). If we want to reverse global warming, we will not only have to adapt but to find measures to reduce the Green House Gas (GHG) emissions which lead to global warming. These measures are called mitigation measures. Mitigation measures in the agriculture sector include improvement of crop and grazing, land management, improved rice cultivation techniques and livestock and manure management to reduce CH4 emissions; improved nitrogen fertilizer application techniques to reduce N2O, CO2, Methane emissions; dedicated energy crops to replace fossil fuel use; improved energy efficiency, conservation tillage, cover cropping and recycling of bio-solids.

**Healthy Environmental transition**

The process of economic restructuring should be aimed at more environmental and social sustainable economy. Ensure cooperation from environmental organizations and trade unions. Environmental transition happens fastest and most efficiently when workers are involved, so that those affected by environmental policy are secure in the knowledge that their views and needs are being fully considered and responded to.

**Environmental information**

Education is important for awareness and knowledge about climate change, especially to make informed policy decisions about adaptation and mitigation measures. It is also important for the re-tooling of skills of the workforce in order to enable workers to adjust to the policies put in place. Timely qualitative disaster management information should be disseminated.

### Reduce Chemicalisation of Agriculture

Land yielding capacity can be maximized and costs can be minimized by using locally produced organic compost, and by adopting labor intensive farming techniques. Organic input has the greatest potential to benefit the health of farmers and consumers. By imparting training in village knowledge centers in the areas like farm management techniques, Water management, conservation of other natural resources, appropriate cropping pattern, use of machineries, chemical fertilizers, pesticides , new variety of seeds, use of information, weather forecasting , soil erosion, protection of fertility will strengthen effective utilization of resources. Constructing dams and canals to prevent floods as well as to make possible multiple cropping.

### Food security

Food security can be ensured, agro based industrial development be augmented by ensuring reasonable price for the produce. Instead of dependence on traditional crops , agriculture diversification in to the areas like livestock, fisheries, animal husbandry, and horticulture will reduce pressure on lands. Linking up the rural production centers with the urban and foreign (export) markets to realize higher returns on the investments for the products

### Human security

Mass killing and mass migration can be averted through timely warning systems, precautionary, remedial and relief measures. Availability timely right information from governmental and nongovernmental organizations. Transporting people from threaten areas to safe areas along with creating employment and other infrastructure at the destination.

**Social protection**

Social protection had multiplier effects, such as generating growth and economic demand, and protecting people. (Mr Juan Somavia, Director-General of the International Labor Office 2010). Social security benefits represented the most powerful, most direct tool for poverty reduction and indispensable investments in social and economic development, and were a key tool to achieving the Millennium Development Goals (MDGs). Social security was not only a universal human right, but also an economic and social necessity. Social protection reduces people dependency on natural resources.

**Harmonious growth**

Global economic development desirable, but not at the cost of the environment. The need of the hour is to strike a balance between the two i.e., development on one side and pollution free environment on the other i.e. measures should be taken to increase Green Gross National Product, and green jobs should be provided.

**Commercial and renewable energy**

Among the tools open to policy makers are tougher energy - efficiency standards, taxes on fossil fuels that are the big drivers of global warming and cap on trade systems on greenhouse gas emissions as well as measures to encourage clean technology. Such measures run into resistance given their potential financial cost and their challenge to established interests.

**Enhance forest coverage**

Forests are playing main role in enhancing the quality of environment by influencing the ecological balance and life support system. Adopt strong conservation measures to preserve forests and reduce carbon emission. Need to adopt a comprehensive approach while dealing with the issue of reducing emissions through deforestation.

## Conclusion

Stabilizing Greenhouse emissions to limit climate change is an insurance strategy for the world as a whole. Emission targets and energy efficiency targets are to be achieved with rational price policy. Successful adaptation coupled with stringent mitigation holds the key to human development. Rich countries have moral obligation to support adaptation in developing nations. Social protection programmes are too implemented as a part of adaptation strategy to help the poor. Social protection programmes like employment programmes, cash transfers, and crisis related transfers, insurance relate transfers, climate monitoring transfers, climate monitoring and disaster risk management infrastructure, dissemination of timely qualitative early warning information. Strengthen global adaptation finance strategy to empower vulnerable to deal with threat. Government integrates adaptation into wider poverty reduction strategies and planning process. Ensure international co-operation on adaptation of climate change. Implement strictly polluter pay price by levying emission taxes.

## References

Acketoft, T (2008).'Environmentally Induced Migration and Displacement. A 21st Century Challenge', *Report of the Committee on Migration, Refugees and Populations,* Council of Europe Parliamentary Assembly, Doc. 11785, 23 December 2008.

Boncour,P (2009). 'The Moment of Truth. Adapting to Climate Change', *Migration,* autumn 2009, IOM, Geneva.

Barnett,J and M. Webber (2009). 'Accommodating Migration to Promote Adaptation to Climate Change', A Policy Brief prepared for the Secretariat of the Swedish Commission on Climate Change and Development and the World Bank World Development Report 2010 Team, Melbourne, Department of

Resource Management and Geography, University of Melbourne.

Barnett, J. (2000).'Destabilizing the environment-conflict thesis'. *Review of International Studies* 26. 271-288.

Barnett, J. and N. Adger (2007). 'Climate change, human security and violent conflict'. *Political Geography* 26. 639-655.

Bhalla (1987). 'Trends In Employment In Indian Agriculture . Land And Asset Distribution' , *Indian Journal of Agricultural Economics* , Oct-Dec , PP 537-560.

Deshingkar, P (2006). 'Internal Migration, Poverty and Development in Asia'. *Asia2015.* http.//www.asia2015conference.org/pdfs/ Deshingkar.pdf

Erza, M (2001). 'Demographic responses to environmental stress in the drought-and famine prone areas of Northern Ethiopia'. *International Journal of Population Geography* 7.259-279.

Field (2007). 'Global and regional drivers of accelerating CO2 emissions.' *PNAS* 104(24). 10288-93.

Hunter, L. M (2005).'Migration and environmental hazards'. *Population and Environment* 26(4). 273-302

Intergovernmental Panel on Climate Change (2001). 'Climate change synthesis report'. contribution of working Group I and III to the Third Assessment of the (IPCC). Cambridge University Press, Cambridge, UK.

International Labor Office (2008).Committee On Employment And Social Policy. Employment And Labor Market Implications Of Climate Change Geneva.

*India Development Report* (2008).Radha Krishna(ed) ,Oxford University Press. New Delhi.

Intergovernmental Panel on Climate Change (IPCC) (2007). 'Fourth Assessment Report, Working Group II. Impacts, Adaptation and Vulnerability, Appendix 1 (Glossary)'.

Lene Olsen (2009). The Employment Effects Of Climate Change And Climate Change Responses. A Role For International Labor Standards? Published by ILO, 32 p. (GURN discussion paper; no.12) Geneva.

Martin,S (2010). 'Climate Change, Migration and Governance', *Global Governance on Migration*,Vol. 16, N° 3, July-September 2010, 397-414.

McLeman, R. and B. Smit. (2006). Migration as an adaptation to climate change.

*Climatic Change* 76 (1-2). 31-53.

Montek, S.Ahuliwalia (1999)." India's Economic Reforms An Appraise". In Jeffrey. S. et al (ed)*India In The Era of Economic Reforms,,* Oxford University Press, New York, PP1-80.

Nordhaus, W (2006). "The Economics of Hurricanes in the United States." NBER Working Paper 12813. Cambridge, MA.

Nicole de Moor(2011). Labor Migration for Vulnerable Communities. A Strategy to Adapt to a Changing Environment, (ed) Jeanette Schade and Thomas Faisted ,Paper presented at the ESF-UniBi-ZiF research conference on 'Environmental Change and Migration. From Vulnerabilities to Capabilities', Bad Salzuflen, Germany, December 5-9, 2010.

Nicole De Moor (2010). Temporary Labor Migration For Victims Of Natural Disasters The Case Of Colombia Paper Prepared For Unu-Ehs Summer Academy On Social Vulnerability Hohenkammer, Germany 25-31 July 2010.

Nordhaus (2006). International Organization for Displacement (IOM), 2008. Displacement and climate change. Geneva. IOM.

Oreskes, N (2004). "Beyond the Ivory Tower. The Scientific Consensus on Climate Change." *Science* 306 (5702). 1686.

Perch-Nielsen, S (2004). Understanding the effect of climate change on human migration. The contribution of mathematical and conceptual models. Department of Environmental Studies. Zurich, Swiss Federal Institute of Technology. M. Sc.Environmental Physics

Reuveny, R. (2007). Climate change induced migration and violent conflict. *Political Geography* 26. 656-673.

Suhrke, A (1993). *Pressure points. Environmental degradation, migration and conflict.* Cambridge, American Academy of Art and Science.

Tacoli,C (2009). 'Crisis or Adaptation? Migration and Climate Change in a Context of High Mobility', *Environment and Urbanization,* Vol. 21(2), p. 513.

United Nations (2010). The Millennium Development Goals Report 2010, New York.

World Bank (2008) '*World Development Report.* Washington D C

World Development Report ( 2010). Development In A Changing Climate Concept Note, World Bank. Washington.

World Commission on Environment and Development (WCED), (1987). Our Common Future. Oxford University Press, New York.

World Migration Report (2010). The Future Of Migration. Building Capacities For Change. International Organisation for Migration, Geneva.

# 10

# Income Levels of Migrant Informal Labor in India

## (A Field Level Investigation)

**Abstract**

*This paper analytically examines wages, income levels and poverty among the informal migrant labor in Jammu and Visakhapatnam cities during pre and post migration scenarios. Rural labor migration has been one of the complex phenomenon in the country. Decline in Public Investment in agricultural sector caused slow/negative growth rate of agricultural GDP coupled with huge rural unemployment, forced rural labor to migrate urban areas. Rural urban migration is the fastest growing type of migration in India . Migrant workers are the most vulnerable section and they are more likely to be found working at very low wages in hazardous physical conditions. Instances of exploitation by employers and contractors are also widespread in the absence of any effective monitoring by government agencies. Poor people migrate from village economy with the hope that the towns and cities have enough opportunities to make them live happy, but what ultimately happened was that, they were moved from rural poverty to urban poverty and from Feudalism to Capitalism. This study is having the theoretical backing of Ravenstein (1885) model of migration, that the migrants move from the areas of low opportunities to areas of high opportunities, migrant's first move to nearby towns and then towards larger cities. Even Post migration, 35% of the households in Visakhapatnam and 30% of the households in Jammu are living below poverty line. The level of poverty is more than that of national poverty line because their wages are less than national minimum wages,* moreover *they don't have work on regular basis, and also cost of living is high in urban areas*

**Keywords:** Informal Labor, Liberalization Privatization Globalization, Decent Work, Distress Migration, Push and Pull Factors, Social Security. Poverty line.

## Introduction

Labor reforms incorporated into economic reforms have resulted in an abnormal expansion of informal sector in most of the developing nations. The larger segment of the population is working in the unorganized sector of the economy, as informal labor (unorganized labor). Informal labor can be defined as those who have not been able to organize themselves in pursuit of common objectives on account of constraints like casual nature of employment, ignorance, illiteracy, small and scattered size of establishments and position of power enjoyed by the employer because of the nature of the industry etc, National Commission on Rural Labor (NCRL 1987-91).

The National Commission for Enterprises in Unorganized Sector (NCEUS 2007) defines unorganized sector and unorganized labor. "The unorganized sector consists of all unincorporated private enterprises owned by individuals or households engaged in the sale and production of goods and services operated on a proprietary or partnership basis with less than ten workers". Unorganized/ informal workers consists of " those working in the informal sector or households, excluding regular workers with social security benefits provided by the employers and the workers in the formal sector without any employment and social security benefits provided by the employers ".

Informal employment is characterized by the temporary, seasonal and changing nature of employment. Informal jobs can be treated as low quality (bad jobs)jobs, in the sense long periods of unemployment, longer working hours , meager earnings, absence of fixed employer and employee relationship, wages and other benefits are lesser than minimum and neither fixed on the basis of collective bargaining nor in accordance with law. Poor working environment, long working hours, irregular incomes, no social security, low productivity, low earnings , no decent work conditions .Decent work is "opportunities for women and men to obtain decent and productive work in conditions of freedom , equity, security and human dignity", International Labor Organisation (ILO 1999).

This paper is organized into six sections. section II deals with methodology of the study, section III focuses on labor migration an observation, section IV gives a light on review of literature, Section V concerns data analysis pertaining Visakhapatnam (Study area I), Section VI deals with data analysis pertaining Jammu (J&K)-(Study area II), Section VII Pre and post migration a comparative analysis, and the final section ends with summary and conclusion.

An increase in the share of informal sector implies deterioration in the quality of employment. Workers displaced from jobs have found alternative employment, mostly in informal sector and large number of new workers have also to resort to this sector for earning their livelihood either as self-employed or wage earners ( Papola 2004). Entry into this sector is easy because it not only requires lesser or no capital, but also requires less or no educational qualifications and formal training. The larger percentage of the informal labor are illiterates and living below poverty line.

People in informal sector mostly do not have formal legally recognized rights over the property they own, therefore these properties are not acceptable as collateral by creditors, is the reason for denial of credit and infrastructural facilities. Transaction costs of entering into formal sector (long procedure, bribes, time consumption, licenses, taxes, red tapism) encourage preference of informal sector (Siddhartha and Mitra 2005). However it should be noted that the incidence of unorganized work status is higher among lower social status groups than the higher social status groups.

The variety of work force including agriculture labor , construction labor, labor in leather tanning, handloom, fishing, forestry, salt making, street vending, domestic work, unorganized service sector, household industry and also village artisans who fall under the generic categories of the unorganized sector ( both wage employed and self-employed) are wholly out of the coverage of legal in the country. The informal workers spread among all the sectors and sub sectors of the economy.

Globalization and liberalization has led to the use of new technology in agriculture resulting in increased unemployment in the countryside. Consequently, this has forced large numbers of the poor from labor and farming communities to migrate from their home to distant places in search of employment (Reddy, 2003). Stieglitz viewed that " The mantra of increased labor market flexibility was only a thinly disguised argument to roll back under the guise of economic efficiency- gains that workers had achieved over years and years of bargaining political activity". This flexibility enhances the welfare of capital class at the expense of workers. Reduction in subsidies, decline in public investment on agriculture, lifting of quantitative restrictions, commercialization of agriculture, crop failure and high cost of credit, has badly affected earnings of rural informal labor, hence caused rural urban migration .

Over the past two decades employment in the informal sector has raised rapidly in all regions of the world. The share of informal sector in nonagricultural GDP is between 45 to 60 percent in developing nations. Informal employment comprises 50 to 75 percent of nonagricultural employment in developing nations. The average income of both men and women are lower in informal sector than in the formal sector. Unorganized sector in India, contributes around 60 percent of total net value added, 60 percent of the total household savings originates from the unorganized sector. Around 30 percent of exports and 41 percent of manufacturing exports are contributed by this sector (Ghatate 1999).

**Table 10.1: Employment (Millions) in organized and unorganized sectors in India 1999-2000 and 2004-2005**

| Year | 1999-2000 (workers) | | | 2004-2005 (workers) | | |
|---|---|---|---|---|---|---|
| Sector | Informal | Formal | Total | Informal | Formal | Total |
| Informal/unorganized | 341.3(99.6) | 1.4(0.4) | 342.6(100.0) | 393.5(99.6) | 1.4(0.4) | 394.9(100.0) |
| Formal /organized | 20.5( 37.8) | 33.7(62.2) | 54.2(100.0) | 29.1(46.6) | 33.4(53.4) | 62.6(100.0) |
| Total | 361.7( 91.2) | 35.0(8.8) | 396.7(100.0) | 422.6(92.4) | 34.9(7.6) | 457.5(100.0) |

Source: - Goi (2006)
Note: - Figures in parentheses are percentage to respective totals

Unorganized sector accounts for 92 percent of the total work force of about 457 million (NCEUS 2007). Table 10.1. Reveals that the total employment in India has increased from 397 million to 457 million between 1999-2000 and 2004-05. Informal employment has increased from 361.7 million to 422.6 million during the same period, whereas formal employment has declined from 35 million to 34.9 million during the same period i.e. the change in the organized or formal employment has been marginally negative.

Table 10.2, reveals that informal workers are not getting even the bottom wage rate of Rs 75 per day. The females' earnings are much lesser when compared to males in all the categories of employment in both formal and informal sectors. Wages of both males and females are lesser than the national commission on labor recommended daily wage rate of Rs 125 in 1996, is a night mare in practice.

**Table 10.2: The average wage rate per day ( in Rs) for regular and casual workers in formal and informal sectors ( 1999- 2000)**

| Nature of employment | Formal sector | | Informal sector | |
|---|---|---|---|---|
| | Males | Females | Males | Females |
| Regular | 196 | 156 | 87 | 56 |
| Casual | 58 | 36 | 60 | 37 |
| All | 175 | 134 | 73 | 46 |

Source:-Computed from the raw data of NSS 55 round employment and un employment survey 1999-2000.

## Methodology of the study

**Problem:-** In the context of economic reforms, Liberalization, Privatization and Globalization (LPG), the employment situation in rural areas is deteriorating .As a result , migration of casual labor from rural to urban areas in search of livelihood has accelerated. Keeping the above aspects under consideration, an attempt is made in the study area to find out wages, income levels, and poverty among migrant labor.

**Selection of the study areas**: - The Visakhapatnam city is one of the fast growing cities of South India, located in Andhra Pradesh. This city has emerged as financial capital of Andhra Pradesh. Jammu city is located in extreme tip of northern India, it is transit tourist centre and summer capital of Jammu and Kashmir.

**Methodology**:- Quantitative research methodology is used.

**Sample selection**:- Clustered simple random sampling method is used in this study.

**Tools**:- Questionnaire , simple Arithmetic mean and factor analysis are used.

## Objectives of the Study

1. To consider wage rates and changes in wage rates of the laborers during the prior and post migration scenario.
2. To consider changes in income levels of migrant labor during pre and post migration and to estimate poverty level.
3. To suggest policy implications for further improvement of the living conditions of migrant labor.

**Data sources: -** This study is based on secondary sources such as various rounds of NSSO and census data, whereas primary data is collected from 625 respondents (375 from Visakhapatnam and 250 from Jammu) .

**Reference period**:- This study has conducted in 2003 in Visakhapatnam and Jammu cities , with the help of specially designed questionnaire.

## Labor Migration an observation

Migration is a socio economic phenomenon, which shapes the urbanization pattern in developing nations. Movement of people from one area to another in search of improved livelihood is a key feature of human history. Migration has become an increasingly important feature in a globalizing world. Migration is defined as a move from one migration defining area to another, usually crossing administrative boundaries made during a given migration interval and involving a change of residence United Nations Organisation (UNO 1993)."A large part of urban growth in the less developed countries has historically been linked to stagnation and volatility of agriculture and the lack of sect oral diversification within the agrarian economy, India is no exception to this phenomenon" India Urban Poverty Report (2009). Increasing transport, communication, industrialization, urbanization, availability of business, employment and educational opportunities in urban areas are the reasons for rural out migration.

Rural urban migration is the fastest growing type of migration in India. Migrants prefer to work relatively at higher wages in non-farm occupations in urban areas. Migrant labor makes enormous contributions to the urban economy by working in major sectors such as construction, textiles, small industries, brick-making, stone quarries, street vending, domestic work, mines, fish and prawn processing and hospitality services (Priya Deshingkar and Shaheen Akter 2009).

In the post-independence period the industrial and economic development in India has led to an increased pace of urbanization resulting in concentration of economic activity in urban areas and the poor migrating in large numbers, to improve their economic lot. Migration of unorganised workers helps themselves and their families to avoid starvation but fails to drastic improvement of their standard of living, so it can be said that it is simply shifting of poverty from rural to urban from Feudalism to Capitalism. Migrant workers are the most vulnerable section and they are more likely to be found working at very low wages in hazardous physical conditions. Instances of various kinds of exploitation

**Table 10.3: Growth of Internal Migrants by Rural Urban Status, India 1971-2001**

| Year | Rural (%) | | | Urban (%) | | | Total % | | |
|---|---|---|---|---|---|---|---|---|---|
| | Persons | Males | females | Persons | Males | females | Persons | Males | Females |
| 1971-81 | 18.0 | 4.5 | 22.6 | 40.2 | 32.1 | 48.4 | 26.30 | 19.43 | 29.40 |
| 1981-91 | 10.9 | -0.2 | 14.1 | 13.8 | 6.5 | 20.7 | 12.04 | 3.21 | 15.72 |
| 1991-2001 | 29.5 | 33.6 | 28.4 | 49.6 | 57.3 | 43.3 | 36.96 | 48.33 | 32.75 |
| 1971-2001 | 69.1 | 69.4 | 68.9 | 162.2 | 156.4 | 169.1 | 93.82 | 82.83 | 98.78 |

Source: Migration tables census of India 1971, 1981, 1991,2001.

by employers and contractors are also widespread in the absence of any effective monitoring by government agencies.

The recent structural change and stagnant percapita GDP in the agriculture sector has further accentuated the distress migration from rural to urban areas. (Patnaik 2010). Per worker earnings of those staying back in agriculture are lesser in relation to that of those getting absorbed in diverse and upcoming , nonfarm activities. The ability of agriculture to absorb additional labor force has considerably declined. Further support for this conclusion is found from the rapidly declining per capita size of land holdings, the increasing proportion of marginal and small farmers and the rising proportions seeking nonagricultural employment.

Table 10.3 shows that the growth of female migrants is greater than those of male migrants. There is 169 percent increase in female migration in urban category during the period1971 to 2001, as against 156 percent increase in male migration during the same period. Moreover except between 1981 to 1991 the percentage of both urban and rural internal migrants has increased

Generally these casual laborers assemble in common places in and around the major working places of towns and cities which are popularly known as labor markets. Various organizations, contractors and the public, who require labor, come to these places and hire the labor from these markets. The casual laborers of these markets constitute newly migrated people and down trodden people, living below poverty line who are mostly slum dwellers and foot path dwellers and people from squatter settlements all of whom are living in miserable conditions.

## Review of literature

Having briefly introduced the topic, objectives and research design it would be fruitful to acquaint ourselves of the findings of the existing studies undertaken by the researchers on the theme of our discussion . Many studies threw a light on the various aspects of migration.

E.G.Ravinstein (1885) stated that the migrants move from the areas of low opportunities to areas of high opportunities, migrant's first move nearby towns and then towards larger cities. Lewis (1954) stated that generally under developed economy consisting of two sectors (1) Traditional agricultural subsistence sector , characterized by zero or low productivity surplus labor and (2) High productivity modern urban industrial sector . Migrants migrate from the low productive subsistence agriculture sector (rural) to high productive modern industrialized (urban) areas. This type of migration continues as long as the surplus labor force exists in rural areas.

Everret, S.Lee (1966), classified forces of migration into push and pull factors. The push factors are negative factors causes migrants to leave their place of origin, while the pull factors are positive factors which attracts migrants to the place of destination in the expectation of improving their socio economic conditions.

Harris and Todaro (1970), risk-neutral individuals migrate in response to a gap between an expected urban and a de facto rural wage. High and institutionally determined urban wages make migration attractive even in the presence of urban unemployment. While wage gaps contribute to explain rural-urban migration in developing countries Lucas (1997). Migration is a collective Endeavour enabling rural households to diversify incomes (Stark and Levhari 1982; Stark 1991). Migrants choose destinations where they are well connected (Lucas 1997).

G.Parthasarathy et.al (1998), observed that in developing nations the impact of economic reforms is seen in two ways. (1) Rapid shift of labor force from agriculture to non-agriculture ( 2) Un employment among agriculture labor and push them towards urban areas Ahluwalia ,M.S.(2002), addressed that the agriculture has suffered most notably from the decline in public investment in areas critical for agriculture growth.

Studies are limited with regarding wages, income levels and poverty of rural urban informal migrant labor in India , hence this study occupies an important place. .

## Data analysis pertaining Visakhapatnam (Study area I)

### *(a) Sample households of casual labor migrants*

The study covers about 4 (Table 10.4) labor markets such as Isukothota, Seethampeta, NAD, Gajuwaka, in Visakhapatnam city, from 375 casual labor. Based on this information, wage, income levels and poverty rate has been analyzed. The maximum proportion of respondents belongs to Isukathota and lesser proportion of respondents belongs to Seethampeta and NAD.

**Table 10.4: Sample households of casual labor migrants of the study area**

| Sample Area | Number of Respondents | % Total |
|---|---|---|
| | I Visakhapatnam city(AP) | |
| 1. Isukathota | 125 | 32.80 |
| 2. Seethampeta | 75 | 20.00 |
| 3. NAD | 75 | 20.00 |
| 4. Gajuwaka | 100 | 26.66 |
| Total | 375 | 100.00 |

Source : Based on field level investigation

### *(b) Pre migration,* daily wage rates

It is evident from table( 10.5) that the maximum proportion of the respondents of about (44.80%) have earned less than Rs 25 per day, followed by Rs 25-50 (41.86%) and Rs 51-100 (11.47 %), while the lowest percentage of labor have earned more than Rs 100 at native place /last place of residence .Similarly a considerable proportion of respondents of about 41.80 percent have earned Rs 25-50 , about 11.47 percent earned in between Rs 51-100, while a lower proportion of respondents of about 1.87 percent have earned more than Rs 100 at their native place /last place of residence.

**Table 10.5: Daily wage rates(in Rupees) pattern of casual labor migrants at last place of residence**

| Wage rate Area | Number of Respondents | | | | |
|---|---|---|---|---|---|
| | < Rs 25 | Rs 25-50 | Rs 51-100 | Rs>100 | Total |
| | Visakhapatnam city (AP) | | | | |
| 1. Isukathota | 36( 28.80) | 68(54.41) | 21(16.80) | - | 125(100) |
| 2. Seethampeta | 45 (60.00) | 25(33.33) | - | 5(6.67) | 75 (100) |
| 3. NAD.(Gopalapatnam) | 37(49.33) | 24(32.00) | 12(16.00) | 2(2.67) | 75 (100) |
| 4. Gajuwaka | 50(50.00) | 157(40.00 | 10(10.00) | - | 100(100) |
| Total | 168(44.80) | 157(41.86) | 43(11.47) | 7(1.87) | 375(100) |

Note :( Figures in brackets indicate percentages to total
Source : Based on field level investigation

### *(c) Pre migration, annual income*

Table (10.6 ) focuses that the maximum proportion of (68.27%) respondents annual income is less than Rs 6,500, followed by income in between Rs 6500-11,500 (22.67%) and in between Rs 11,500 -20,000 (7.73%), while the lowest (1.33%) of respondents income is between Rs 20,000-30,000. Interestingly no body earn annual income more than Rs 30,000.

### *(d) Post migration daily wage rates*

Table (10.7) exhibits that the maximum proportion of the respondents of about (68.53 percent), have earned daily wages in between Rs 50- Rs 100, whereas (27.73 percent) have earned less than Rs 50. While the lowest are found to earn more than Rs 100 (3.73 percent) in the sample as a whole.

### *(e) Post migration annual Incomes*

Table (10.8) presents that the maximum proportion of respondents of about (49.30 percent ) have income in between Rs 11500 to 20,000 per annum, followed by Rs 20,000 to 50,000 (25.60 percent ) between Rs 6,500- 11,500 (24.00 percent ), while the lowest percentage of respondents (1.07 percent ) earns income of more than Rs 50,000 per annum in this sample as a whole.

## Data analysis pertaining Jammu (J&K)-(Study area II)

### *(a) Sample households of casual labor migrants*

The study covers about 4 labor markets (Table, 10.9) such as Kaluchak, Raipur, Satwari, and Sanjuwan in Jammu city. The information was collected from 250 casual labors in Jammu. Based on this information, wage, income levels and poverty rate has been analyzed.

**Table 10.6: Pattern of annual income (in Rupees) of casual labor migrants at last place of residence**

| Income Area | Number of Respondents | | | | | |
|---|---|---|---|---|---|---|
| | Rs<6,500 | Rs6,500-11500 | Rs11,500-20,00 | Rs 20,000-30.000 | Rs>30,000 | Total |
| | | | Visakhapatnam (AP) | | | |
| 1. Isukathota | 56(44.80) | 51(40.80) | 18(14.40) | - | - | 125(100) |
| 2. Seethampeta | 59(78.67) | 11(14.66) | - | 5(6.67) | - | 75 (100) |
| 3. NAD. (Gopalapatnam | 49(65.33) | 23(30.67) | 3(4.00 ) | - | - | 75 (100) |
| 4. Gajuwaka | 92(92.00) | - | 8( 8.00) | - | - | 100(100) |
| Total | 256(68.27)) | 85 (22.67) | 29(7.73) | 5(1.33) | - | 375(100) |

Note :( Figures in brackets indicate percentages to total
Source : Based on field level investigation

**Table 10.7: Pattern of Daily wage rates (in Rupees) of casual labor migrants- post migration**

| Daily wage Area rate | Number of Respondents | | | |
|---|---|---|---|---|
| | < Rs 50 | Rs 50-100 | Rs>100 | Total |
| Visakhapatnam city(AP) | | | | |
| 1. Isukathota | 24( 19.20) | 97 (77.60) | 4 (3.20) | 125(100) |
| 2. Seethampeta | 37 (49.33) | 38 (50.67) | - | 75 (100) |
| 3. NAD.(Gopalapatnam | 14(18.67 ) | 58 (77.33) | 3 (4.00) | 75 (100) |
| 4. Gajuwaka | 29 (29.00) | 64 (64.00) | 7 (7.00) | 100(100) |
| Sub total | 104(27.73) | 257 (68.53) | 14 (3.73) | 375(100) |

Note :( Figures in brackets indicate percentages to total
Source : Based on field level investigation

**Table 10.8: Pattern of annual income(in Rupees) of casual labor migrants-post migration**

| Income Area | Number of Respondents | | | | | | |
|---|---|---|---|---|---|---|---|
| | <6,500 | 6,500-11,500 | 11,500-20,000 | 20,000-50,000 | >50,000 | Total | Average income per annum |
| Visakhapatnam city(AP) | | | | | | | |
| 1. Isukathota | - | 49(39.20) | 57(45.60) | 15(12.00) | 4 (3.20) | 125(100) | 14,885 |
| 2. Seethampeta | - | 22 (29.33) | 41 (54.67) | 12 (16.00) | - | 75 (100) | 14042 |
| 3. NAD. (Gopalapatnam | - | 12(16.00) | 44(58.67) | 19(25.33) | - | 75 (100) | 17,459 |
| 4. Gajuwaka | - | 7 (7.00) | 43(43.00) | 50(50.00) | - | 100(100) | 19,700 |
| Total | - | 90(24.00) | 185(49.3) | 96(25.60) | 4(1.07) | 375(100) | 16,215 |

Note :( Figures in brackets indicate percentages to total

Source : Based on field level investigation

**Table 10.9: Sample households of casual labor migrants of the study area**

| II. Jammu (J&K) | Number of Respondents | % Total |
|---|---|---|
| 1. Kaluchak | 75 | 30.00 |
| 2. Raipur | 50 | 20.00 |
| 3. Satwari | 75 | 30.00 |
| 4. Sanjuwan | 50 | 20.00 |
| Sub Total | 250 | 100.00 |

Source : Based on field level investigation

### *(b) Pre migration,* daily wage rates

It is evident from table (10.10) that the maximum proportion of the respondents of about (45.20%) have earned Rs 25-50, followed by 44.40 percent respondents earned less than Rs 20 per day whereas 20.40 percent workers earned Rs 51-100. While the lowest percentage of labor have earned Rs more than 100 at native place /last place of residence in the sample as a whole.

### *(c) Pre migration, annual income*

Table (10.11 ) focuses that the maximum proportion of (71.60 percent) respondents annual income is less than Rs 6,500, followed by income in between Rs 6500-11,500 (18.40 percent) between Rs 11,500 -20,000 (8.00 percent), and in between Rs 20,000 –Rs 30,000 (1.20 percent) while the lowest (0.80 percent) of respondents income is more than Rs 30,000.

### *(d) Daily wage rates (in Rupees) pattern of casual labor migrants- post migration*

Table (10.12) exhibits that the maximum proportion of the respondents of about (77.20 percent), have earned daily wages less than Rs 50, whereas (18 percent) respondents have earned between Rs 50-100. While the lowest are found to earn more than Rs 100 (4.80 percent) in this sample as a whole.

**Table 10.10: Pattern of Daily wage rates of casual labor migrants- pre migration**

| Wage rate Area | Number of Respondents | | | | |
|---|---|---|---|---|---|
| II. Jammu (J&K) | < Rs 25 | Rs 25-50 | Rs 51-100 | Rs>100 | Total |
| 1. Kaluchak | 38(50.66) | 32(42.67) | 5 (6.67) | - | 75 (100) |
| 2. Raipur | 15 (30.00) | 21 (42.00) | 14(28.00) | - | 50 (100) |
| 3. Satwari | 40 (53.33) | 31 (41.33) | 4(5.34) | - | 75 (100) |
| 4. Sanjuwan | 18(36.00) | 29(58.00) | 3 (6.00) | - | 50 (100) |
| Sub total | 111(44.40) | 113(45.20) | 12(10.40) | - | 250(100) |

Note :( Figures in brackets indicate percentages to total
Source : Based on field level investigation

**Table 10.11: Pattern of annual income( in Rupees) of casual labor migrants- pre migration**

| Area Income | Number of Respondents | | | | | |
|---|---|---|---|---|---|---|
| II. Jammu (J&K) | Rs<6,500 | Rs 6,500-11500 | Rs 11,500-20,000 | Rs 20,000-30.000 | Rs>30,000 | Total |
| 1. Kaluchak | 65(86.67) | 5(6.67) | 5(6.67) | - | - | 75(100) |
| 2. Raipur | 18(36.00) | 21 (42.00) | 9(18.00) | - | 2(4.00) | 50(100) |
| 3. Satwari | 60(80.00) | 12(16.00) | - | 3(4.00) | - | 75(100) |
| 4. Sanjuwan | 36(72.00) | 8(16.00) | 6(12.00) | - | - | 50(100) |
| Total | 179(71.60) | 46(18.40) | 20(8.00) | 3(1.20) | 2(0.80) | 250(100) |

Note :( Figures in brackets indicate percentages to total.

Source : Based on field level investigation

**Table 10.12: Daily wage rates (in Rupees) pattern of casual labor migrants- post migration**

| Area Daily wage | Number of Respondents | | | |
|---|---|---|---|---|
| II. Jammu (J&K) | < Rs 50 | Rs 50-100 | Rs>100 | Total |
| 1. Kaluchak | 64 (85.33) | 6 (8.00) | 5(6.66) | 75 (100) |
| 2. Raipur | 38 (76.00) | 12 (24.00) | - | 50 (100) |
| 3. Satwari | 59 (78.67) | 11 (14.67) | 5 (6.67) | 75 (100) |
| 4. Sanjuwan | 32 (64.00) | 16 (32.00) | 2 (4.00) | 50 (100) |
| Sub total | 193(77.20) | 45 ( 18.00) | 12(4.80) | 250(100) |

Note :( Figures in brackets indicate percentages to total)
Source : Based on field level investigation

### *(e) Post migration annual Incomes*

Table 10.13) presents that the maximum proportion of respondents of about (78.80 percent ) have income in between Rs 20,000 to 50,000 per annum, followed by Rs 11,500 to 20,000 (12.40 percent ) between Rs 6,500- 11,500 (5.60 percent ), while the lowest percentage of respondents (2.40 percent ) earns income of more than Rs 50,000 per annum in this sample as a whole. On average annual per capita earnings of each worker is Rs 26,952 only.

## Pre and post migration a comparative analysis.

### *(a) Pre and post migration wage rates: A comparison (changes in daily wages)*

Table (10.14) focuses that the share of respondents who earn less than Rs 50 per day is showing decline from (87.84) to (47.52%). While the share of respondents who earn in between Rs 51 to Rs 100 per day has increased from (11.04%) to (48.32%) and more than Rs 100 has increased from (1.12%) to (4.16% ) during prior and post migration scenario in the sample as a whole. Post migration large number of workers (302 i.e. 48.32 percent) earn between Rs 51 to 100 in both the cities.

**Table 10.13: Pattern of annual income (in Rupees) of casual labor migrants post migration**

| Income Area | Number of Respondents | | | | | | |
|---|---|---|---|---|---|---|---|
| II. Jammu(J&K) | Rs<6,50 | Rs6,500-11,500 | Rs11,500-20,000 | Rs20,000-50,000 | Rs>50,000 | Total | Average income per annum |
| 1. Kaluchak | - | 11(14.67) | 5(6.67) | 59(78.66) | - | 75 (100) | 26,470 |
| 2. Raipur | - | - | - | 47(94.00) | 3(6.00) | 50 (100) | 32,058 |
| 3. Satwari | 2(2.67) | - | 21(28.00 | 49(65.33) | 3(4.00) | 75 (100) | 23,577 |
| 4. Sanjuwan | - | 3 (6.00) | 5(10.00) | 42(84.00) | - | 50 (100) | 25,952 |
| Sub total | 2(0.80) | 14 (5.60) | 31(12.40) | 197(78.8) | 6(2.40) | 250(100) | 26,952 |

Note :( Figures in brackets indicate percentages to total.
Source : Based on field level investigation

**Table 10.14: The pattern of the extent of changes in the daily wages(in Rupees) of casual labor migrants during prior and post migration scenarios**

| Sample area | Visakhapatnam city(AP) | | | Jammu city(J&K) | | | Sample as a whole | | |
|---|---|---|---|---|---|---|---|---|---|
| Daily wages | Prior migration | Post Migration | % change | Prior migration | Post Migration | % change | Prior migration | Post Migration | % change |
| < Rs 50 | 325(86.67) | 104(27.73) | -68.00 | 224(89.60) | 193(77.20) | -13.84 | 549(87.84) | 297(47.52) | -49.90 |
| Rs 51 to100 | 43(11.47) | 257(68.53) | 497.67 | 26(10.40) | 45(18.00) | 73.08 | 69(11.04) | 302(48.32) | 337.68 |
| > Rs100 | 7(1.86) | 14(3.73) | 100.00 | – | 12(4.80) | – | 7(1.12) | 26(4.16) | 271.42 |

Note: - (1) Total sample respondents from Visakhapatnam are 375 and from Jammu are 250.
(1) Figures in parenthesis are percentage of the total respondents of the respective city

Source : Based on field level investigation

Regarding sample areas, a considerable number of respondents who earn less than Rs 50 per day are in almost all the sample areas in Jammu in post migration scenario. In respect of growth , the proportion of respondents who earn less than Rs 50 per day are showing decline of about 45.90 percent, while the respondents who earn Rs 51- 100 per day (337.68 percent ) and more than Rs 100 per day (271.42 percent), are showing increase in the sample as a whole.

### *(b) Pre and post migration annual income: A comparison (changes in income levels)*

Table (10.15) indicates that the maximum proportion of about ( 69.60%) of the respondents annual income is less than Rs 6000 in prior migration, whereas during post migration a higher proportion of respondents annual income is in between Rs 11501 to 20,000 (34.56). Where-as 46.88 percent of respondents annual income is in between Rs 20,001 to 30,000 .During post migration scenario a considerable decline is found in the proportion of respondents who earns income in between Rs 6501 to 11500 (20.96% to 16.64% ), interestingly no one is earning income less than Rs *6000* in the sample as a whole.

Regarding growth, relatively higher growth is found in the respondent's income. In the income groups of Rs 11,501 - 20,000 (36.82 percent ), Rs 20,001 to Rs 30,000 (3562.50), and more than Rs 30,000 (50.00 percent ), while a considerable proportion of decline is found in the respondents income of Rs 6,501-11,500 (-20.61 percent ) during the prior and post migration scenario in the sample as a whole.

### Interpretation of results

Post migration wage rates are higher in Visakhapatnam when compared to wage rates prevails in Jammu, but daily work availability is the main reason for higher income levels in Jammu. In both the cities because of the availability of daily

**Table 10.15: The pattern of the extent of annual income of casual labor migrants during prior and post migration scenarios**

| Sample area | Study area I Visakhapatnam city(AP) | | | Study area II Jammu city (J&K) | | | Sample as a whole | | |
|---|---|---|---|---|---|---|---|---|---|
| Annual income | Prior migration | Post migration | % change | Prior migration | Post migration | % change | Prior migration | Post migration | % change |
| < Rs 6500 | 256(68.27) | – | – | 179(71.60) | – | – | 435(69.60) | – | – |
| Rs 6501 to11,500 | 85(22.67) | 90(24.00)) | 5.88 | 46(18.40) | 14(5.60) | -69.56 | 131(20.96) | 104(16.64) | -20.61 |
| Rs 11,501to 20,000 | 29(7.73) | 185(49.33) | 538.16 | 20(8.00) | 31(12.40) | 55.00 | 49(7.84) | 216(34.56) | 340.82 |
| Rs 20,001 to 30,000 | 5(1.33) | 96(25.60) | 1820.0 | 3(1.20) | 197(78.80) | 6466.67 | 8(1.28) | 293(46.88) | 3562.50 |
| Rs >30,000 | – | 4(1.07) | – | 2(0.80) | 8(3.20) | 300.00 | 2(0.32) | 12(1.92) | 500.00 |

Note: - (1) Total sample respondents from Visakhapatnam 375 and from Jammu 250.
(2)Figures in parenthesis are percentage of the total respondents of the respective city.

Source : Based on field level investigation

work, post migration annual income is more than pre migration level. The annual percapita income of respondents in Visakhapatnam is Rs 16,215 where as it is Rs 26,952 in Jammu and Rs 26379 in the sample as a whole.

**Alternative poverty measure (Capability poverty Index (CPI):-** There is a growing opposition for poverty measurement based on income or calories, so an attempt is made to measure poverty through an alternative poverty measure .To prepare capability poverty index, 12 variables are taken into consideration viz caste, education, occupation, number of workers in a family , family size , house type, number of rooms , electricity facility, toilets, type of cooking fuel, income , expenditure. For constructing the index weights are assigned to all the 12 variables. It is found that any household may have a maximum weight of 12 or minimum weight is (0) or in between these two extremes. Each household weight is converted into percentage in the maximum weight 12. All the households who got less than 50% of the weight are treated as poor by poverty index. Thus in Visakhapatnam 35% of the households , in Jammu 30% of the households are living below poverty line. The level of poverty is more than that of national poverty line among the migrant labor working in both the cities.

This study reveals that if labor move far away from their native place , their earnings are better than those labor migrated nearer to their actual place of origin. Further it can be stated that nowadays labor migrate to distant nations to increase their income levels.

## Summary and conclusion

Solution to rural poverty must be found within the rural areas. In order to safeguard the economic and social safety interests of the migrant laborers, govt enacted migrant labor act in 1979, this act is to be implemented without lapses. Wages for the casual laborers are to be fixed according to price index in the region in question migrant workers are working. All the migrant labor are to be enrolled and identity cards (smart cards) and Ration cards should be issued to ensure food security. Adequate compensation may be provided for casual laborers if injured or dead while in work or in connection with the work. Scholarships and hostel facilities may be provided for the children's of migrant labor. Micro finance may be provided by forming SHGs by fixing cap on the interest rate being charged by MFIs.

Identify villages from where migrations are taking place, as those are backward in character and give priority to those villages for the implementation of various developmental programmers through DRDA, SC, BC, social welfare organizations. Implement Programme of Urban amenities in Rural Areas (PURA) to stop further migration. Increase the role of NGOs to create awareness about anti-poverty programmes. Contractor should not recruit migrant labor without obtaining license from the government. Ensure no discrimination of wage payment on the basis of gender. Ensure implementation of social security act (2007) for informal workers. Guarantee employment to all the adults in the family under MNREGA and reduce corruption in its implementation. Labor participation is required in design and implementation of anti-poverty programmes. Employment oriented agricultural growth, rural industrialization and creation of other off farm jobs are more important to stop rural urban migration. Perceptions should be changed as migrant labor is source but not burden for urban development.

### References

Bose, Ashish (1967): 'Migration Streams in India', *Population Review*, 11: 39-45.

Bala Krishna Pulapri (2000): 'Agriculture and Economic Reforms, Growth and Welfare'. *Economic and political weekly* xxxv (12) March 12-18: pp 999- 1003.

Census of India (2001). Soft copy, India D-series, 'Migration Tables'. *Registrar General and Census Commissioner, govt of India*

Everett, S.Lee (1966): ' A Theory of Migration', *Demography*, No.3 pp 47-57.

Govt of India (2008) 'Eleventh five year plan 2007-2012 ,Vol-1' ,*Planning Commission Govt of India*, Oxford University Press .New Delhi.

Govt of India (2008): *Economic Survey 2007-2008*, Oxford University Press, New Delhi.

Harris, J. R. and Todaro (1970): 'Migration Unemployment and development: A two sector analyses, *American Economic Review*, 60. No 1.pp126-142.

Kannan, K.P (2008): 'Dualism, Informality and Social Inequality'. *Presidential address at 50th annual conference ISLE*, Lucknow.

Kundu, Amitabh and Shalini Gupta (1996), 'Migration, Urbanisation and Regional Inequality' '*Economic and Political Weekly*, Vol. 31, No. 52, Dec. 28.

Lewis, W. Arthur (1954), 'Economy Development with Unlimited Supplies of Labor', *The*

*Manchester School*, Vol. 22, pp.139-91.

Montek, S.Ahuliwalia (1999): 'India's Economic Reforms an Appraisal'. In Jeffrey. S.et.al (Ed) *India in the Era of Economic Reforms*, Oxford University Press, New York, pp .1-80.

Narayana murthy, A et al (1999): 'Agricultural growth and migration search for new evidence'. *Indian journal of Agriculture Economics* 54 (3) July- Sept: pp 402- 410.

Popola, T S (1986): *Urbanization, Rural Urban Migration and growth of informal sector*. Working paper No 51, Giri Institute of Development Studies.

Partha Sarathy, G. et al. (1998): 'Determinants of Rural Non Agricultural Employment, the Indian Case'. *Indian Journal of Agricultural Economics*. No 53 (2) April- June: pp139-145.

Reddy, D. Narasimha (2003), 'Economic Reforms and Travails of Circulating Labor of Dry Regions: A Case Study of Palamur Labor in Andhra Pradesh', *Labor& Development*, Vol. No.2, December.

Srivastava (1998):' Migration of Labor in India', *Indian Journal of Labor Economics*, Vol 41, no 4.

Vijay Joshi (1998): *Indian Macro Economics and Political Economy 1964-1991*, Oxford University Press, Delhi.

Zacharia, K.C. (1968): *Migrants in Greater Bombay*, Asia Publishing House, Bombay.

# 11

# Informal Labor in India
## (A Historical Perspective)

**Abstract**

*This paper is an attempt to analyze socio economic conditions of informal (unorganized) labor during ancient times. Those who engaged in farming, cattle rearing, hunting, fishing, poultry farming etc. come under the category of labor. All societies were primarily agriculture based in earlier period throughout the world. This was not different as far as Indian society was concerned. The rate of progress in agricultural labor was, of course, difficult to estimate and hence, in this paper an attempt is made to analyze one aspect i.e. the transformation of the labor class in various periods such as Indus valley, early Vedic, later Vedic, epic period, Buddhist period, period of Alexander's invasion, Mauryan period, Gupta period etc. An attention is given to the activities of the agricultural laborers of the south Indian regions too. Vedas, epics and other literary texts of ancient India provide several references to the agriculture labor of ancient India. In the age of Brahmanas too the agricultural labor played a significant role. Labor centered activities contributed much to the development of trade relations between Kerala and other European countries. Bible testifies this fact. This tradition of high production of spices continued in the modern period also due to the active participation of the labor. We can aptly say that the laborers were indirectly responsible for the occurrence of many battles in the southern regions. The present study helps us to assume that in each and every culture the animal labor played a significant role as it was strong support to the agriculture laborers in many ways.*

## Introduction

Labor class constitutes not only cultivators but also those who engaged in farming, cattle rearing, hunting, fishing, poultry farming etc. Almost all the societies were primarily agriculture based in earlier period throughout the world. This was not different as far as Indian society was concerned. Hence, in this paper an attempt is made to analyze the transformation of the labor class in various periods such as Indus valley, early Vedic, later Vedic, Epic period, Buddhist period, period of Alexander's invasion, Mauryan period, Gupta period etc. An attention is given to the activities of the agricultural laborers of the south Indian regions too. In India, the Paleolithic[1] men had no idea of agriculture. Yet, it is interesting to note that they lived on the flesh of animals and such fruits and vegetables as grew wild in jungles. But the civilization of the Neolithic men shows a distant phase of advance. They started cultivation and grew fruits and corn. Consequently, as years rolled by, men acquired greater knowledge and skill in mastering the cultivation process. The rate of progress in agricultural labor was, of course, difficult to estimate. It may be assumed that it may have been hundreds or thousands years before a distinctly higher type of agricultural labor evolved in India.

This paper is organized into 8 sections. The second section focused on labor in epics period. The third section gives a light on labor in the Indus Valley Civilization, fourth section deals with Labor in the Vedic Period, fifth section focused on later period and the sixth section dealt with labor in south India and the concluding section presents a summary of the paper .

## Labor during the Epics period

Vedas, Epics and other literary texts provide several references to the agriculture labor in ancient India. It is learnt from various sources that the economy in ancient India was mainly rural and agricultural in nature. There are numerous references to the agricultural labor and various crops in the *Atharva Veda* too. Other labor that chiefly contributed to the economy of ancient India included pottery, carpentry, metal-work, glass-work, jewellery making, weaving and leather-work. Besides cultivators, there were the carpenter, goldsmith, blacksmith, weaver, barber, woodcutter laborer , fighter, dancer, hunter, fowler, beggar, usurer, oil maker, garland-maker, stonecutter, pearl cutter, armor-maker, attendant, merchant, trader, chariot-maker, metal-worker and craftsmen.

In the age of *Brahmanas* too the agricultural played a significant role as agriculture was the principal occupation. The *Shatapatha Brahmana* mentions the different agricultural operations, such as ploughing, tilling, sowing, reaping, threshing etc. The word *Panchakrsti* literally means either rotation of five crops in the same field or the growing of five kinds of crops in different fields. Besides paddy, barley and sugarcane several other agricultural products are evident through the Vedic texts. *Rig Veda* appears to be familiar with the irrigation canals and the *Atharva Veda* describes the excavation of a canal from a river. Furthermore, cattle-rearing also contributed to the labor of ancient India. It was an essential occupation in the ancient society. Domesticated animals were known as *gramya* (rural). In a labor based society, which was mainly agricultural and pastoral, huge significance was attached to the cattle. Moreover, in several places described in *Shatapatha Brahmana,* cattle are stated to be the source of prosperity, fortune, goods, riches, food and even of home. *Atharva Veda* mentions the natural manure of animal. In the age of *Brahmanas,* various other arose to suit the needs of mixed castes. Brahmins performed rituals, rites and other religious practices along with the teaching duties. Kshatriyas were mainly engaged in the army. Trade, commerce and agriculture were the occupations of Vaishyas. Service of the upper classes was the livelihood of Sudras.

**Labor during the period of Indus Valley Civilization**

In recent years many archaeological excavations have been carried on at Mohenjo-Daro, Sind, Harappa, Baluchistan and different parts of Punjab including the Union Territory Chandigarh. These excavations have proved beyond that some four or five thousand years ago a highly civilized culture flourished in these regions. The valley of Indus thus takes its rank with the valleys of the Nile, the Tigris and the Euphrates as having contributed to the most ancient phase of human civilization of which we are yet aware. The antiquity of the civilization in India is thus carried back nearly to the same period which witnessed the growth of ancient civilizations in Egypt, Assyria and Babylonia. We see that in these cultures agricultural labor played an important role in the daily life of the common people. Little do we know about the agricultural labor of the Indus people. The difficulty is that we have no contemporary sources as to the actual method of agriculture practiced by the Indus valley people. The oldest known description of the Indus agricultural labor on flood-irrigated lands comes from Alexander's captains. The existence of such big cities as Mohenjo-Daro and Harappa clearly indicates that food must have been available in an ample measure. Workmen's quarters was discovered at Harappa which comprised of fourteen small houses built in two blocks separated by a long narrow lane. The remains unearthed at Mohenjo- Daro demonstrate the existence of the learned class, warriors, traders and artisans, and finally manual laborers, corresponding roughly to the war *varnas* of the Vedic period.[2] The learned class probably comprised of priests, physicians, astrologers and sorcerers constituted the first group. They were entitled to rule and administer the city. The existence of the armed people and watchmen's quarters at Mohanjo-Daro points to a class similar to the Kshatriyas, whose duty was to protect the people. A commercial class and various artisans such as the mason, engraver, shell -worker, weaver, gold smith etc. formed the third class. Domestic servants and manual laborers like leather workers, basket makers, peasants, fishermen etc., belonged to last group.[3] The prevalence of the distinct social groups in the Indus valley civilization indicates the importance given to them . It is mainly noted here that both the third and fourth group consisted of the who worked in the city. They also included the farmers who cultivated wheat and barley as their main crops. The examination of the specimens of wheat and barley discovered from the ruins indicates that they were not of the wild species. The same variety of wheat is cultivated in Punjab even today.[4] From the evidences we understand that they did not use plough instead, only a toothed harrow was in use. Bullock carts were found among the toy models, denoting the use of animal in the field, where there was neither plough harness nor a plough proper.

The farmers of ancient India depended upon rainfall. Scholars believe that in olden days Sind and Punjab received copious rainfall, and this, as also the presence of many rivers, must have made the problem of irrigation easy of solution. Though in considerable part of India irrigation was not regular or common, yet canal irrigation was very popular and widely practiced in the ancient Punjab. This might be due to the easy availability of plentiful cheap labor to work for the irrigation related activities. Moreover the prevalence of fertile silt deposits left on the river-banks by natural floods, the Indus method of irrigation i.e. damming of the rivers on the smaller branches etc, also helped to produce a regular crop. The specimens of wheat, barley and cotton have been found there, indicating Indus valley people cultivated these crops on large scale. The valley made real agriculture, yielding a substantial surplus, possible, as well as necessary. This facilitated the search for material with exchange of commodities along the great trade route. The surplus production might have led to a revolution in the population, life style, art, literature and architecture of this culture.

## Labor in the Vedic Period

When we consider the early Vedic age we see that the principal occupation of the village folk was cattle breeding. Agriculture was their second main occupation. They cultivated mainly wheat, rice and barley. The cultivated fields were known as *Urvara* or *Kshetra.* They were often watered by irrigational canals. Water was drawn from out of wells or from rivers. They used sickle, digging tool and plough, which was drawn by bulls. Ploughing appears to have been an old practice of the Aryans. All these indicate the highly developed labor activities of this period. There was no evidence of the division of land, or land ownership, selling or buying of land, or for that matter any commodities during this period. The wealth of a man was measured by the number of cattle he processed. The wide use of manure was also was known.

In later Vedic period agriculture continued to be one of the main occupations of the people and hence the role of agricultural labor was very dominant which led to great progress in agriculture in this period. During this period labor contributed considerable improvement in the use of agricultural implements. The quality and size of the plough was improved and the use of manure was well understood to increase the production. New kinds of grain and fruit trees were grown. Barley, rice, wheat, beans and sesame were cultivated in their due seasons. The exchange of food surplus for commodities led to the development of a new labor based social organization. This new organization of the society made available for the first time a supply of labor whose surplus was easily expropriated, and with the aid of which new territories could be settled.[5] Thus we see that the agricultural labor activities in the fertile plains increased the material prosperity of the Aryans and this gave rise to a variety of occupational groups and occupations to meet the various needs of the people. There were evidences of the division of labor during this period.

The principal change that took place after the invasion of the Aryans was in the productive relations. It was due to the formation of a servile class from the conquered *dasa* population. The *dasa* by caste had no property and were treated as same as the cattle. The word *pasu,* which applies generally to the beasts and particularly to the cattle, was once applied to human beings also.[6] It may be assumed that these *dasas* were the descendants of the Indus valley people who had provided the surplus for the Indus cities. This was considered as the beginning of caste system in India. The post Vedic period witnessed great structural changes and also changes in physical measurements, structure of the labor class, birth rates and population ratios due to the superior methods of food production. The initial stage of Aryan transition in India from pastoral raider to agrarian food producing labor was represented by sources like rituals, legend, myth, fable and sermons. As soon as take to regular food production from a previous irregular food gathering mode, they breed more rapidly. In earlier stage Aryan lived by the labor of cattle breeding supplemented by plough cultivation. But in the crucial stage they realized that plough would produce much more than cattle. So what spread was a new method of life and labor. The plough agriculture greatly increased the food supply, and made it more regular. Thus both quality and quantity of life and labor changed together. The Aryans advanced eastwards, burnt over the forest along the Himalayan foothills only through the physical labor. So we can say that the Aryans were able to settle in the east by the method of land clearing i.e. well utilization of the physical labor.[7]

### Labor in Later Periods

In the epic age also agriculture was the main stray of the mass of the people. The bulk of the population lived in villages around forts, tending cattle and practicing agriculture. The villages were autonomous in ordinary affairs, but the king as the overlord administered justice and exacted taxes, which were perhaps paid mostly in kind. *Manusmriti* gives details of the tax collections.[8] This indicates the significance of the as the perennial source of income and the best means to meet expenditures. It was during the period of Buddhism and Jainism the situation remained unchanged. The *Jatakas*, the *Pitakas* and other *Pali* works furnish detailed account of the village life and agricultural of this period. The village folk had common rights over the adjacent forest and grazing ground, where the cattle belongs to various house holders, were sent under the charge of a collectively hired herdsman called *gopalaka*. The rural economy was based on what may be called peasant proprietorship. But no owner could sell or mortgage his land without the consent of the village council. He cultivated the fields himself, but often employed labor and slaves to work. There were no big estates or landlords. The laborers of the village united of themselves in such undertakings as laying irrigation channels, building rest houses etc. The clan subsisted on the produce of the rice-fields, and the cattle grazed in the village common or the forests. The laborers of the villages were grouped together, and the laborers following particular crafts and occupations generally lived at one place. On the whole, each village was self-sufficient, and life was simple and unsophisticated. It was during the time of Alexander's invasion the number of the agricultural labor was very large in every kingdom. Agriculture and cattle breeding were important occupations of the people of Punjab and the North West during this period. The bigger holdings were rare, which were owned by the Brahmins and nobles and were managed with the help of hired labor. Many irrigational canals and reservoirs were constructed in this period with the help of hired labor .

In the Mauryan period the state had a large part of the agriculture of the country directly in its own hands. It was specially the state's business and responsibility to organize and extend the agricultural productivity of the country by schemes of colonization, encouraging the surplus population to settle new or abandoned tracts, and also by assisting the emigration of foreigners to settle in the country ( in Sanskrit it is said: *bhutapurvam abhutapurvam va janapadham paradesapavahanena swadesabhishyandavamanena va nivesayet*).[9] Each village had its full apparatus of agricultural life. Fields with crops (*kedara*), horticultural gardens (*pushpa vata*), plantations of bananas and sugarcane (*mula vapa*) and fields of roots like ginger, turmeric (*ardrakaharidradhi*) etc. were developed and prospered due to the hard work of the agriculture of the villages in the Mauryan period. The recorded and registered area was known as *nibandha* of the village. After deducting from it the area covered by boundaries were known *simavarodhena*. It consists of following parts:(1) Cultivated area (*krishta*), (2) Uncultivated wastes (*akrishta*), (3) High and dry ground (*sthala*), (4) Fields with crops (*kedara*), (5) Grove (*arama* also known as *upavana*), (6) Plantations of fruits like plantains (*shanda* also known as *kadalyadi kshetram*), (7) Sugarcane plantations (*vata* or *ikshvadibhumih*), (8) The source of the firewood for the village and other requisites (*vana*), (9) Area under houses (*vastu*), (10) Sacred trees (*chaitya*), (11) Temples (*devagriha*), (12) *Setubandha* (embankments), (13) Cremation grounds (*smasana*), (14) Almshouse (*sattra*), (15) Store-house of drinking water (*prapa*),(16) Holy places (*punyasthana*), (17) Grazing ground for village cattle (*vivita*), and (18) Area covered by roads (*pathi*).[10] The played a significant role in managing and supervising these lands and hence we can proudly say that they were actually responsible for the prosperity of these lands.

## Agricultural labor in South India

Even in south India too we see that society was primarily agricultural labor based. It is said that the trade relations between south India and the west countries started in ancient period itself due to the labor based activities in the south Indian region. South Indian ports had been frequently visited by the merchant ships from the Red sea and Persian Gulf in search of spices and valuable products from very early times. The credit for developing south Indian region as an emporium for international commercial and trade activities goes to the labor. The Sangam literature gives adequate proofs regarding the activities of the labor in various fields: It says that labor brought war horses that came through sea, bags of black pepper brought overland by cart, gems and gold from northern mountain, sandal and *akil*[11] wood from the western mountain, pearls of the southern and corals of the eastern sea, the produce of the Ganga basin and Kaveri valley, foodstuffs from Ceylon and luxuries from Kadaram.[12] It validates the multi-phase of the labor based activities. It is clear from the descriptions that the service of the was available in each and every phase of south Indian life. Bible and early Greek-Roman records also testify to this fact. King Solomon built a fleet of ships...[13] Hiran sent his servants with the fleet, sailors who were familiar with the sea, together, with the servants of Solomon.[14] The arrival of the Greeks including the labor in ships is clearly validated in *Akananuru* also.[15]

In Kerala, the production of spices was dominant from ancient period onwards and hence always on high demands.[16] Labor centered activities contributed much for the development of trade relations between Kerala and other European countries. Bible testifies this fact: The queen Sheba (Ethopia) came to Jerusalem with a very great retinue, with camels bearing spices, and very much gold, and precious stones....[17] It is believed that the spices might have been reached Ethopia and other western countries from south Indian region especially Kerala through trade relation. This tradition of high production of spices continued in the modern period also due to the active participation of the labor. The magic of the spice trade lured traders from the western world to this region. Vasco da Gama's triumphant voyage intensified an international power struggle over spices.[18] Among the spices, the pepper was the centre of attraction to the foreigners and,[19] thus, the south Indian regions became the arena of many battles[20] and we can aptly say that the laborers were indirectly responsible for the occurrence of many battles in the southern regions.

## Conclusion

In short, in India the feudalization of the state can be traced from the close of the sixth century and beginning of seventh century A.D. Division in the labor, agrarian expansion, deforestation etc. of the ancient period led to the growth of private farming, improvements in techniques of agriculture and increase in crop production, all of which ultimately led to the growth of market economy even during the ancient period. The features of the developments, which characterized the growth of rural economy in and around these focal points, were summed up as: attempts to increase the production of food crops by reclaiming new lands and felling and burning forests, converting old dry land into wet rice field through consolidation of drainage facilities, development of new modes surplus collection etc. by the landlord class.

## Footnotes

1 The wordPaleolithic has been derived from Greek words signifying old stone.

2 K.N Dikshit, *Pre-historic Civilization of the Indus Valley*, pp.31-32.

3 R.C.Majumdar and A.D. Pusalker, *The History and Culture of the Indian People: The Vedic Age*, 1957, p.179.

4 R.C.Majumdar and A.D. Pusalker, *The History and Culture of the Indian People: The Vedic Age*, 1957, p.174.

5 D.D. Kosambi, *An Introduction to the Study of Indian History*, p. 91.

6 *Rig Veda*, 3, 62, 14. It is assumed that the word *pasu was* generally applied to call the ;abour especially agricultural labor.

7 The method of land clearing was confirmed by many adjectives for *Agni* mentioned in *Rig Veda*: The swallower of forests, the axe etc. were described in *Rig Veda*. Though this method was not a principal one for bringing land under cultivation in historical times, land burning was mentioned in *Mahabharat, Khandavadaha Parva*, 1.214-225 too.

8 *Manusmriti*, VII, 130-132.

9 M. P. Radha Kumud Mookerji, *Chandragupta Maurya and His Times*, 1952, p.197.

10 M.P. Radha Kumud Mookerji, *Chandragupta Maurya and His Times*, 1952, pp.197-198.

11 Neem tree (*Azadiracht indica*), also known as margosa tree or aloe wood.Elamko Atikal, *Chilappatikaram*, Vol. XIV, pp. 104-112 says thatthe rulers of Tondi dispatch vessels loaded with *akil* wood (eaglewood), silk, sandal and spices and all sorts of camphor (*Cinnamomum camphora*), indicating the role of as carpenter and textile worker. They even engaged in dealing with sandal and spices also.

12 *Pattinappalai*, II. pp. 185-191.

13 *The Holy Bible, 1 kings, 9. 26, 2 Chronicles*, 8.17-18. The descriptions in the Bible regarding the buildings of the ships indicate the availability of the class, who were expert in ship building in thousands and thousands years back. Moreover it also validates the service of the labor in the ships, fleet and also as sailors.

14 *The Holy Bible, 1 kings*, 9. 27. The sailors of Solomon are believed to have arrived at Kodungallur in Kerala.

15 *Akananuru*: 149: 7-11.

16 W.H. Schoff, Ed., *Periplus of the ErythreanSea*, pp. 210- 215; E.H. Warmington, *Roman Trade with India*, pp. 181-183.

17 *The Holy Bible, 1 Kings* 10. 2. 2, Chronicles 9.1- 28, *1 kings*10:10, 2, Chronicles 9.1- 28.

18 S.L. Kochhar, *Economic Botany in the Tropics*, p. 27,

19 The travellers like Yaqut, Al Kaswini, Al Idrisi, Marco Polo and Marignolli give elaborate accounts of pepper cultivation and its trade in southern region. For details see, M. H. Nayinar, *Arab Geographers Knowledge of Southern India*, pp. 34, 41, 46, 206. The details of the extensive and intensive cultivation of paddy, different crops, vegetables and fruit trees practiced by the agricultural are also available.

20 It is reported that special watchmen were appointed as in the palaces to protect them. In ships crews were instructed to use shirts and pants without pockets. Velayudhan Panikkassery, *Marko Polo Indiayil*, pp. 80- 82.

## References

Dikshit .K. N.(1939), *Pre-historic Civilization of the Indus Valley*, Madras,

*Holy Bible*(1987) The Bible Society of India, Bangalore,

Jha, D.N (2000) *The Feudal Order*, Manohar Publications, New Delhi,

Kochhar S.L., *Economic Botany in the Tropics*, Delhi,

Krishnaswami Aiyangar, S(1980), *History of Ancient India*, Seema Publications, Delhi,

Majumdar R. C. and Pusalker A.D (1957); *The History and Culture of the Indian People: The Vedic Age*, George Allen & Un win Ltd., London.

Nilakanta Sastri, K.A(1966) ;*A History of South India*, Oxford University Press, Madras,

Panikkar, K.M.(1947); *A Survey of Indian History*, The National Information and Publication Ltd., Bombay,

Panikkar, K.M.,(1963); *Studies in Indian History*, Asia Publishing House, Bombay,

Radha Kumud Mookerji, M.P.(1952); *Chandragupta Maurya and His Times*, Rajkamal Publications Limited, Bombay,

Raghuvanshi, V.P.S.(1969); *Indian Society in the Eighteenth Century*, Associated Publishing House, New Delhi,

Ramaprasad Chanda, B.A.(1978); *The Indo-Aryan Races*, Cosmo Publications, New Delhi, 1978.

Singh, Yogendra,(1977); *Social Stratification and Change in India*, Manohar Publications, New Delhi,

Thapar, Romila(1993); *From Lineage to State*, Oxford University Press, Delhi,

Thapar, Romila,(2002); *History of Early India from the Origins to A.D. 1300*, Penguin Books India (P) Ltd., New Delhi.

Thapar, Romila(1995); *Recent Perspective of Early Indian History*, Popular Prakashan, Bombay.

Tharoor, Shashi,(1995); *India from Midnight to the Millennium*, Penguin Books India (P) Ltd., New Delhi..

Tripathi, R.S.(1942); *History of Ancient India*, Motilal Banarsidass, Delhi.

# 12

# Changing Employment Patterns in Informal Manufacturing Sector in India

**Abstract**

*The present paper attempts to analyze the changing trend, pattern of employment in the unorganized manufacturing sector based on three rounds (51$^{st}$, 56$^{th}$ & 62$^{nd}$) of National Sample Surveys (NSS) on unorganized manufacturing sector. Although there has been increase of employment in the unorganized manufacturing during the first study period i.e. 1994-95/2000-01 but it has declined the second period i.e. 2000-01/2005-06. Further, there is a positive growth of female employment in both the periods. The female employment has largely been concentrated in low-productive and labor intensive industry groups; large part of female employment are of part-time and contractual in nature and preponderant majority of female are engaged in tiniest enterprises, i.e. OAMEs. The present paper makes an attempt to understand the emerging pattern of employment in the unorganized manufacturing sector.*

**Keywords:** Unorganized manufacturing, employment.

## Introduction

Employment has been an issue of serious concern in India, especially after economic reform. This concern is underlined not just by the fact that even the economy is growing at a fairly high rate, the employment situation has been discouraging. The overall employment has been growing at a very slower pace and the conditions of employment have also been far from satisfactory. Another serious concern relating to employment has been the rise of employment opportunities only in the unorganized or informal segment of the economy, which is largely characterized by low levels of wages, insecure and poor quality of employment. In such a scenario, the issue related to employment in the unorganized manufacturing poses another dimension of the challenge which is not frequently discussed in the Indian context.

The globalisation process has deregulated and liberalised the labor market in the developing countries. It is argued that the process of globalization leads to informalisation, feminisation and casualization of employment. However, under deregulated and liberalised market system, the new industries targeted to make quick profits to become 'a world class company'. In pursuit of this objective these industries introduced changes in their organisational, managerial, technological and operational set up. These changes are so designed that they prefer low skills, female workers and opt for informalisation and segmented employment. Some of these jobs are contractual, casual, insecure, flexible, result in informal work relations (Vanamala 2001).

The globalization process in India led by reforms in different sectors has contributed to the enlargement of unorganized, informal sector in the economy. In the post-reforms period most of the employment is generated in the unorganized sector with informal work relations (Deshpande and Deshpande 1992). Reforms such as abolition of all industrial licensing policies reduction in public expenditure, the disinvestment policy, the 'Exit' provisions are all a part of this process. This is fast catching up in the corporate world as an important instrument for enforcing changes in employment size, its mix and total wage bill. These together contributed to the enlargement of the informal sector.

In India, it is not informal, but unorganized sector that is more often used and official data refer to the sector as unorganized or unregistered units. More precisely, unorganized sector refers to the collection of those operating units whose activities do not come under any statutory Act or legal provision and/or which do not maintain any regular accounts. As in the case of other developing countries, in India too, the unorganized sector occupies a prominent place. This sector contributes to about 60 percent of total Net Domestic Product (NDP) and provides livelihood to nearly 93 percent of the work force (Kulshreshta and Singh, 2001) and over a period of time its presence and extent have been growing (Sakthivel and Joddar, 2006).[1]

Since a large part of India's manufacturing is comprised of unorganized segment, an incisive and elaborate understanding of this category of workers is thus essential to comprehend India's labor market especially from the point of view of income generation and poverty reduction. The present paper thus attempts the emerging pattern of employment in the unorganized manufacturing sector in India. In this context, section I reveals a brief introduction followed by section II analyses the overall trend of employment in the Indian economy; section III briefly discusses the size, structure and growth of the unorganized manufacturing sector; section IV describes the trend, pattern and growth employment in unorganized manufacturing sector. The concluding section, (Section V) presents a summary of the paper .

The data source for the study is National Sample Survey Organization (NSSO) survey on unorganized manufacturing in its 51st (1994-95), 56th (2000-01) and 62nd (2005-06) rounds. A major problem that needs to be solved while comparing the NSS rounds is the choice of National Industrial Classification (NIC). The concordance table has been used to compare different NSS rounds and the nineteen 2-digit industries are reclassified into 15 industry groups across various rounds following the NIC 1987. The concordance table is given in appendix.

## Employment situation: Recent trends

Recent data shows that overall employment increased in the Indian economy, both in terms of usual principal status (UPS) and usual principal status plus subsidiary status (UPSS). Total employment has increased from 334.4 million in 1993-94 to 416.3 million in 2004-05, as per UPS estimates. Similarly, total employment has increased from 374.3 million in 1993-94 to 459.0 million in 2004-05 (Table 12.1).

The rise in employment is often explained by improvement in educational attainment. There had been significant progress in the performance of education attainment as revealed from rising literacy rates over time. Secondly, last decade has witnessed the rise of micro finance institutions and self-help groups (SHGs) which have not only opened greater employment for female but also enhance their empowerment. Ramesh (2007) observed that over thirty million women are linked to banks through over 2.2 million SHGs. Third, increase employment opportunities in services sector due to higher growth of this sector.

Growth of employment in the labor market did show some signs of comfort, but does it reflect a demand-led expansion of productive employment opportunities or an outcome of the search for survival strategies? Sadly, a large part of the expansion in employment is mostly subsistence in nature and distress-driven due to lack of gainful employment opportunities. Because agriculture, the largest employer has witnessed serious employment setbacks especially after economic reforms. The rise in the share of female employment in manufacturing and services is therefore partly due to poor performance of agriculture. Further, during recent period, increase in subcontracting and outsourcing activities in manufacturing has promoted the role of home based work especially for women. But these employments are of part time and contractual and low productive in nature. Nearly 36 % of female own account proprietors were homeworkers, operating on contract or sub-contract arrangements (NCEUS, 2007). In addition, service sector provides a significant employment to

**Table 12.1: Latest Trends in Work Force (in Millions)**

| Gender | Usual Principal Status (UPS) | | | Usual Status (UPSS) | | |
|---|---|---|---|---|---|---|
| | 1993-94 | 1999-00 | 2004-05 | 1993-94 | 1999-00 | 2004-05 |
| Males | 246.2 | 267.3 | 304.3 | 252.3 | 271.4 | 310.1 |
| Females | 88.2 (26.4) | 95.4(26.3) | 112.0(26.9) | 121.9(32.6) | 121.8(31.0) | 148.9(32.4) |
| Total | 334.4 | 362.7 | 416.3 | 374.3 | 393.2 | 459.0 |

Growth of Workforce across Various Years

| Gender | Usual Principal Status (UPS) | | Usual Status (UPSS) | |
|---|---|---|---|---|
| | 1993-94/1999-00 | 1999-00/2004-05 | 1993-94/1999-00 | 1999-00/2004-05 |
| Males | 1.38 | 2.18 | 1.47 | 2.70 |
| Females | 1.32 | 2.71 | -0.02 | 4.10 |
| Total | 1.36 | 2.32 | 0.99 | 3.14 |

Note: Figures in the parentheses are the share of female to total employment.
Source: Neetha (2010).

women workers, but their concentration in personal services in urban areas points towards distress driven employment growth (Mehta, 2010).

**Size, structure and growth of unorganized manufacturing sector**

The manufacturing sector contributing 15.6% to GDP (organized = 10.4 and unorganized= 5.2 percent) is growing at a rate of 8.9% and emerged as a fast growing segment of India's domestic economy in 2008-09 (NAS, 2010). The unorganized manufacturing sector contributing one-third of value added and nearly 80% of manufacturing employment also accounts for the bulk of manufacturing exports[2].

The total number of enterprises in unorganised manufacturing sector has increased from 9.34 million in 1994-95 to 12.12 million in 2005-06 in rural area (Table 2). During the same period of time, the total number of enterprises in unorganised manufacturing sector has increased from 2.96 million to 4.94 million in urban areas. Enterprises of all sizes have grown at varying rate both in rural and urban areas. However, more than 90% in rural and nearly 70% of urban enterprises constituted of Own Account Manufacturing Enterprises (OAMEs) which is the smallest among the three types of units in the unorganised manufacturing sector.

As far as the employment in unorganised manufacturing sector is concerned, the total number of workers engaged in rural areas has increased from 20.52 million in 1994-95 to 23.45 million in 2005-06 (Table 12.2).

During the same period of time, the employment in urban areas has also increased from 9 million to 12.9 million. It shows that a significant section of population in rural and urban areas depends on unorganized manufacturing sector. Unorganized manufacturing has thus emerged as a major source of income and livelihood for rural population.

During 1994-95 to 2005-06 the share of workers employed in OAME units in rural areas has declined and that of NDME and DME has increased. In fact, the share of workers in OAME

**Table 12.2: Number and Distribution of Enterprises and Workers in Unorganised Manufacturing Sector by Enterprise Type**

| Year | | No. in 'Millions' | | Percentage share | | | | | |
|---|---|---|---|---|---|---|---|---|---|
| | | | | Rural | | | Urban | | |
| | | Rural | Urban | OAME | NDME | DME | OAME | NDME | DME |
| 1994-95 | Enterprises | 9.34 | 2.96 | 90.56 | 6.31 | 3.14 | 66.69 | 22.14 | 11.17 |
| | Workers | 20.52 | 9.00 | 80.18 | 7.92 | 11.9 | 42.03 | 25.11 | 32.86 |
| 2000-01 | Enterprises | 11.93 | 5.08 | 92.65 | 5.28 | 2.07 | 70.88 | 21.26 | 7.86 |
| | Workers | 23.98 | 13.09 | 79.83 | 8.06 | 12.12 | 45.16 | 27.71 | 27.12 |
| 2005-06 | Enterprises | 12.12 | 4.94 | 91.6 | 6.14 | 2.26 | 70.9 | 20.74 | 8.36 |
| | Workers | 23.45 | 12.98 | 76.82 | 10.16 | 13.01 | 43.64 | 26.15 | 30.21 |

Source: Computed using NSS unit level data 51st, 56th and 62nd Round on unorganized manufacturing

units has marginally declined from 80.18 percent in 1994-95 to 76.82 percent in 2005-06 and the share of workers in NDME units has increased from 7.92 percent to 10.16 percent during the same period of time. Further, the share of rural workers employed in DME units has increased from 11.90 percent in 1994-95 to 13.01 percent in 2005-06.The same pattern is followed in case of urban areas. This may be due to modernization of small scale industries.

## Employment in Unorganized Manufacturing Sector

Workers in unorganized manufacturing activity in India constitute a large and significant section of our population. However, there is an expansion of the unorganized sector in India since the implementation of the new economic policy. The reasons may be the rate and pattern of growth, including the labor-intensity and sectorial composition of growth, economic restructuring or economic crisis, including privatization of public enterprises and cut-backs in public expenditures, and global integration of the economy, including the restructuring of global production characterized by outsourcing or subcontracting. In today's globalizing world, various demand factors are also at work. An increasing share of unorganised work is subcontracted from the formal sector; the low costs of subcontracted work contribute to profits in the formal sector. In their pursuit of global competitiveness, employers in a wide range of key export industries favor the kinds of employment relations associated, rightly or wrongly, with women, namely those with insecure contracts, low wages, and few benefits. Given the rapid shifts in market demand, both domestically and globally, self-employed women producers find it difficult to retain their traditional market niche or negotiate access to emerging markets. There is also evidence to suggest that global integration and competition are associated with the erosion of both the employment arrangements of workers and the competitiveness of micro businesses.

There is evidence of feminization of workers in unorganized manufacturing sector both in rural and urban areas. In fact, the rural female workers employed in unorganized manufacturing sector have increased from 37.85 percent in 1994-95 to 43.92 percent in 2005-06. During the same period of time urban female workers has increased from 17.46 percent to 27.26 percent (table10.3). There is a general views in the literature that the rate of economic growth and level of education have a significant positive impact on female employment. But it is also argued that female participation in the labor market has been low due to various factors such as limited entitlement to resources and assets, social institutions, inadequate access to education and training, limited freedom to move and so on. Women are generally discouraged to acquire relevant skills and human capital required to enter into the labor market (Papola, 1999). Therefore, the presence of female in well-paid and regular jobs in the organized sector is very low (Mitra, 2006).

**Table 12.3: Share of Female Workers in the Unorganised Manufacturing Sector, 1994/5-2005/6**

| Year | Rural | Urban | Total |
|---|---|---|---|
| 1994-95 | 37.85 | 17.46 | 31.05 |
| 2000-01 | 38.69 | 24.58 | 33.71 |
| 2005-06 | 43.92 | 27.26 | 37.98 |

Source: Computed using NSS unit level data 51st, 56th and 62nd Round on unorganized manufacturing

There is a sharp decline of male employment during 2000-01/2005-06 in both rural and urban areas (table 12.3). The decline of male employment during the same period in rural and urban areas may be due to low remuneration which discourages the male workers to engage in this sector. The other reason may be due to available of employment opportunities in other sectors.

There has been a faster growth in the employment of female than male during 2000 to 2005 years in both rural and urban areas, thus raising the proportion of women workers in this sector. In fact, female workers employed in unorganised manufacturing sector were growing at 7.23 percent in rural

**Table 12.4: Growth of Workers by Gender across Rural and Urban Areas in the Unorganised Manufacturing Sector, 1994-94/2005-06**

| | Rural | | | Urban | | | Total | | |
|---|---|---|---|---|---|---|---|---|---|
| | Male | Female | Persons | Male | Female | Persons | Male | Female | Persons |
| 1994-2000 | 1.12 | 1.73 | 1.35 | 1.29 | 8.86 | 2.83 | 1.19 | 3.26 | 1.86 |
| 2000-05 | -6.87 | 7.23 | -0.44 | -18.55 | 24.02 | -0.17 | -10.85 | 12.58 | -0.35 |

Source: Computed using NSS unit level data 51st, 56th and 62nd Round on unorganised manufacturing

areas and it was growing at 24.02 percent in urban areas during 2000-05 (Table 12.4). The growth of female worker in both rural and urban areas is both for full time and part time workers. Employment prospects for women are also found to be associated with flexibility. Flexibility of enterprises implies of subcontracting form of production.

The feminization of employment in unorganised manufacturing sector followed two ways. First, increase in the share of female workers compare to male workers. Table12.5 shows the percentage share of female employment in rural and urban areas by industry divisions of the National Industrial Classification (NIC) 1987 workers into two successive period 2000-01 and 2005-06.

Agro based industries are dominated by providing female employment and its share has increased over time in rural and urban areas. These industries include manufacture of tobacco & beverage (22), manufacture of textile product (23+24+25), manufacture of paper & paper product (28). On the other hand, female employment in non-agro industries has declined in rural and urban areas which include manufacture of nonmetallic mineral product (32), basic metal alloys (33), machinery & equipment's (35-36), transport equipment's (37). Hence, non-agro industries are capital intensive and it requires regular skill formation. Further, female workers were unable to manage the burden of work in non-agro industries. Second, some employers reduced male employment and increased female employment. In addition, feminization of workers in the unorganised manufacturing sector is supported by the analysis of type of work.

First, when we look at distribution of overall employment by nature , the share of female in both full time and part time work have increased. Table 12.6 shows that the percentage of female full time worker has increased from 23.91 % in 2000-01, though by a small extent, to 26.42 % in 2005-06. During the same period the percentage of female part time workers has increased from 9.80 % to 11.56 per cent. The same trend is observed both in rural and urban areas. However, the incidence of part time employment for female is higher as compared to their male counterpart.

**Table 12.5: Share of Female Workers across Industries in Rural and Urban Areas**

| NIC | Rural | | Urban | | Total | |
|---|---|---|---|---|---|---|
| | 2000-01 | 2005-06 | 2000-01 | 2005-06 | 2000-01 | 2005-06 |
| 20-21 | 28.04 | 28.85 | 21.47 | 23.70 | 26.43 | 27.68 |
| 22 | 64.31 | 72.14 | 71.20 | 71.27 | 65.68 | 71.98 |
| 23+24+25 | 49.30 | 52.46 | 33.17 | 30.27 | 42.71 | 40.87 |
| 26 | 41.64 | 51.84 | 28.34 | 38.05 | 35.88 | 46.33 |
| 27 | 34.47 | 34.69 | 10.95 | 11.57 | 30.20 | 30.36 |
| 28 | 34.54 | 67.26 | 16.35 | 22.66 | 19.29 | 36.65 |
| 29 | 9.49 | 11.03 | 11.67 | 13.00 | 10.94 | 12.62 |
| 30 | 45.64 | 72.40 | 60.64 | 63.74 | 52.61 | 69.75 |
| 31 | 28.87 | 31.85 | 17.11 | 18.36 | 20.65 | 23.07 |
| 32 | 34.71 | 29.42 | 31.68 | 24.02 | 34.22 | 28.56 |
| 33 | 8.23 | 7.87 | 2.82 | 6.81 | 4.60 | 7.12 |
| 34 | 12.89 | 8.40 | 4.08 | 3.86 | 7.84 | 5.81 |
| 35-36 | 10.58 | 8.49 | 8.70 | 5.49 | 9.20 | 6.25 |
| 37 | 5.46 | 3.52 | 2.26 | 3.84 | 2.71 | 3.74 |
| 38 | 35.84 | 27.22 | 18.26 | 16.65 | 24.62 | 19.97 |
| ALL | 38.69 | 43.92 | 24.59 | 27.26 | 33.71 | 37.98 |

Source: Computed using NSS unit level data 51st, 56th and 62nd Round on unorganised manufacturing

The male-female division of full and part time employment also suggests that there has been a faster increase in full time than part time employment of workers as is shown by a large variations in their share in the former than latter. While the share of female in full time employment increased from 28.36 % to 32.26 % and that of part time employment increased from 62.38 % to 63.93 % during 2000/2006. This holds true both for rural and urban areas (Table 12.7)

Does increase in female employment relate to increase in subcontracting? Subcontracting represents a form of inter-firm relationship where large firms procure manufactured components, sub-assemblies and products from a large number of small firms. In some cases, subcontracting is associated with 'job work' where a parent firm provides the necessary raw materials to small firms which return these

**Table 12.6: Share of Female Workers by Nature of Employment**

| | 2000-01 | | | | | 2005-06 | | | | |
|---|---|---|---|---|---|---|---|---|---|---|
| | Female | | Male | | | Female | | Male | | |
| | Full time | Part time | Full time | Part time | ALL | Full time | Part time | Full time | Part time | ALL |
| Rural | 27.01 | 11.68 | 53.91 | 7.4 | 100 | 30.55 | 13.37 | 48.08 | 8 | 100 |
| Urban | 18.22 | 6.37 | 72.23 | 3.19 | 100 | 18.97 | 8.29 | 68.89 | 3.85 | 100 |
| Total | 23.91 | 9.80 | 60.38 | 5.91 | 100 | 26.42 | 11.56 | 55.5 | 6.52 | 100 |

Source: Computed using NSS unit level data 51st, 56th and 62nd Round on unorganised manufacturing

**Table 12.7: Distribution of Female Workers by Nature of Employment in Unorganized Manufacturing Sector**

| | 2000-01 | | | | 2005-06 | | | |
|---|---|---|---|---|---|---|---|---|
| | Full time | | Part time | | Full time | | Part time | |
| | Female | Male | Female | Male | Female | Male | Female | Male |
| Rural | 33.38 | 66.62 | 61.21 | 38.79 | 38.85 | 61.15 | 62.56 | 37.44 |
| Urban | 20.14 | 79.86 | 66.64 | 33.36 | 21.59 | 78.41 | 68.28 | 31.72 |
| Total | 28.36 | 71.64 | 62.38 | 37.62 | 32.26 | 67.74 | 63.93 | 36.07 |

Source: Computed using NSS unit level data 51st, 56th and 62nd Round on unorganised manufacturing

materials after turning them into a required form (as per the technical specification), at a pre-determined rate. The percentage of unorganised manufacturing enterprises operating on contract basis has increased from 30.66 percent in 2000-01 to 31.68 percent in 2005 (Table 10.8).

It is evident that the incidence of subcontracting is more for smaller sized enterprises, i.e. OAME and those located in rural areas (Table 12.8). The fact that there is a possibility of penetration by merchant capital in search of cheap home-based production sources that ensures the required returns. Most of the units are getting inputs from the parent enterprise and there is little choice for the household units to bargain.

One of the common exploitative practices adopted by the middlemen is to deduct wages for 'rejection'. Many a times, the middlemen withhold partial payment to maintain a hold on the worker and to discourage him/her from leaving for competitors. The strategy of denying work to the most vocal leader amongst the workers is often adopted by the traders. The home workers tend to remain with the same contractor, even in the absence of written agreements or benefit payments. The inertia in seeking alternatives is accounted for by the high opportunity costs of change (lack of alternative or excess supply of labor), debt bondage, delayed payments, and contractors preferring to keep workers isolated (Mehrotra and Biggeri 2007). The majority of these home workers are women.

**Table 12.8: Percentage of Enterprises Working on Contract Basis**

| | 2000-01 | | | | 2005-06 | | | |
|---|---|---|---|---|---|---|---|---|
| | OAME | NDME | DME | Total | OAME | NDME | DME | Total |
| % of enterprises working under subcontracting | | | | | | | | |
| All | 26.43 | 2.91 | 1.32 | 30.66 | 27.82 | 2.63 | 1.22 | 31.68 |
| Distribution of subcontracting enterprises (%) | | | | | | | | |
| Rural | 94.25 | 4.11 | 1.64 | 100 | 94.06 | 4.47 | 1.47 | 100 |
| Urban | 72.51 | 18.65 | 8.84 | 100 | 74.44 | 16.55 | 9.00 | 100 |
| All | 86.21 | 9.49 | 4.30 | 100 | 87.84 | 8.30 | 3.86 | 100 |

Source: Computed using NSS unit level data 56th and 62nd Round on unorganised manufacturing

Table 12.9 presents the percentage of female workers engaged in subcontracting units by industry groups for each category of enterprises. The figures indicate that the importance of female employment in subcontracting units varies across industry groups.

Agro-based industries have dominated in terms of female employment in Indian unorganised manufacturing industry which operates under contract basis. Dominance of agro-based industries in terms of providing female employment (with more than 30 percent of share) belongs to manufacture of food & food product, beverage & tobacco product, textile, textile product industries. It is thus evident that industries extensively using subcontracting include the ones that have female labor intensive production processes such as textiles and tobacco products. Correlation between total worker engaged in unorganised manufacturing sector and female workers in sub-contracting enterprises has increased from 0.91 to 0.94.

**Table 12.9: Percentage of Female Workers Working in Sub-Contracting Enterprises**

| NIC | OAME | | NDME | | DME | | ALL | |
|---|---|---|---|---|---|---|---|---|
| | 2000-01 | 2005-06 | 2000-01 | 2005-06 | 2000-01 | 2005-06 | 2000-01 | 2005-06 |
| 20-21 | 4.57 | 7.80 | 11.73 | 3.87 | 7.51 | 0.87 | 5.40 | 5.74 |
| 22 | 84.68 | 66.93 | 10.18 | 46.28 | 10.37 | 26.11 | 80.83 | 66.53 |
| 23+24+25 | 55.82 | 52.64 | 66.05 | 65.38 | 52.85 | 46.81 | 56.12 | 53.52 |
| 26 | 31.83 | 40.87 | 44.55 | 26.99 | 51.27 | 45.84 | 33.66 | 40.52 |
| 27 | 5.65 | 3.92 | 10.29 | 6.40 | 7.37 | 55.76 | 5.73 | 4.71 |
| 28 | 41.46 | 73.62 | 48.86 | 28.40 | 40.69 | 57.77 | 42.26 | 67.91 |
| 29 | 42.18 | 64.89 | 27.95 | 34.69 | 65.10 | 53.51 | 46.72 | 59.89 |
| 30 | 79.73 | 80.58 | 8.03 | 0.15 | 28.11 | 11.64 | 69.51 | 69.93 |
| 31 | 50.38 | 38.58 | 29.13 | 45.13 | 35.29 | 18.81 | 41.93 | 31.89 |
| 32 | 4.43 | 10.01 | 13.67 | 6.14 | 3.73 | 1.87 | 4.50 | 7.56 |
| 33 | 50.79 | 21.01 | 60.49 | 54.37 | 42.16 | 34.47 | 51.38 | 33.22 |
| 34 | 10.67 | 13.72 | 39.00 | 31.09 | 35.18 | 48.41 | 15.94 | 21.66 |
| 35-36 | 44.51 | 39.77 | 36.64 | 75.96 | 35.96 | 27.74 | 38.51 | 45.14 |
| 37 | 9.12 | 66.23 | 29.74 | 16.52 | 64.51 | 72.92 | 39.74 | 64.56 |
| 38 | 40.96 | 50.54 | 39.73 | 42.09 | 48.84 | 26.35 | 41.61 | 46.82 |
| All | 38.45 | 43.02 | 35.05 | 36.04 | 24.88 | 21.26 | 36.97 | 40.70 |

Source: Computed using NSS unit level data 56th and 62nd Round on unorganised manufacturing

Further, women workers in unorganised manufacturing sector suffer under highly insecure and vulnerable working conditions. There are no social security measures to provide risk coverage and ensure maintenance of basic living standards in times of crises such as unemployment or health issues. There are no laws to ensure they work under suitable working conditions and are not subject to any health hazards. There is no fixity of working hours, no compliance to minimum wages and in most cases these are governed by local factors (NCEUS 2007). The insecurity, lack of safety, occupational hazards and incidence of exploitation is even more in the case of migrant laborers and forced labor. This is because of lack of organization and unionization among the group, which is mainly on account of poor literacy and awareness levels and high levels of poverty prevalent among the groups. There is also very little legal protection available.

## Conclusion

The present paper attempted to examine the changing structure of employment in the unorganised manufacturing sector. Analysis shows that the changing policy environment has augmented the feminization employment in unorganised manufacturing sector. Increased presence of female employment is visible only in agro-based industries and those operating under subcontracting system. This may be due to increase in the sub-contracting method of production in the unorganized manufacturing sector. female are absorbed more in the tiniest enterprises, i.e. OAMEs and a large part of this employment opportunities are of part time and contractual in nature. Thus it reflects the precarious conditions of women in the unorganised manufacturing sector. The optimism about the current pattern of female employment is cause for concern and rather than cheer.

**Appendix**
**Concordance Between 2-digit Level Of Nic-87 & Appropriate Level Of Nic-98(for Converting Nic-98 Based Data In Terms Of Nic-87)**

| NIC 1987 | Industry description | NIC 1987 | NIC 1998 |
|---|---|---|---|
| 20-21 | Food & food product industry | 20-21 | 151 + 152 + 153 + 154 |
| 22 | Beverage & Tobacco Industry | 22 | 155 + 16 |
| 23 + 24 + 25 | Textile industry | 23 + 24 + 25 | 171 |
| 26 | Textile product industry | 26 | 172 + 173 + 181 |
| 27 | Wood & wood product industry | 27 | 20 + 361 |
| 28 | Paper & paper product industry | 28 | 21 + 22 |
| 29 | Leather & leather product industry | 29 | 182 + 19 |
| 30 | Chemical & chemical product industry | 30 | 24 |
| 31 | Rubber, petroleum & petroleum product industry | 31 | 23 + 25 |
| 32 | Nonmetallic mineral product industry | 32 | 26 |
| 33 | Basic metal alloys | 33 | 27 + 371 |
| 34 | Metal product | 34 | 2811 + 2812 + 289 |
| 35-36 | Machinery & Equipment's | 35-36 | 2813 + 29 + 30 + 31 + 32 |
| 37 | Transport equipment's | 37 | 34 + 35 |
| 38 | Others | 38 | 33 + 369 |
| 39 | | 39 | 725 |

Source: National Industrial Classification, 1998, CSO.

## Footnotes

[1] According to Sakthivel and Joddar (2006), employment in the unorganized sector increased from 276 million in 1983 to 371 million in 1999-2000.

[2] The National Sample Surveys on the unorganised manufacturing sector cover (I) All manufacturing enterprises except those registered under section 2m (i) and 2m (ii) of Factories, Act, 1948 and Bidi Cigar Workers (conditions of employment) Act, 1966.(ii) All manufacturing enterprises except those run by Government (Central Government, State Governments, Local Bodies)/ Public Sector Enterprises.Further this unorganised manufacturing sector is divided into three types of enterprises namely, Own Account Manufacturing Enterprises (OAME), Non Directory Manufacturing Establishment (NDME) and Directory of Manufacturing Establishment (DME).

## References

Deshpande, S and Deshpande, L.K. (1992). New Economic Policy and Female Employment. *Economic and Political Weekly,* 27(41): 2248-225.

Ministry of Finance. 2009-10. *Economic Survey 2009-10.* Government of India, New Delhi.

Mehrotra, S. K. and Biggeri, M. (2007). *Asian Unorganised Workers: Global Risks, Local Protection.* New York: Rutledge.

Mehta, Niti (2010). *Female employment in India: Trends and underlying processes in the Era of Reforms.* Sardar Patel Institute of Economic and Social Research, Working Paper No.3.

Mitra, S.(2006). Pattern of Female Employment in Urban India: Analysis of NSS Data 1983 to 1999-2000. *Economic and Political Weekly* 41(48): 5000-5008.

NAS (2010). *National Accounts Statistics 2010.* CSO: Govt. of India.

NCEUS. (2007). *Report on Condition of Work and Promotion of Livelihood in Unorganised Sector.* Government of India.

Neetha, N. (2010). *Women Work in Post-Reform Period: An Exploration from Macro Data".* CWDS Occasional paper No.52.

Neetha, N. (2009). Changing Dimensions of Female Employment in India: Insights from

NSSO Data. *Labor and Development* 15(1): 22-47.

Papola, T. S and Sharma, A.N (1999). *Gender and Employment in India.* New Delhi: UBS Publisher

Ramesh, J.(2007). Self-help Groups Revolution: What Next?. *Economic and Political Weekly*, 42(36): 3621-3624.

Sharmila N. and A. Christoper (2010). *Development of Women Education in India*, MPRA working paper No. 20680.

Sunder, P. (1981). Characteristic of Female Employment: Implication of research and Policy., *Economic and Political Weekly*. 16(19): 863-871.

Vanamala, V (2001). Informalisation and Feminsation of a Formal Sector Industry, A Case Study, *Economic and Political Weekly*. 36(26):2378-2389.

# 13

# Part-Time Paid Domestic Workers: An Exploration of their Gendered Relations at Home Sphere in Delhi

**Abstract**

*This paper explores some important gender concerns which are related to the women's world of work especially focusing on the private life of part-time paid women domestic workers in Delhi. Workers being a woman face several constraints in their private life. Part time domestic work provides women of several poor households an opportunity to earn and live. But the selection of this work itself has a gender linkage. The present study clearly pointed out that house work i.e. cleaning, washing, cooking and caring are women's task and thus women selected this work mainly because it helps them to perform their own household tasks and also gives them an opportunity to earn for the family, however in doing so they suffer from dual burden of work. It is also cleared in this study that women workers in Delhi participate significantly in household expenditure and their income cannot be seen as subsidiary in nature. In spite of their significant contributions, majority of them do not have any decision making power in their households and domination of husbands is more prominent. The unequal distribution of workers' household resources and their experience of domestic violence are also explored in this study by conducting a primary survey in Delhi.*

## Introduction

In India, paid domestic work is considered as an important occupation for majority of women and girls of different poor households who steps in the world of work in unorganized economy. [1] According to NCEUS (2009:145), migrant women with no skill and assets from poor rural households often become domestic 'servants' in the urban areas. This informal sector in the urban area provides several work opportunities for the women who are unskilled, illiterate and poor. The irregular nature and low earnings of male members in the family compel women to enter in several low paid and insecure (work and environmental status) occupations, which serves as the only source of a supportive earning for the entire family. As per NCEUS 'among women 90 percent of wage workers are engaged in either some kind of manufacturing, construction activities or just domestic services'(2009:142). Thus, domestic work is one of the important occupations of the women in urban informal sector. Issues which are related to the insecure work status, long working hours, lack of decent work terms and conditions, exploitation (economic, physical and mental) faced at the workplace and the struggle of ILO and other organizations to bring domestic workers under labor legislation all over the world are some of the aspects which are widely explored. However there are other issues related to the workers' private sphere, which are yet not being explored much. Women's paid and unpaid work performed at home has several links with the domain of gender.

Thus the present paper explains some important aspects concerning women's work and its relation to gender aspects taking part-time domestic workers as a case study. The issues like their reasons to prefer part-time domestic work, double work burden, gender division of house work, experience of violence at home, household divisions of resources, workers' economic contribution to their household expenditure and whether their involvement in the waged work really empowers them to take decisions at home are explored.

## Sample design

### *Data source*

In India, there are two data sources, which collect information on domestic workers, namely Census and NSSO. NSSO is the most comprehensive data source, where Employment and Unemployment Survey gives information on all employed persons by "Private households with employed persons" which is considered as Domestic workers (Luebker.M and S. Y. 2011). In Census, domestic work is considered under 'Community, Social and Personal Services', within this category six services are combined (L to Q).[2] Thus employers under '(P) Private households with employed persons' cannot be segregated to get domestic workers (Census of India 2001, B-10 and B-19 General note: 2). Thus, NSSO is the only national statistical source which is preferably use to estimate domestic workers in India. But there are several qualitative aspects which are unable to explain with NSSO data.

For this study Census-2001 and DDA-1994 (slum wing Municipal Corporation of Delhi) are used to design the samples of part time domestic workers. Delhi is an interesting case study because it lacks labor protection for domestic workers and is a favorite destination of several migrants from different backward regions of the country where women seek to enter in paid domestic work to earn their livelihood. Thus, data from field survey according to the requirements of the study have been used. The sample area is East-Delhi, which is rather representative of Delhi on the basis of female work participation of slums, literacy rate and share of female slum population.

Individual as well as household based questionnaire was prepared for the primary survey. Total 152 samples were selected for the survey with the help of purposive sampling technique. The responsive category, with women aged between 20 to 58 years, ever married were interviewed.[3] Data was collected between November 2010 to January 2011.

## Selection of the survey area

Slum data from census 2001 was collected for nine districts of Delhi. Three socio-economic indicators like slum female work participation rate, female literacy rates and percentage of female slum population to the total slum population were calculated for the districts as well as for Delhi. [4] These indicators for each district were further matched with the state average to select the district, which represent the state. Thus, in doing so East Delhi was selected for the survey (Table 13.1).

Each district has several constituencies according to which DDA (1994) - *slum wing Municipal Corporation of Delhi* provide information of slums in Delhi. East Delhi has ten constituencies (Jangpura, Okhla, Trilokpuri, Kondli, Patparganj, Laxmi Nagar, Vishwas Nagar, Krishna Nagar, Gandhi Nagar and Shahdara) (2009-10). Each constituency has several clusters of *jhuggi-jhopries* (slums). According to 1994, DDA list two constituencies were selected based on their similar number of *jhuggies* as well as based on feasibility to the study area. From Okhla Gandhi Camp, Pahari no-1and 2 was surveyed. In Jangpura Pratap Camp, Jal-Vihar, Madrasi Camp was surveyed. The total sample from Okhla is 80 and Jangpura is 72. Thus, the total sample size for the study is 152.

## Brief socio-demographic profile of the women workers in Delhi

The mean age of women workers in Delhi is 38 years. Majority of them belong to lower caste and the proportion of Hindu is highest among all other religion in Delhi. Currently married women constitute the highest proportion of domestic workers followed by the widowed women in Delhi. Illiteracy among the workers is very high and majority of the workers have migrated from Uttar Pradesh, Bihar and West Bengal. Nepal and Bangladesh also contribute significant proportion of

**Table 13.1: Basic socio-demographic and economic characteristics of Delhi and respective districts: 2001**

| Census codes | Districts | Slum pop | Slum pop | Total female literates | Total female workers | Female slum literacy rate | Female slum work participation rate | Share of female slum pop |
|---|---|---|---|---|---|---|---|---|
| 1 | North West | 315975 | 13409 | 46279 | 12525 | 35 | 9 | 42 |
| 2 | North | 408649 | 18481 | 113179 | 14035 | 61 | 8 | 45 |
| 3 | North East | 84113 | 37787 | 12288 | 3302 | 33 | 9 | 45 |
| 4 | East | 113530 | 50792 | 21182 | 5703 | 42 | 11 | 45 |
| 5 | New Delhi | 35573 | 14829 | 4961 | 1343 | 33 | 9 | 42 |
| 6 | Central | 456839 | 20796 | 129950 | 16820 | 62 | 8 | 46 |
| 7 | West | 248345 | 10416 | 39966 | 13182 | 38 | 13 | 42 |
| 8 | South West | 113435 | 44540 | 15798 | 6085 | 35 | 14 | 39 |
| 9 | South | 253296 | 92927 | 38679 | 12316 | 42 | 13 | 37 |
| | Delhi | 202975 | 87194 | 422282 | 85311 | 48 | 10 | 43 |

Note: 1. T- Total, F- Female
2. Female work participation rate of slum= Total female workers of slum/ Total female population of slum.
3. Female literacy rate of slum= Total female literates of slum/ Total female population of slum.
4. Share of female population of slum= Total female population of slum/Total population of slum.

Source: Computed from census 2001

migrant workers in Delhi. Most of these women migrated mainly with the purpose of reunion and the second largest proportion migrated mainly due to the push factor of the origin i.e. Un-employment and poverty. Migration experienced by these workers is a secondary phenomenon which is dependent on the husband. However, this move has both economic as well social consequences.

**Work preferences and the constraints faced by the workers being a woman**

This section would mainly focus on the reasons which encourage women to take up part-time paid domestic works in private households. This is followed by another concern i.e. the constraints face by these workers at their home sphere focusing on the issue of dual burden of work.

From the field experiences it is found that most of the domestic workers suggested a particular combination of reasons (Fig-1) which encourage them to engage in paid domestic services. Among them flexible working hours is one of the important reasons cited by most of the women at almost six combinations that encourage them to pursue part-time domestic work. This aspect clearly shows that most of women in the surveyed urban poor localities choose part-time paid domestic work because it allows them to carry out their own household tasks/ responsibilities as well as to earn outside home. Deshpande (2001) reports a parallel situation in his work on Mumbai slum, which reveals that most of the women opt for such economic activities which are an extension of housework as such occupations allow them to carry out their economic activities along with their domestic work. Mitra (2005) in his work put forth similar observation that many women workers are not able to engage themselves in full time and regular jobs due to household responsibilities.

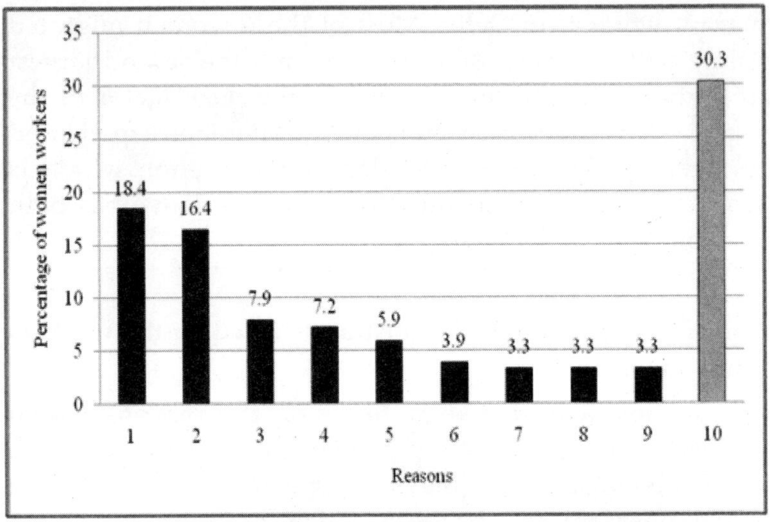


**Figure: 13.1 Reasons to Enter In Domestic Work**

Note: Reasons 1-Low/ no education and skills and flexible working hours, 2-Flexible working hours, 3-Safe workplace and flexible working hours, 4-Low/ no education and skills, 5-Low/no education and skills, safe work place and flexible working hours, 6-Low income of Husband and flexible working hours, 7-Low/no education and skills and safe work place,8-Flexible working hours, low /no education and skills and low income of the husband, 9-Lack of other options, 10-Others (Sample size of several reasons are very small (below five; which is statistically Insignificant), thus they are clubbed together to form a group called 'Others').

Source: Field survey 2010-2011

The previous discussion opens yet another horizon of women's work where they constantly have to carry out dual burden of responsibilities. Their being in the paid workforce outside homes does not absolve them from household chores. Caring, cleaning, washing, cooking etc are activities that women are never allowed to escape from. In this context, Lutz (2002:96) commented, 'women remain responsible for care work anyway and thus acquire a double burden or seek domestic help privately' (Figure 2). Infant or small child is an important obstacle for women who go out for work. Babies need a constant care of mothers. Most of the families are nucleated even in slums, and therefore majority of women who have infants at home do not go for work until their child grows older.

In the survey [5] a large proportion of women – housewives - were willing to work only after their babies grow older enough to walk so that children can manage themselves or supervised usually by family members, especially other women bear the care responsibility of the children. Many a times the elder sibling has to accept the responsibility and in this due course, they even drop out from schools. One of the respondents has this to say *"My daughter does not go to school because her brother is very small and she has to look after him, otherwise who will take care of the child…once he grows older she will start going to school"*.

Similar observation is also made by Rana whose work focuses on women workers in different informal economy in Delhi. She observes that women in the unorganized sector start working only after their family responsibilities are completed and children have grown up, when they can manage on their own or when the eldest siblings can take care of the younger children (2009).

Most of the women workers in the survey had their children at home only if they are not less than a year old. Neighbors (31 percent), female family members such as mother or mother-in-law or sister, sister-in-law etc emerge as important helpers (25 percent); about 16 percent children are left back home under the supervision of different members of the family. The rest grouped under 'others'[6] comprises 29 percent. Kaur (2007:207) has also observed a similar situation about child care responsibilities of domestic workers. In her study in Delhi, friends and neighbors were seen as playing an important role in caring for the children of domestic workers. Other solutions were obtaining someone, usually young girls from worker's village or hiring child-minding team for a small fee.

Women reported that their working day starts at about 9 to 10 am when other members i.e., their husbands and children go to work and to school respectively. The children return back around 12.30 to 1 pm which is the time for most of the workers to return home (some also go in the evening to finish rest of the chores). Such a time-table helps them easily manage their children and household chores. Somewhere they manage to take some rest. According to Kaur (2007:207), part-time domestic workers fit their own housework, domestic lives (family duties), childcare, socializing, leisure and their children's schooling into their work routines.

Thus it can be concluded from the above observation that housework is women's work and most of the women opt for part-time domestic work only because it allows them to carry their tasks at home as well as offer opportunities to earn to support their families. It is another matter that in doing so the overall work burden increases tremendously.

The next section would concentrate on the women's economic contribution to their own household expenses.

### Workers' income and their contribution to household expenditure

Wage structure of domestic workers are not fixed, it varies by different activities performed by the workers. Though there is no definite wage, system maintained is the localities. Wages varies from one locality to another, it differs from one constituency to another and even within that specific locality and constituency, the wage structure varies. Neetha (2010:14) makes similar argument that domestic workers have wage structure, which varies, across regions and even by locality in the same town/city. The mean monthly wage of part-time domestic workers in Delhi is rupees 2474. To understand women workers' economic contribution to the household expenditure it is also important to understand their husbands' economic status and the nature of work they performed. Most of the workers' husbands are engaged in low-ended regular salaried or waged works. In this category most of the men work as guards in the private households, as sweepers and

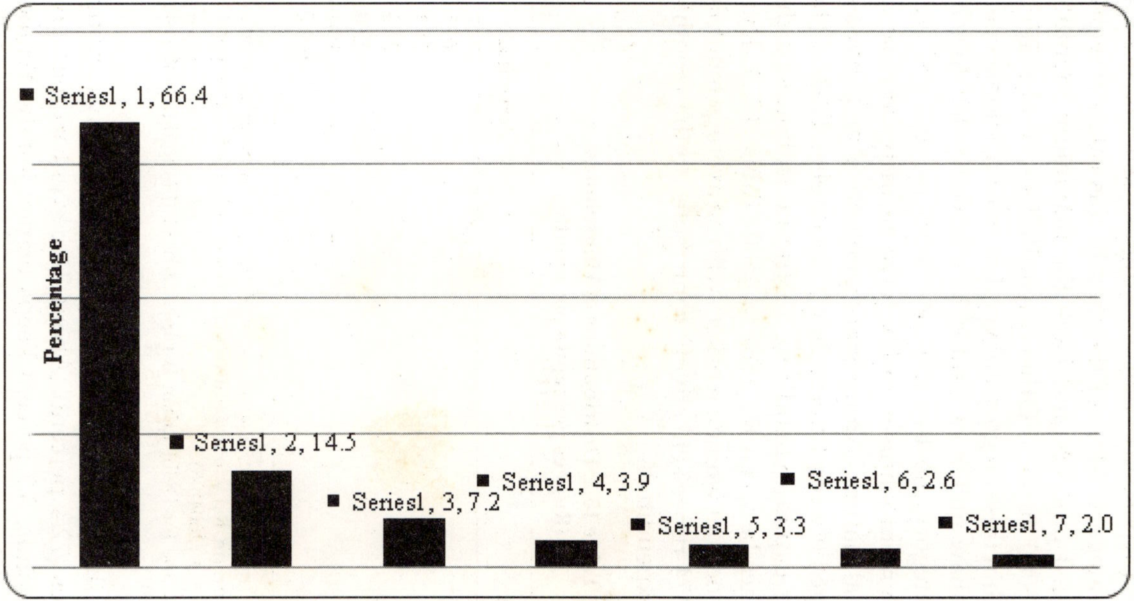


Note: 1-Self (domestic worker), 2 Self and daughter, 3- Self and mother/other in law/daughter in law/other female members, 4- Only daughter in law, 5- Only daughter(s), 6- Self and daughter(s), 7-Self and son.

Source: Field survey 2010-2011

**Figure 13.2: Household Tasks Performed by women workers and her Family Members**

domestic workers in the formal work place (any factory, office or schools), as cooks in hotels, as driver in private households and as peons (51percent). Men working as casual labors are next to this category. Most of the men in this category work as daily waged laborers and have the maximum monthly earning of 3000 rupees. Other unskilled or semi-skilled activities within this category are vendor, mason, shopkeeper, painter, rickshaw puller, carpenter, Kawariwalla etc.[7] In self-employed category most of the men work as vendors. All these employment statuses rarely have security because of their informal nature. About sixty percent of men have a monthly wage between Rupees 2630/- to Rupees 4032/-. The monthly per capita expenditure of the households of the workers ranges between Rs. 1667 to 4500 (Table- 13.2). Thus it is understood that women workers with an average monthly income of 2474 rupees effectively contributes to the monthly household expenditure.

**Table 13.2: Distributions of Households (Rupees per capita per month)**

| MPCE (in Rs.) | Percentage |
|---|---|
| 600 and below* | 10.5 |
| 625 to 833 | 21.1 |
| 834 to 1200 | 24.3 |
| 1200 to 1600 | 25.0 |
| 1600 to 4500 | 19.1 |
| Total | 100.0 |

Note: 1. MPCE (monthly per capita expenditure) = Number of monthly expenditure (in Rs) /total family members of a household as per 61st round NSSO (2004-05).
2. Poverty line for Delhi urban is rupees 612.91 (Planning commission: March 2007)

Most of the women workers keep their monthly earnings to themselves (72.4 percent). About 24 percent women give to their husbands, 3.3 percent keeps money jointly. Women engaged in different informal economy in the urban labor market often make a significant contribution to the households' incomes and survival by bearing significant chunk of household expenditure on food, clothing, shelter, education etc (Joshi, n.d.). A parallel situation is evident among part-time women domestic workers in Delhi where workers share significantly in household expenditure. Majority of them spend their earning on all household affairs, also shared by their husbands (73 percent). About eight percent women are the sole spenders of their income on household expenditure, majority of them are widowed (83.3 percent) followed by those who are separated (16.7 percent). Thus, it is clear that women workers participate significantly in household expenditure and therefore their income is not subsidiary in nature.

### Decision-making in household affairs

Despite of women's significant contribution to the household expenditure, about five out of ten workers have no power in decision making in their households. Husbands (40 percent) and other family members (6.6 percent) mostly control the households. As one worker commented while asking her role in decision making within her own household as: *Aadmi jo kehete hai waise hi karna padta hai, mera kuch bhi nahi chalta* (Whatever my husband says, I have to obey, I have no voice).

Thirty-one percent women workers participate in making decision in their household with their husbands. The dominance of males mainly husbands in the households is clearly visible. Only 22.4 percent of paid domestic workers have the sole power to take decision of their own house and it comprises widowed (41.2 percent), separated (8.8 percent) but fifty percent are currently married.

### Unequal distribution of household resources and experience of domestic violence by the members of the family

Alcohol consumption is a regular practice of several household members of domestic workers; about 54 percent

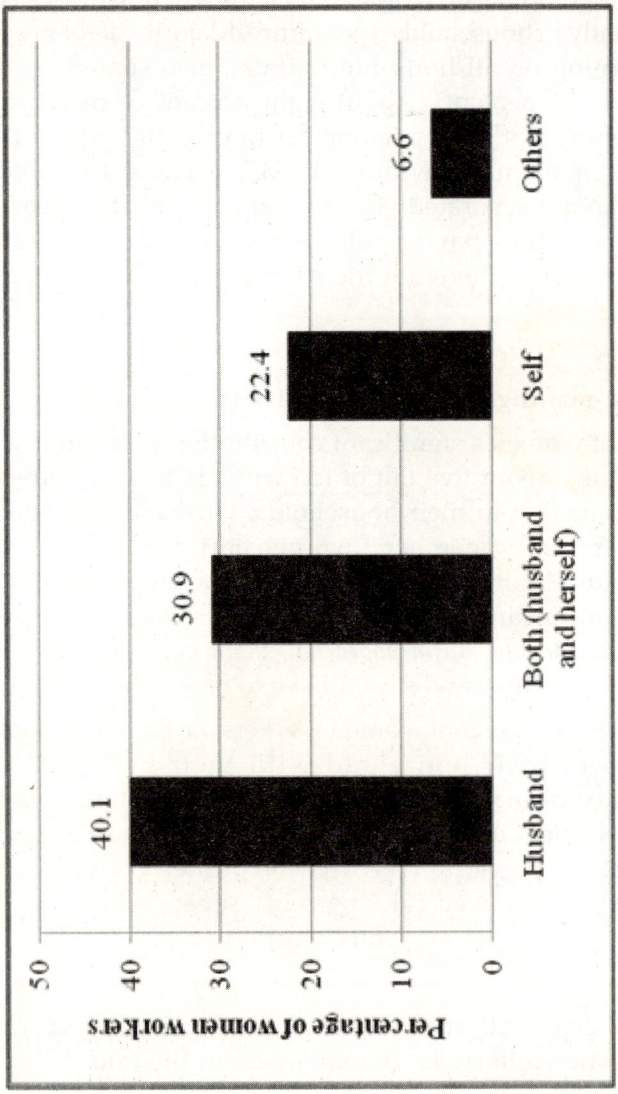


Note: * In-laws (2), Son (s) (2), Parents (mother/father) (3), Brother(s) (1); both brother (s) and herself (2) are clubbed as Others.
Source: Field survey 2010-11.

**Figure-13.3. Decision Making in Household Affairs**

of domestic workers' family members are alcoholic in nature and are all males. Among them 79.3 percent are husbands of domestic workers, 12.2 percent constitutes both husband and other male members of the family who consumes alcohol followed by the other groups (Fig 4).

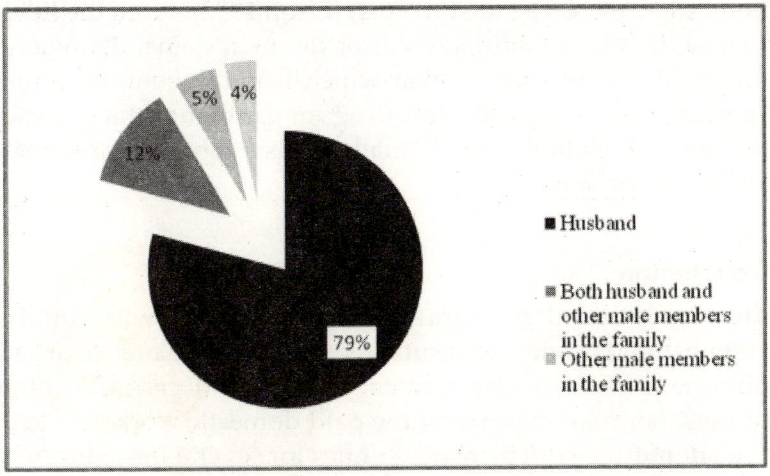


Note: Other groups include son and other male members in the house.
Source: Field survey 2010-11

**Figure: 13.4: Consumption of Alcohol by Family Members**

Among all the groups, frequency of husband's daily consumption is the highest due to which considerable share of household income is spend on husbands' means of entertainment i.e. on alcohol. Joshi (n.d.) also observes that considerable amount of husbands' income of women workers is spent on their own expenses such as tobacco, alcohol and intoxicants. She pointed out about the existence of unequal distribution of resources within household further substantiated by what is pointed out by Roy (2003 cited in Joshi n. d.) where she talks about the unequal spread of resources - an outcome of structural imbalance which is gender based.

Information on domestic violence on women workers in Delhi suggests that about forty-four percent of male members of the family reported both physical and mental violence on women workers. Most husbands, who consume alcohol every day, have higher tendency of wife beating than others. Among all men (spouses of workers) who consume alcohol, forty-eight percent fight and abuse their wives. As alcohol, consumption leads to domestic arguments, it often leads to domestic violence against women (Elson 1992). From the field survey, it is revealed that most of the men demands money for the drink(s) from women which leads to conflict; some spend their money on alcohol, drugs or gambling which create dispute in the family which finally leads to physical or verbal abuses of women.

**Conclusion**

This study has demonstrated that negotiation with family responsibilities and the insufficient low income are the most important factors which influence women's decision to enter in the labor market as part-time paid domestic workers. Part-time domestic work provides venues for several less educated and economically disadvantaged women to be gainfully employed which in turn helps them to support their family. However, on a flip side, these workers constantly suffer from the insecurity and informality in work conditions.

Part-time paid domestic work provides women with flexible work life where they can combine the benefits of paid working along with responsibilities of child rearing and managing own household tasks. In this course these women suffers from dual burden of work as they do most of their household tasks by themselves. Unequal sharing of domestic chores by men is evident whereby most women carry the burden of household responsibility.

Women workers in Delhi participate significantly in household expenditure and thus their income cannot be seen as subsidiary in nature. In spite of their significant contributions, majority of them do not have any decision making power in their households and domination of husbands is more prominent. Much of the household income of these workers is spend on alcohol consumption of male members of the house. Forty-four percent workers experiences physical as well as verbal torture by different male members of the house after their alcohol consumption. Forty-eight percent of women reported an experience of physical and verbal torture from their husbands after their consumption of alcohol.

## Endnotes

1 Paid domestic work and workers will further be termed as domestic work and workers will be identified as domestic workers

2 Tabulation Category of NIC 98: L-Public Administration and defense, compulsory social security, M- Education, N- Health and social work, O-Other community, social and personal Activities, P-Private households with employed persons, Q-Extra-territorial Organizations and Bodies(Census of India 2001, B-10 and B-19 General note:2).

3 Prior to the survey, sample for the controlled groups, where women working in other un-organized sector apart from paid domestic work were thought to be collected, but the samples for controlled group in the surveyed areas were very few. Thus, the present study will not consider any control group.

4 Female work participation and share of female population in slums are mainly given importance to select the district as to get women workers.

5 Pilot survey 2010-2011.

6 'Others' – This variable comprises Husband, daughter (s), son (s), relatives, self, anganwari, and crèche. As independently each variables does not consists statistically sufficient sample size (i.e. less than 5), thus they are clubbed together into one.

7 Most of the men in Okhla, works as *Kawariwalla,* which means they collect solid waste from different places and separate it, then sell it according to its monetary value.

## Reference

Deshpande, S.(2001). 'Impact of emerging Labor Market on Women and their households: A tale of three slums in Mumbai', in A. Kundu and A.N. Sharma, eds. *Informal Sector in India: Perspectives and polices,* Ch.18. New Delhi: Institute for human Development and Institute of Applied Manpower Research.

Elson, Diane. (1992). 'From Survival strategies to Transformation Strategies: Women's Needs and Structural Adjustments': 26-48 in Loures Beneria and Shelley Feldman (eds.). *Unequal Burden: Economic crises, Persistent Poverty and Women's work.* Boulder, Co: Westview Press.

Joshi, Seema.(n.d.) 'Marriage, Migration and Labor Market-A case study of Slum Area in Delhi': 1-22.

Kaur, Ravinder.(2007). 'Migration for work: Rewriting Gender Relations' in: Arya Sadhna and Roy Anupama, eds. *Poverty, Gender and Migration India*. Volume 2. Chapter-9. Sage Publication.

Luebker, Malte and Simonovsky, Yamila. (Travail). (2011). *Global and regional estimates on domestic workers*. Domestic work policy brief 4. ILO. Geneva: 1-12.

Mitra, Arup.(2005). 'Women in the urban informal sector: perpetuation of Mearge *earning'*. *Development and Change*, 36(2): 291-316, Blackwell publication.

NCEUS. (2009). *The challenge of Employment in India: An Informal Economy Perspective*, 1: 1-393.

Neetha N. (2010). 'In defense of the rights of domestic workers', *Labor file*, 8 (1-3): 13-15.

Rana, Rachita. (2009). *Working women in informal urban economy*. Sunrise publication, New Delhi: 1-235.

Roy, Ananya. (2003). *City Requiem, Calcutta: Gender and the Politics of Poverty*. University of Minnesota Press, Minneapolis: 1-288.

# 14

# Working Conditions of Informal Labor in IT &BPO Sector

## (A case study of Gujarat)

### Introduction

India grew at Hindu growth rates for more than half a century after independence. It is known more for poverty, backwardness and exploding population, but it has witnessed revolution in growth of service sector during the reforms period. The credit for partial success of economic reforms will goes to information technology sector. During the last decade, India is at the forefront of the rapidly evolving global IT-Business Process Outsourcing (BPO) market and is well established as a 'destination of choice'. Today, the superlatives as, for instance, 'Soft Superpower', 'IT Hub' and 'World's IT-Capital' have become synonymous with India for its Information Technology revolution.

The present study aims at studying emergence and transformation of the IT sector in India in general and Gujarat in particular in the context of economic reforms which caused in formalization of the labor force in IT sector. The focus of the study would be to identify the complex issues related to work and workers revenue, etc. in the computer hardware, software services and IT-BPO sector in Gujarat.

**Objectives of the research paper:**

i. To map the economic reforms brought in after 1991 by the government of India exclusively aimed at making the IT industry more competitive in the country/Gujarat.

ii. To estimate the growth of computer software services and IT-BPO sector in India/Gujarat.

iii. This would also include analyzing issues concerning earnings, social security benefits, labor attrition, training, career opportunities in the IT/ITES sector, etc in Gujarat.

iv. To discuss future challenges to the software services and IT-BPO sector in India in general and Gujarat in particular.

**Research Methodology**

This study is principally based on both primary as well as secondary data sources.

**Primary data**

Primary data which is collected from employees (about 25) and their employers (about 6). Primary Data is collected from about 25 young students who have/had hand experience with the ITES sector-call centers, BPO, KPO etc. in Ahmedabad.

**Secondary data**

Secondary data have been collected from different sources such as NASSCOM, NIC, DATAQUEST, GESIA etc. Secondary data would mostly relate to the reforms period, which had been collected from 1991 onwards from India/Gujarat. Secondary data is collected from available policy documents/reports, annual reports of relevant ministries both at the central and state levels databases.

**Variables for the study**

The following variables/aspects related to the labor force in the IT sector in Gujarat has been taken into consideration such as:

- Nature and terms of employment
- Earnings, incentives and promotions of workers
- Socio-economic and demographic profile of the employees
- Educational qualifications of employees
- Nature and duration of training
- Problem of labor attrition and reasons
- Work environment
- Transportation facilities
- Health related problems of the labor
- Social security and other benefits for employees
- Gender specific issues as safety, discrimination, etc.

**Information from stakeholders**

The employers, policy makers, bureaucrats, researchers etc are the important stakeholders in the IT sector. They are fully aware of and are well versed with developments taking place in the IT/ITES sector. Hence, their opinions were collected through discussions. Broadly the concerned stakeholders were.

- Entrepreneurs/employers
- Officials of relevant industry associations like NASSCOM, GESIA
- Concerned bureaucrats/government officials
- Civil society members
- Social scientists/researchers

Some of the crucial themes for interaction through discussions with the stakeholders principally in Gujarat were as follows:

- What benefits have accrued to the IT/ITES sector through policy initiatives of the governments from time to time?
- What are the expectations of the IT/ITES entrepreneurs from the government to remove hurdles both at the Centre and Gujarat state levels?
- Are there, if any, social security benefits and labor rights proposed or in the pipeline for the employee of the IT/ITES sector?
- What are the possible opportunities and challenges before the IT/ITES sector especially in a situation of growing global competition and economic crisis?

**Review of Literature**

India occupies right place in the computer software services in the world. In the beginning of the 1990, it was the domestic segment of India's IT industry which was contributing 80 percent of total output while export segment was 20 percent. On the other hand, by 2000-01, contribution of domestic segment declined to 40% while export segment increased to 60% (Desai, 2005).

India, with 44 per cent of the global offshore outsourcing market for software and back-office services, has stood as the most dominant outsourcing destination in the world. Its outsourcing industry generated revenues of US$17.2 billion and provided direct employment to 1.05 million programmers and other skilled workers in the year ended March 2005. This apart, it has generated indirect employment to about 2.5 million people in support services such as transport and catering. As many as 400 of the Fortune 500 companies either have their own centers in India or are currently outsourcing work to Indian outsourcing firms (Pradhan and Abraham, 2005).

A report by E-value service predicts that India will capture more than 70 per cent of the KPO sector by 2010. It can lead to Indian IT-BPO revenues of USD 225 billion by 2020. The industry also has the potential to transform India by harnessing technology for inclusive growth. According to a report by Global Sourcing, the Global Knowledge Process Outsourcing industry (KPO) is expected to reach USD 17 billion by 2010, of which USD 12 billion (almost 70%) would be outsourced to India alone.

India has a vast workforce of young, college going, urban, educated, English-speaking, tech-savvy personnel which is readily available to work in the IT industry in odd hours. Indian costs are roughly one-third of international costs and efficiencies are of international standards. These factors have made obstacle free journey for India to reach the pinnacle of the software services and ITES industry. The companies from the US and the EU outsource businesses to save their time, cost and resources etc. But there are possible challenges to India to compete with for retaining its present position at the top and therefore, there is an urgent need to identify the same with the help of the proposed research.

According to the task fragmentation theory, activities in the software production process are divided into conception and execution tasks. Conception tasks involve preliminary analysis and designing of software and conception workers perform high skill activities as project managers and project leaders. The execution tasks involve coding, testing, maintenance etc and the execution workers perform low skill activities as developer, module leader etc. The low level workers have limited career growth opportunities which deprive them to upgrade their skill and they experience only a horizontal movement or virtual promotions (Ilavarasan, 2008).

The evidence for a link between skill up-gradation and worker stability suggests that skill up-gradation policy may have a role to play in creating greater employee stability in

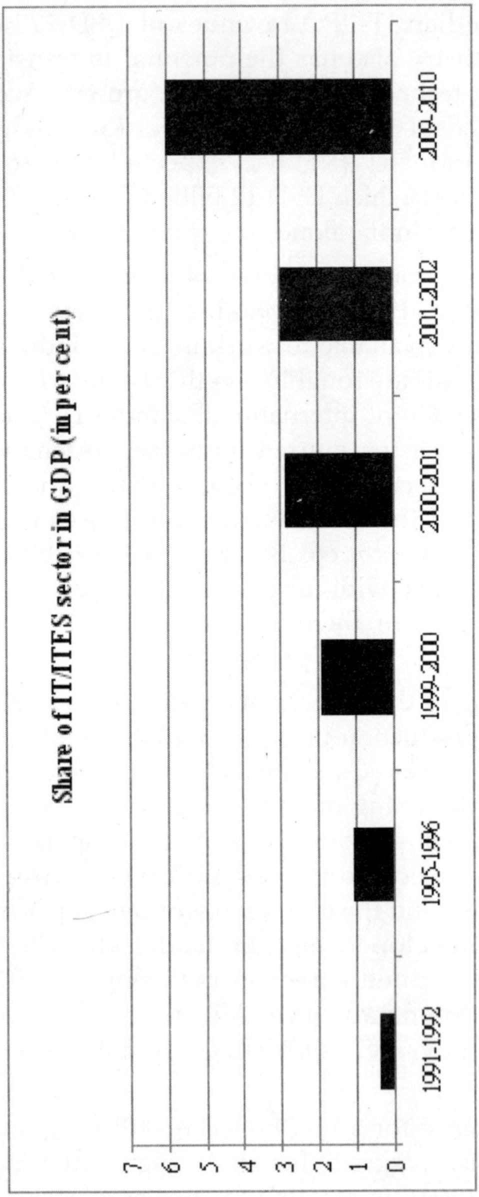


Source: Dataquest for IT Industry Output

**Figure 14.1: Share of IT/ITES sector in GDP (in percent)**

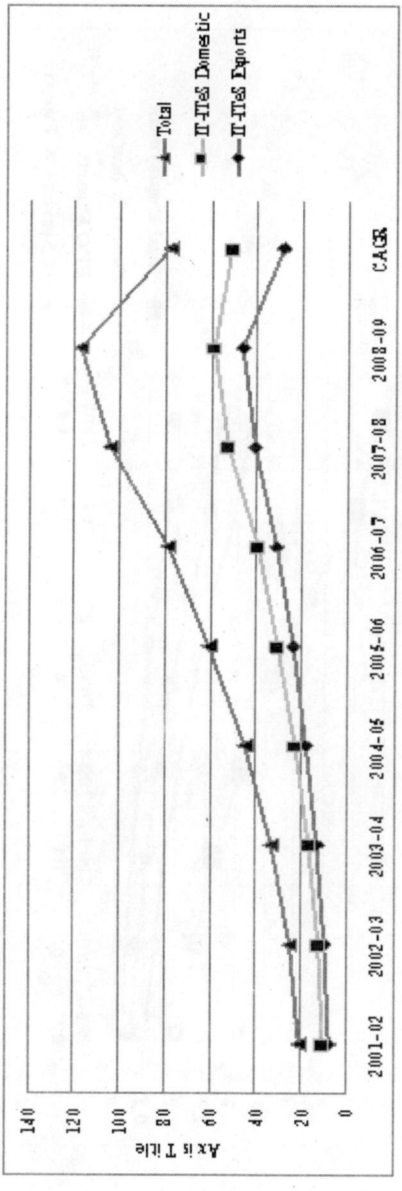


Source: Ministry of Information and Communication Technology, India

**Figure 14.2: Revenue of IT/ITES sector (in Billion US Dollars)**

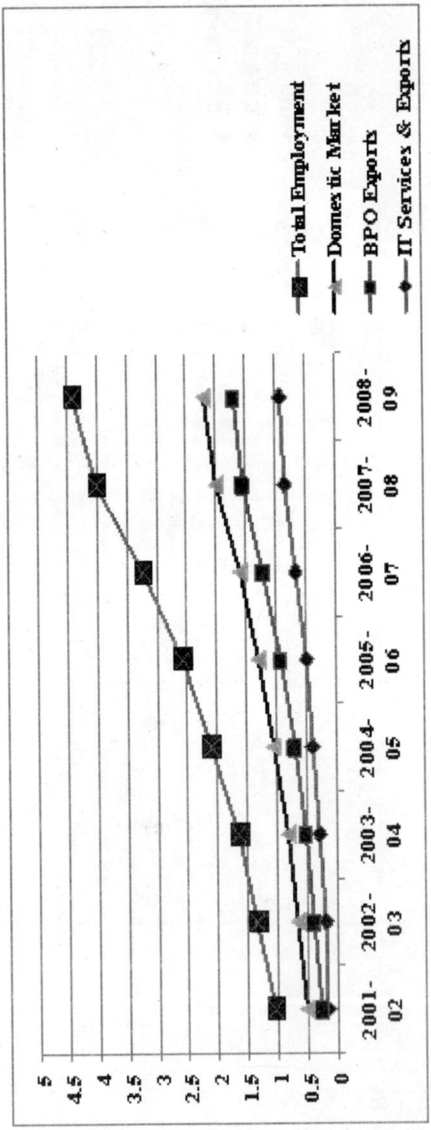


Source: Ministry of Information and Communication Technology

**Figure 14.3: Employment in millions**

software firms. Abundant life-long learning opportunities at low cost may keep attrition rates lower. Similarly, standardized pay packages across the industry and skill levels may discourage workers from their quitting behavior. Reducing the quitting behavior and attrition rates are very important to control the spiraling efficiency wage for workers which, in turn, would keep the software industry internationally competitive (Abraham, 2007).

The Indian information technology industry is often represented as providing employment opportunities to a wider cross section of society than has been the case with other professional and white collar jobs. However, available data suggest that the social composition of the IT workforce is more homogeneous than is often supposed, in that the workforce is largely urban, middle class, and high/middle caste. The processes of exclusion that operate in the educational system and in recruitment as also the ideology of "merit" in the context of elite opposition to reservation, create this relative social homogeneity in the IT workforce (Upadhya, 2007).

NASSCOM is the premier trade body and the chamber of commerce of the IT-BPO industries in India. NASSCOM is a global trade body with more than 1200 members, which include both Indian and multinational companies that have a presence in India.

## IT and the Role of Government in India

The state policies in 1980's, for the first time, acknowledged the importance of software development and underlined the needs for institutional and policy support. Policy shift towards the market mechanism began in 1986 that gradually reduced government control and a larger role was given to Indian private corporations. Accordingly, an explicit software policy was announced underlining the importance of an integrated development of software for the domestic and export markets giving more incentives for the industry to grow, such as tax holidays, tax exemption on income from software exports, export subsidies, and duty-free import of hardware and software.

Initiation of economic reforms from 1991,and number of other policy initiatives have facilitated the growth of IT. The new policy included the provision to finance software development through equity and venture capital, measures to make available faster and cheaper data communication facilities, removal of entry barriers for foreign companies and reduction and rationalization of taxes, duties and tariffs. But it was the creation of a series of software technology parks under the aegis of the Software Technology Park of India (STPI) that soon revolutionized the development of the software industry, which led to the mushrooming of several local IT companies (Taganas and Kaul, 2006).

Government of India has formulated a national IT policy in 1998 and also set up a National Task Force on Information Technology and Software Development with the objective of making India an 'IT superpower'.

### *Labor Laws and the IT Industry*

The call centers in Bangalore city are housed in multi-purpose buildings such as the gleaming International Tech Park (ITPL) complete with a granite-façade waterfall, gym, coffee shop, restaurants, and the modern look and feel of the call centre, with neon-lit coffee shops and MTV stand as a stark contrast to the surrounding semi-urban villages and slums (McMillin, 2006). The superior work environment, use of state art technology in day-to-day work, better salary structure, catchy designations, smart and young peer workers and so on tend the workers to believe that the job being carried out is that of an executive or professional. (Remesh, 2004).

Organisations in the ITES sector have been extremely successful in using both the exclusivist and exclusivist strategies to keep unions at bay. These strategies have reinforced the notion of corporate culturalism that aims at winning the "hearts and minds" of employees by managing what they think and feel, and not just how they behave (Noronha and D'Cruz, 2006).

Employment in IT industry implies a host of insecurities and vulnerability, which is partially reflected in the high attribution rate. The work is too demanding, depressing and demeaning. Most of these youngsters are in fact burning out their formative years as 'cyber coolies'. The other blatant insecurity is the complete absence of organization activities, as the philosophy of work organization is based on individualization. The young employees represent a group of expensively educated cheap labor and the long term opportunity could be very high (Remesh, 2004).

**GESIA and IT/ITES sector in Gujarat**

In 1995 a group of Eight Chief Executives of companies located in GIDC Electronics Estate in Gandhinagar formed a group called Action Group Electronics (AGE). This group's main concern was why Gujarat has been lagging behind in the field of Electronics and what steps are needed to be taken to catch up. On 14th December, '96 GEIA (Gujarat Electronics Industries Association) was formed with initial membership of around 40 members. In 1997 GEIA was rechristened as GESIA (Gujarat Electronics & Software Industries Association) to widen scope to include software industries. GESIA is a not-for-profit, industry-led and industry-managed association. After a decade, GESIA has become the only nodal representative association of ICT Industry in Gujarat having 240+ members from various parts of Gujarat. GESIA works in partnership with the Government of Gujarat for the promotion of Software, BPO / KPO, Telecom / ISP and Electronics industry in the State of Gujarat.

Since inception, GESIA has achieved many milestones, including, establishment of EQDC (Electronics & Quality Development Centre) and STTL (Software Testing Training Laboratory), under STQC Directorate, Ministry of Information

Technology - New Delhi, partnerships with various National Level Industry associations, working with the Government of Gujarat for State level IT policies, seminars and programs based on relevant industry topics, etc.

Government of Gujarat IT Policy 2006-2011. Salient features of this policy are as following:

- The State government will initiate steps to enhance the supply of skilled manpower for IT/ITES such as industry-institute partnerships for enhancement of industry relevant skills, optimum use of existing educational infrastructure including distance learning through satellite communication facilities available at Bhaskaracharaya Institute for Space Application and Geo-informatics (BISAG).
- Collaboration with NASSCOM for conducting NAC test for facilitating benchmarking of BPO manpower.
- Promotion of Mega IT projects on case to case basis. Promotion of IT parks / SEZs for enhancing availability of ready built up space for IT/ITeS sector.
- Provision of self-certification under Labor Laws. In addition of relaxation of Labor Laws Gujarat's SEZs law provides host of exemptions from state specific taxes and cess etc.
- The State Government has already set up Gujarat IT venture fund under the aegis of Gujarat Venture Finance Ltd., Ahmedabad.
- All new Information Technology Industry units have been exempted from the payment of Electricity Duty for a period of 5 years from the date of which the said unit commences its commercial operation.
- The captive power unit set up by eligible IT / New IT & TIeS units will be exempted from payment of electricity duty as per provision of section 3 of the Bombay Electricity Duty Act, 1958. IT & ITES unit will be considered eligible for exemption from power cuts.

- In order to facilitate adequate availability of floor space to IT/ITES units in the urban centers, the government will permit more than the permissible (Floor Space Index) FSI to IT Parks subject to payment of premium of such additional FSI at market rate.
- Gujarat Informatics Ltd. has been identified as nodal agency for promotion of IT in the State.

**Findings and conclusions**

State government has been proactive in making the IT sector boost to parallel the states like Karnataka, Andhra Pradesh, Tamil Nadu, and Maharashtra. The government has initiated reforms ranging from tax exemption to labor laws to venture capital for the firms in the IT/ITES sector. Though late, the role of government has been extremely positive.

Gujarat Government has been trying very hard to attract investments in the IT sector from realty, finance, banking sector companies through the highly propagated Vibrant Gujarat Summits every year. Many memorandum of understanding are signed between the stakeholders but only a few of them actually invest. It means the amount of FDI or local investments claimed by Government in Vibrant Summits remain substantially on papers. Lately, many companies who have applied for, identified land, or even made initial investments in the SEZs; IT parks are withdrawing increasingly, looking at the slowing down of the world economy.

**a) The factors that make Gujarat better off compared to other states in growth of the IT/ITES sector in India are given as follows:**

1) Entrepreneurial nature of Gujaratis and high level professionalism in them
2) Best IT infrastructure for Growth of IT sector, in terms of bandwidth, network etc.

3) Surplus and uninterrupted 24X7 power supply
4) Lower cost of operations particularly in purchase of land
5) Highly safe and friendly state even for women even during nights
6) High telephone or mobile density is quite reasonable
7) Excellent connectivity to both domestic and international centres through airways and waterways.
8) Prohibition policy makes Gujarat a business friendly place
9) In addition to a vast army of English medium graduates, there is a pool of professionals like CA, CS, and MBAs etc. Therefore, Gujarat is sometimes rightly called CA Hub.
10) Proactive and encourage state government machinery
11) Old and reliable linkages between Gujaratis living and Gujarat and the NRG (Non Resident Gujarati)
12) So Gujarat as an IT location is selected on basis of five parameters
    a) Business minded people,
    b) Business friendly environment,
    c) Easy market access,
    d) Modern infrastructure &
    e) General competitiveness.

Gujarat state has done immensely well as far as implementation of the information technology is concerned from cities to villages in terms of e-governance. The government records, certificates, documents are being converted into e-formats for their easy accessibility as well as for bringing transparency. So, Gujarat stands at higher levels in the implementation part of information and communication technology (ICT) ranking table. But, Gujarat is definitely lagging behind in IT/ITES or BPO sector compared to the southern states. Moreover, the outsourcing business is concentrated in twin cities of Gandhinagar and Ahmedabad. Vadodara, Surat, Rajkot etc cities have only sparsely spread call centres. So, one can say Gujarat has missed the first IT/ ITES bus.

There is both domestic and international call centres stationed in Ahmedabad particularly. Gandhinagar's Info city is exclusively meant for IT/ITES. Large IT/ITES firms like AZURE, MOTIF, AEGIG, SIS etc operate in both categories. Many IT/ITES companies have offices in Gujarat on one hand and elsewhere on the other. The offshore outsourcing is done to USA, EU, Chinese, Singapore clients, but near-shore outsourcing is done for customers from Madhya Pradesh, Rajasthan, etc.

Principally, Gujarat IT/ITES business is more in services related to finance, loan recovery, software customization and software solutions, web designing and maintenance, data mining, data entry and data processing, outsourcing consultancies, AutoCAD accounting etc. The small IT firms have very limited and time bound outsourcing projects compared to the larger ones which work with MNCs from the West.

**b) Work and work environment in IT sector in Gujarat**

There are two categories of BPO firms or call centres in Gujarat, large firms which operate on several outsourcing projects at a time and small ones which deal with one or two contracts at a time. The clientele is largely from the West. The small sized call centres with less than 10 employees, (which are run from home or a small shop) are fast coming up everywhere in cities like Ahmedabad and Rajkot, but they get shut down equally fast for financial, quality maintenance or other reasons.

Gujarat IT firms have relatively good demand for both hardware and software products. Therefore, hardware trading is coming up as a big business, though manufacturing is not at all taking place in the state. The IT firms in the state are more into software customization, website development and website maintenance, mobile applications, etc. The local demand for the software and hardware products is showing a rising trend in the state.

Employees working in call centres in Gujarat are mostly young English knowing urban population. The international call centres have mostly convent educated workers but the domestic ones manage with Gujarati or sometimes Hindi medium learnt youth. Discipline and etiquettes at work place are utmost important as they are constantly and regularly kept watch on while dealing with clients in the voiced based call centres.

The entrepreneurs in IT/ITES sector in Gujarat are young risk takers who have worked in some call centre or BPO firm in the past for a few years and now they want their own firm. The starting salary for a call centre representative as they are commonly known as would be Rs 5000/month for a domestic BPO but may be around Rs 9000/month in an international call centre. There are increments and incentives for meeting the targets in case of telemarketing call centres. Some big BPO/KPO firms have their own transportation facilities particularly during night shifts. The work environment in corporate type call centres is reasonably conducive and generally liked by the employees working over there compared to their small counterparts where exploitation of workers persists extensively.

A very visible process is being repeated in Gujarat also, as it has happened in case of the IT/ITES sector in IT forward states. And it the process of in-formalization in the IT/ITES sector which is characterized by flexible labor laws, absence of job/old age/social security, absence of trade union activities etc for the ITES employees. Therefore, there is job dissatisfaction and so, attrition rate in BPOs, is around 25% on annual basis. The labor frequently switches over to others for a better pay and perks, promotion, work environment. The opportunities to grow vertically for an employee within the firm are less, though monetary rewards continually rise. No one joins this sector to work on a permanent basis but it is a make shift arrangement for those who want to earn handsomely while studying or till he/she does not get hand on a fair employment.

There is increasing number of cases among the IT/ITES workers related to loss of sleep and appetite, indigestion, depression, break up of friend/ social circle etc. The employees seem frustrated, showing lack of interest in social activities, narrowing their friend circle and so on. One remarkable observation was that some of the small sized call centers, though their number is very less, are indulged into illegal activities like financial frauds, fraudulent loan recovery, fake credit card/loan sale etc. The profit margins are extremely high and young collegiate are tempted towards such assignments which fetch them more returns. But, no large well established IT/ITES firms are into such malpractices.

The labor force working in the BPO/KPO would be more than 10 lacks all over the country and less than 1 lack in Gujarat. But, one can arguably say that the ITES workers employed anywhere in India are not getting any social security and employment related benefits as they deserve for being employed in the industry which made India poised in terms of exports, employment and economic growth. But, one astonishing fact visible from this research is that neither the central government nor its state level counterparts are interested in formalizing or regulating this sector for the benefit of the employees.

Trade Unions are at bay as far as the IT/ITES sector is concerned. The young labor force is so much involved every minute to fulfill their business targets, taking up call after call that they do not have time for such activities. Employees also take this as a part time assignment or a make shift arrangement for the time being, till they can shift permanently to a better and secure profession. The traditional Trade Unions are losing their grounds at their own home fronts, so they seem to be less interested in the college going work force which is neither going to stick to one firm or city nor is going to sustain in the long run. No such efforts of regulation of workers in the IT/ ITES sector are being taken by Government/NGOs/Trade Unions.

Government has not shown interest in this industry beyond proudly showing the amazing data on exports, GDP growth, and employment. Despite the fact that this completely privately dominated and immense profit making business does have grey areas in employment terms and conditions from the employee point of view, but the state has not started any company or venture so far to get a share of profit (as it has done in cases of no so lucrative sectors), neither has it formulated any legal policy framework which can benefit the workers and regulate the employers in the BPO sector. It has been proved by different studies undertaken by researchers that the government initiated reforms have worked wonders in facilitating and in expansion of this sector during the reforms period. But, the sector gets all types of tax sops, incentives and exemptions more than what industry in India used to get during the pre-reform period. The government at both levels is more interested in further growth of this sector through liberal policies rather than labor reforms in favor of the BPO workers, this makes an easy way for the IT/ITES firms to adopt hire and fire labor policies which are always at benefit of employer and at the cost of the employees. Gujarat government is offering more to the IT/ITES firms and expecting least from them for the workers.

## References

Abraham, Vinoj and R.K. Sharma (2005), 'New Technology and the Emerging Labor Market: A Study of Indian IT Industry', *Indian Journal of Labor Economics*, Vol. 48, No. 4.

Abraham, Vinoj (2005), 'Labor Productivity and Employment in the Indian Information and Communication Technology

Industry', unpublished Ph.D. thesis submitted to the Jawaharlal Nehru University, New Delhi.

Abraham, Vinoj (2007), 'Employee Attrition in Indian Software Industry: Patterns and Proximate Factors', *Labor and Development*, Vol. 12, No. 2 and Vol. 13, No. 1.

Basant, Rakesh and Uma Rani (2004), 'Labor Market Deepening in the Indian Information Technology Industry: An Exploratory Analysis', *Working Paper No 2004-06-06*, Indian Institute of Management, Ahmedabad.

Basant, Rakesh, (1998), Review of Richard Heeks, '*India's Software Industry: State Policy, Liberalisation and Industrial Development*', Sage Publications, 1996, in *The Journal of Entrepreneurship*, Vol. 7, No. 1.

Desai, R.G. (2005), *Information Technology and Economic Growth*, Rawat Publications, Jaipur.

Gorden, Jim and Poonam Gupta (2003), 'Understanding India's Services Revolution', paper presented at the IMF-NCAER Conference on "A Tale of Two Giants: India's and China's Experience with Reforms", New Delhi, November 14-16.

Ilavarasan, P. Vigneswara (2008), 'Software Work in India: A Labor Process', in Carol Upadhya and A.R. Desai (Eds.), *In an Outpost of the Global Economy: Work and Workers in India's Information Technology Industry*, Routledge, New Delhi.

*IT and ITES Policy*, Government of Maharashtra, (for the years 2003 and 2009).

*IT and ITES Policy*, Government of Rajasthan (for the year 2007).

Kumar, Nagesh and K.J. Joseph (Eds.) (2007), *International Competitiveness and Knowledge based Industries in India*, Oxford University Press, New Delhi.

Lall, S. (2005), 'Rethinking Industrial Strategy: The Role of the State in the Face of Globalization', in Kevin Gallagher (Ed.), *Putting Development First*, Zed Press, London.

McMillin, Divya C., (2006), 'Outsourcing Indian Identity: Call Centres and Cultural Transformation in India', *Economic and Political Weekly*, Vol. 41, No. 3.

Noronha, Ernesto and Premilla D'cruz (2006), 'Organising Call Centre Agents: Emerging Issues', *Economic and Political Weekly*, Vol. 41, No. 21.

Pradhan, Jaya Prakash and Vinoj Abraham (2005), 'Cultural and Social Impact of Outsourcing: Emerging Issues from India's Call Centres', *Harvard Asia Quarterly*, Vol. 9, No. 3.

Remesh, Babu P. (2004), '"Cyber Coolies" in BPO: Insecurities and Vulnerabilities of Non-Standard Work', *Economic and Political Weekly*, Vol. 39, No. 5.

Rothboeck, S., M. Vijayabaskar and V. Gayathri (2001), *Labour in the New Economy: The Case of the Indian Software Industry*, International Labour Organisation, New Delhi.

STPI Annual Report (2009-10), Ministry of Information and communication Technology, Government of India.

Taganas, Rey A. L. and Vijay Kumar Kaul (2006), 'Innovation Systems in India's IT Industry: An Empirical Investigation', *Economic and Political Weekly*, Vol. 41, No.39.

Upadhya, Carol (2007), 'Employment, Exclusion and "Merit" in the Indian IT Industry', *Economic and Political Weekly*, Vol. 42, No. 20.

**Websites**

NASSCOM Event India, 'BPO Study Roadmap 2012', *www.nasscom.in*

STPI (1991), Ministry and Information and Communication Technology, Government of India, *www.mit.gov.in*

*www.gesia.org*

# Index

**D**

P



Q



R